· significance of the finger in the wound.

· the wound is not just the result of trauma, the existence and awareness of the wound becomes the portal for the "razors" to come out.

"Shelly Rambo forges a powerful—and necessary—theology of resurrection wounds that unflinchingly addresses the trauma of contemporary woundedness even as it celebrates and claims the victory of life that followed the cross. In so doing, she presents a profound vision of the resurrection, bears witness to suffering, and offers hope for healing."

—Serene Jones, *President, Union Theological Seminary*

"*Resurrecting Wounds* is challenging—Rambo requires us to face the social and personal traumas and woundings that reveal the fraying edges of our theologies and life together. Her writing is elegant and painful. Such witnessing does not remove scab or wound; it makes us reread the Gospel narratives, in community, with the reality and theology of wounding in the foreground."

—Phillis Isabella Sheppard, *Associate Professor of Religion, Psychology and Culture, Vanderbilt University*

"Shelly Rambo combines theology, philosophy, feminism, and trauma studies in this highly original reading of wounds and scars. Ranging from Macrina of Nyssa and Calvin to contemporary veterans and trauma victims, she shows how the resurrection of bodies is more about this life than the next, more about communal survival than private salvation."

—Richard Kearney, *Charles B. Seelig Chair of Philosophy, Boston College*

Resurrecting Wounds

Living in the Afterlife of Trauma

Shelly Rambo

BAYLOR UNIVERSITY PRESS

Scripture quotations are from the New Revised Standard Version Bible, copyright 1989, Division of Christian Education of the National Council of the Churches of Christ in the United States of America. Used by permission. All rights reserved.

Cover design by Will Brown
Cover image by unknown artist
Interior image by Michelangelo Merisi da Caravaggio (1571–1610), *The Incredulity of Saint Thomas*, 1602–1603, Schloss Sanssouci, Potsdam, Brandenburg, Germany

Library of Congress Cataloging-in-Publication Data

Names: Rambo, Shelly, author.
Title: Resurrecting wounds : living in the afterlife of trauma / Shelly Rambo.
Description: Waco, Texas : Baylor University Press, [2017] | Includes bibliographical references and index.
Identifiers: LCCN 2016042031 (print) | LCCN 2016046080 (ebook) | ISBN 9781481306782 (hardback : alk. paper) | ISBN 9781481306812 (ebook-Mobi/Kindle) | ISBN 9781481306805 (ePub) | ISBN 9781481306829 (web PDF)
Subjects: LCSH: Suffering—Religious aspects—Christianity. | Jesus Christ—Appearances.
Classification: LCC BT732.7 .R33 2017 (print) | LCC BT732.7 (ebook) | DDC 248.8/625—dc23
LC record available at https://lccn.loc.gov/2016042031

Contents

Acknowledgments

I am grateful to many companions in thought, writing, and life.

With each draft, Julie Meadows prodded me to sharpen my thinking, and her keen editorial eye drew out my best thoughts. Since our doctoral days at Emory, we have communed amid the wonder of words, and I am so grateful that she inhabited the space of this book with me. Ordinary practices of academic life can become soul nourishing, and I am grateful to Mayra Rivera for mulling over the meaning of all of these activities with me—teaching, writing, and theologizing.

It is an immeasurable gift to have a life-partner who drinks in the world of ideas alongside me. Thank you, Michael Yuille, for listening to multiple iterations of these ideas and buffering my self-criticism by reminding me that I have important things to say. Thanks to Jody Rambo, Ty, Helena, and Wyeth Buckman, for reminding me daily of the joys of family. Special thanks to Anastasia and Chad Kidd for your fun-filled and steady friendship.

Dale Andrews, Phillis Sheppard, and Diana Swancutt helped me work out some knots in my thinking and added a few along the way. Thank you for being fearless scholars and telling truths that are difficult to hear. John Schluep and Warriors Journey Home welcomed me into their healing work, and I am grateful for their truth telling. I want to thank the students in multiple iterations of my "Trauma and Theology" courses at Boston University School of Theology who bring their lives to the topics that we discuss and commit themselves to the work of healing.

Special thanks to Nicole Smith Murphy for first introducing me to Baylor University Press and to Carey Newman for coaching this project to completion. His stories and plotlines fueled me at each stage. Thanks, as well, to Ashley, David, Kathryn, and Stephanie, for tracking down materials and fine-tuning footnotes.

The deaths of my mother and my father bookend this project. A theology of resurrection is birthed amid these losses. Just before my mother's final medical procedure, the nurse pulled back her hospital gown, revealing the scars of her early heart surgeries. I imagined tracing the surface of that scar as I worked through Gregory of Nyssa's account of *The Life of Saint Macrina*. "Do not pass by this miracle," Vetiana whispers to Gregory. In those scars, I had my beginning, and by those scars I continue to know myself in this world. My father, a lifelong preacher, insisted that the gospel should be preached like Garrison Keillor—in story form. Punkin' Ridge, Pennsylvania, was the Lake Wobegon that my dad returned to throughout his life. He insisted that the good news often carries you far from home, but that, at its best, it brings you home. In my parents' absence, my questions about the afterlife are profoundly shaped by the textures of the lives that they lived. Their spirits are still participating.

This book is dedicated to Ruth and David Rambo.

Introduction
Reenvisioning Resurrection

What is the nature of a life that continues beyond trauma?

——*Cathy Caruth*[1]

Amid the surge of zombie apocalypse and dystopian films, there is a quieter yet perhaps more eerie vision of the dead returning in the French series *Les Revenants* (*The Returned*).[2] The series opens with the image of a tour bus winding along a steep mountain road, filled with schoolchildren going on a field trip. As they approach a turn, the bus swerves into the other lane and drives over the edge. The accident is fatal, but the image is still and quiet, conveying a tone that carries throughout the series. Moments later, viewers witness members of a grief group gathered in a circle, processing the loss of their loved ones. A woman, Sandrine, announces to the group that she is expecting a baby. Having lost her child, presumably in the bus accident, she is reticent to make the announcement. She offers these words: "Perhaps we don't get over the loss, but life *continuer, avancer.*" Then she follows with the statement, "C'est la vie qui est la plus forte." The English translation provides an important inflection, presented to English-speaking viewers in this form, "Life always prevails." As the group moves to discuss the public memorial to commemorate the collective loss, Jerome, a father of another victim, comes back to Sandrine's comment, responding with

1

what could be read as a mix of despair and biting sarcasm: "Maybe life will bring me marvelous gifts, too."

Jerome is interrupted moments later by a call from his wife, as she announces that unusual things are happening. They are separated, presumably as a result of their loss. Claire tells him that Camille, their daughter, is standing in the kitchen, rummaging through the refrigerator as she would on any ordinary day. Yet Camille was seated on the bus that went over the cliff; she has been dead for four years. And so the dead begin to return to the living, appearing to their loved ones with no awareness that time has passed or that they are, in fact, dead. Eerily, the dead return seemingly as they were. They are literally unmarked—unwounded—by death. In *Les Revenants*, the returns are not triumphant. The returned do not appear to come back with any mission. They are, in fact, disturbed by their own returns. Not realizing that they are dead, they, too, seek explanation for the encounters they have with the living. While each of the departed returns to his or her familiar setting—one by one—the returns start to link persons in the community, and a more collective picture emerges.

These visions of the return provide a compelling commentary on resurrection. In Christian accounts, resurrection is the promise of life *after* death that rests on the figure of the resurrected Jesus who triumphs *over* death. Christ's resurrection ensures a future and forecasts a resurrection for all believers. Sandrine's statement, "Life prevails," can be understood to express a familiar trajectory of resurrection—that life overcomes death, and that it wins out in the end. And yet the undertow of Sandrine's comment suggests that *"la vie continue"* is something different, something less triumphant. Jerome's sarcasm counters the notion that life prevails, underscoring a more complex picture of life following experiences of loss that the series will put forward.[3] While the plotline is recognizable, the characters in *Les Revenants* improvise along the tangled lines of what it means to remain, *continuer*, in life in the aftermath of loss. And yet addressing these losses within the genre of the supernatural brings them into the rich territory of religious claims about the afterlife and the resurrection of the body, more particularly within Christianity.

Les Revenants directly appeals to the story of Thomas' encounter with the resurrected Jesus in the Gospel of John.[4] These appeals to the biblical story juxtapose the returns to the resurrection appearances. A local detective named Thomas approaches the village priest, asking questions about the returns. He has just viewed video-surveillance tapes of Simon, one of the returned, appearing to Adele, Simon's bereaved fiancée. Thomas is invested in more than this investigation, because he is Adele's current fiancé, and Simon's return is an obvious threat to his upcoming marriage. Thomas enters the sanctuary, surrounded by the symbols of Christian faith. Thomas knows that Adele has consulted with the priest and wants to discern from him whether Simon's return could be real. The priest assures him that Simon is nothing but a ghost and that Adele will soon forget him. According to the priest, his appearances are merely the product of her grief. Simon is just a figment of her imagination; he is not real. Thomas replies, "Wasn't Jesus considered a ghost when he came back?" He is appealing to the part of the narrative in which Jesus moves through the locked doors of the Upper Room appearing to the group of disciples gathered there.[5] The priest responds, "Why do you ask?" Thomas replies, referring to Simon, "He was here. Physically speaking. In flesh and blood."

The priest dissuades him from taking the story so literally. But Thomas insists on a response, saying, "I'm a detective, not an intellectual. . . . I need to understand." Thomas asks the priest, "Do you believe it?"—"it" meaning belief in Jesus' resurrection—to which the priest replies, "Of course." And yet Thomas pursues his line of questioning, pressing the connection between the biblical story of resurrection and the return of Simon. At this point, the priest retorts with this biblically inflected statement, drawn from the Thomas narrative in John 20: "Believing is more important than seeing." This Thomas responds to the priest's appeal to mystery by insisting that he, as a detective, solves mysteries for a living. The priest refuses to follow Thomas' line of inquiry. The sphere of faith, as the priest presents it, does not have anything to say on what is taking place. Faith, he conveys to Thomas, serves other purposes. We witness a familiar interaction between believing and seeing, as the priest immediately reaches for this biblical language and yet relegates it to the realm of faith, shutting down Thomas' line of questioning.

Thomas presses the question of belief a second time. The priest defers, responding, "You don't ask the right questions," to which Thomas responds, "You don't give the right answers."

The Posttraumatic

David Morris opens his biography of PTSD, *The Evil Hours*, by stating that trauma has moved from the sidelines of public awareness to its center: "Over the past four decades, post-traumatic stress disorder has permeated every corner of our culture."[6] It has become, he says, the lingua franca of suffering in our times. Moving from a diagnosis that identified the suffering of a few, trauma has become an overarching term. A growing awareness of trauma and its effects has also contributed to the expansive use of trauma to speak not only to the experience of particular persons and communities but also to a broader cultural ethos in which we live. The use of the term "trauma" to name the pathos and pathologies of American culture should be approached critically, but it is also important to ask why it has taken hold. Images in popular culture of the dead returning and of wounds resurfacing are worthy of our attention. These depictions as well as those within popular novels and films accompany theories of trauma and can serve not only to figure violence and its effects but also potentially alternative approaches to it. The dead are living and the living dead. The contemporary Thomas in *Les Revenants* is asking about life in its *continuer*. And he is met with reproach. When this ancient narrative comes to life for Thomas, can it speak?

The emerging discourse of trauma at the end of the twentieth century provided a new framework in which to interpret suffering. A new understanding of trauma, as distinct from other forms of loss, dispelled existing assumptions that trauma follows a timeline of healing—that *in time* one can just get over or beyond it. Instead, trauma came to be identified as what does not get integrated in time and thus returns or remains, obstructing one's ability to engage the world as one did before. Both individually and collectively, trauma marked a problem of living in the present, given that the past was still a "living" and intrusive reality. As neurobiological studies narrated the limitations of language to articulating and bringing to light the story of trauma, so, too, theories of trauma drew attention to the breakdown of assumptions about the knowability of experience. This was reflected in the negative and apophatic language that emerged around trauma—trauma is an unknowing, unclaimed, unassimilable, unsayable experience. The therapeutic challenge was how to diagnose and treat such experiences, while the theoretical challenge, expanding to the interdisciplinary study, was how to identify and ethically respond to trauma.

Trauma makes it impossible to think that traumatic experiences are over. It turns us to think of bodies as the loci of trauma. It turns us to think about the porousness of experience and the complex ways that another's trauma, trauma that we view as external to us, comes to live within us. It also means that if we are oriented posttraumatically, we interpret events with epistemological humility and a wariness about how easy it is to dismiss them, to cover them over, to render them invisible. Both the vulnerability of such experiences internally and the difficulty translating such experiences externally require a unique set of capacities for those who seek to witness trauma. Judith Herman's early and influential text *Trauma and Recovery* insisted that the public dimension of trauma was complex and, in many respects, insidious. The internal vulnerabilities coalesced into external mechanisms by which those in power desire to deny trauma. Addressing trauma entails attending to layers of covering and uncovering, appearing and disappearing, surfacing and receding. This underscores Cathy Caruth's statement that the challenge lies not only in the structure of the experience but also in witness to it.[7] The concept of witness, as forged through trauma literatures, offers a way of thinking about a relationship to, and responsibility for, the past in its *ongoingness*.

More recently, studies of trauma have extended beyond analysis of the aftereffects of an event of "death" (*aftermath*) to describe forms of life arising given the impact, and, might we say, the ongoingness of forces of violence (*afterlife*). The aftermath presented a landscape of survival, emphasizing the impossibilities of conceiving of life beyond an event of death.[8] The emerging language of life points to something *more than* survival. While there is an acknowledgment that life can never be restored to its previous condition, terms within the clinical communities such as resilience and posttraumatic growth suggest a reworking of life in ways that press beyond descriptions of the aftermath.[9] This research demands a language of life that can account for the ruptures of experience and history without succumbing to despair. For many working within the field of trauma, this articulation of life does not come in any pure form.[10] They insist that the marks of death remain. The gesture toward something *more* or *beyond* does not come at the expense of denying suffering. Instead, it focuses attention on how people refigure their lives, given their experiences of trauma. Is life, following "death," improved life? Do people grow and develop desirable capacities through experiencing trauma?

These questions prompt a return to familiar conversations within Christian theology about the meaning of suffering and its usefulness in bringing about a more desirable end. This returns, again, to difficult questions that are still contested within Christian theology. It also

presses for reenvisioning of the *afterlife* within Christian theology, and
what the meaning of life following death entails.[11]

The Afterlife of the Cross

Christian believers often speak of their faith in terms of following in
the footsteps of Jesus, of patterning their lives after his life. The way of
the cross, as articulated throughout the tradition, shapes the Christian
imagination, providing a way for believers to map their relationship to
suffering. They make sense of their wounds through his.

In the twentieth century, the meaning of the symbol of the cross
was radically challenged by Christian theologians witnessing the horrors of war and contending with the historical realities of oppression
and enslavement. Theologians called attention to how the symbol of
the Christian cross functions to sanction violence and glorify suffering,
raising the question of whether the cross was a symbol of redemption
or whether it was a symbol that needed to be redeemed. No longer can
the Christian cross be read apart from the genocide of Jewish peoples,
Jürgen Moltmann notes. No longer can the crucifixion be read apart
from the crucifixion of black lynching in the United States, James Cone
declares. No longer can the crucifixion be read apart from the surrogacy
of black women in history, writes Delores Williams. No longer could
the salvation of women come about by way of a male savior, argues
Rosemary Radford Ruether.[12] Instead of the traditional understanding
of Christ's suffering and death, each theologian contested a dominant
narrative of wounds as the means by which redemption is enacted.

This theological energy around reenvisioning the meaning of the
cross continues to inform Christian theology. Yet, in turning away from
interpreting the cross redemptively, there is a danger in not theologizing
suffering at all, in avoiding any moves to narrate human suffering by
way of the Christian story. While keen attention was paid to rethinking
the suffering *on the cross*, it is critical to think *after the cross*. And yet conceiving the "after" involves contending with the perplexing return of
death within the sphere of life. The challenges of interpreting suffering
now reside in providing critical reflection on—and response to—what
we might call the traumatic afterlife of the cross. The return of unintegrated suffering as narrated in trauma not only sheds light on how we
make sense of recurring, intrusive symptoms and the reemergence of
forms of oppression, such as racism and sexism; but also it presents an

invitation to reconceive the story that we tell about life in the aftermath of the cross—the story of resurrection.

Christianity is rife with images of the afterlife and with accompanying practices that shape a vision of what lies beyond death. These visions are largely focused on describing life beyond this world and a future place set apart for Christians who profess belief in Jesus as the Christ. The afterlife signals the otherworldly—a space and time outside this present life. And yet when we conceive of resurrection as otherworldly, we miss opportunities to talk about resurrection in this world.[13]

Turning to the meaning of resurrection in Christian theology via the study of trauma calls into question assumed divisions between the natural and the supernatural, the earthly and the heavenly. It draws out the ways in which the biblical text complicates these divisions, probing whether the dead are living and the living are dead. To probe the afterlife via the trajectory of trauma provides a different entrance into the classic questions of Christian faith. The visions of life in the aftermath of death emerging both within the discourses of trauma and in popular culture press theology to articulate anew responses to questions at the heart of faith: What is the promise of life given the ongoingness of "death"? What forms of life might arise in the afterlife? Many Christians place their hope in the resurrection of Christ as a triumphant new beginning.[14] And yet these proclamations of newness are situated within a context in which endings and beginnings, the old and the new, are much more porous. There is no clear-cut line separating the two; life is not a departure from death but, instead, a different relationship to death and life. In a posttraumatic age, they exist simultaneously rather than sequentially.[15] The return of Jesus reveals something about *life in the midst of death*. If we take the line between death and life to be more porous, as the context of trauma suggests, then resurrecting is not so much about life overcoming death as it is about *life resurrecting amid the ongoingness of death*. The return of Jesus marks a distinct territory for thinking about life as marked by wounds and yet recreated through them.

Christian theologians reinterpret the story of crucifixion and resurrection, reflecting on how the story is transmitted and received in new contexts and within changing historical situations. Revisiting the plot, tracing its dramatic structure, inhabiting the movements of the central actors is all part of the work of theology. If, as trauma suggests, death and life are coterminous rather than sequential, entangled rather than clearly delineated, biblical narratives of life after death—the resurrection accounts—might attest to a powerful vision of life, albeit disentangled from some of the theological interpretations attached to them. The aim of this book is to configure a theology of resurrection that links the promises of Christian theology to the realities of trauma that we are witnessing in our time. Thus, the challenge is to rethink the trajectory of the major plotline of the Christian story and to revisit its central assumptions: that life triumphs over death, and that resurrection hope points to the future. The language of the afterlife of trauma thus signals new opportunities within Christian theology to articulate the relationship between death and life, cross and resurrection. Instead of reaffirming the way of the cross, there is a need to imagine *ways of resurrecting.*

Resurrecting Wounds

He returns with wounds on the other side of death. Witnessing his violent death, they awaken, disoriented and filled with grief. The way ahead is not clear; they are left to make sense of their lives without him and to continue the work, accompanied by the spirit he promised to them. In one account, he told them, just before he left, that they would not understand all of the events that were about to occur. They would not be able to take in all that his death meant, but they would be guided into truth in the aftermath. They should not mistake his departure for abandonment. He would be with them by way of this spirit, their advocate, who would accompany them, "presencing" him even in his absence. It was a mystifying departing speech that he offered them, and they reach for its meaning now in his absence.

And yet, he returns, standing in their midst just days later. They gather around him, this time on the other side of death. Thomas missed the first appearance. He was not clear about the return as his friends conveyed it to him. He heard them talking about the return, about how Jesus had miraculously appeared to them. They say he appeared without entering through the door; instead, he came through the walls, like a ghost. He knew that they had locked themselves in a room together, afraid of what would happen to them in the aftermath of Jesus' death. Thomas insists on seeing for himself. This second time, the others gather around Thomas, as if waiting to see what this second appearance will bring. Jesus approaches him. Thomas is invited to come closer, to touch, and to plunge his finger into the wounds on Jesus' side. Other disciples move closer, accompanying Thomas as he witnesses the marked skin.

Readers familiar with this biblical narrative may step in at this point, noting how elements of the story have changed, noticing different points of emphasis that may alter the story altogether. The standard plotline of the story reads as follows: Thomas, one of the disciples, is the doubter who comes to belief only after witnessing evidence of the resurrection. The encounter features his doubt and the invitation extended to him by the risen Christ to receive the evidence that he needs. He professes his belief with the exclamation—"My Lord and my God."

Some of these elements—Thomas missing, the disciples' second approach, the context of fear, the spectral skin of one returning from the dead—have been folded into the standard reading—known, in short, as the story of doubting Thomas. These elements are read as incidentals on the way to the climax of this account—the moment in which Thomas proclaims belief in Jesus as the Christ. That is the point of the story, after all. But is it? When read within our present context, these incidentals are not so incidental. They resonate with sensibilities within the culture, with a posttraumatic ethos in which things are not what they appear to be and truths do not surface. Instead, the wounds return, surfacing and receding, in ways that call for a new understanding of the resurrection. This return of wounds, within our present context, necessitates a rereading of the narrative.

The Gospel of John's account of the resurrection features the return of Jesus to his disciples. He appears as one who is both familiar to them and yet unfamiliar. He appears to them as they once knew him and yet in ghostly form, as one who can enter a room through locked doors. From the gospel's account of Mary mistaking him for the gardener to the Thomas encounter in which he makes his identity known by inviting Thomas to touch his wounds, resurrection is a period of disorientation and reorientation. He is both returning and ascending. He is both spectral and carnal. He is both recognizable and unrecognizable to those whom he meets, and it is the process of coming to recognition, through the strangeness—and misrecognition—that makes this narrative of resurrection both consonant with trauma's afterlife and open to a reinscription of it in Christian theology. The fact that the gospel narrative provides testimony to the challenges of recognizing the risen Christ underscores how difficult it is to resurrect, to come to life again. The testimony to the challenges of locating the body, of determining whether the body is there or not there, can be read as a sacred witness to the complexities of healing.

Resurrection is often viewed as the event that secures the truth
of Christian faith. If the resurrection did not occur, if Jesus did not
rise, then the truth of Christianity goes without verification, and, as
Christians profess, their hope is in vain (1 Cor 15:12-18). There is a
lot riding on resurrection. And it is precisely because it bears so much
weight, that interpretations of resurrection have been, like the disciples,
on lockdown. But what if this encounter is not a matter of belief? What
if we have missed the point of this story altogether? And what if this
"missing" is part of the truth of it all?

This project aims to defamiliarize readers from what is taking place
in order to offer it anew. This estranging work is not for the sake of
refuting one interpretation so much as it is to reopen the plot, the characters, and the action (its dramatic structure) to interpretation. It invites
theology, by way of the literary, to refigure resurrection.

While many will acknowledge that resurrection refers to the return
of Christ, the notion of a miraculous return catapults this return in
a supernatural direction, often ignoring the specific elements of the
return itself. The resurrection is both extraordinary and yet profoundly
ordinary, as Jesus returns to his disciples and, at several points, does
everyday and recognizable things. The marks of resurrection provide
both a commentary on death and life that has yet to be unearthed. It is
the very fact that we think we know what this encounter means, what
each character represents, and how it ends, that it ceases to speak meaningfully and to offer anything new to our lives. The event of resurrection appears to us, via a return, as a stranger who beckons to us from
a familiar place, as the skin of a healer now marked by death. So the
process of interpreting this story is to suspend what we think we know
in order to give way to a rearrangement of the familiar. This might be
identified as the work of theological imagination.

Each of the chapters that follow provides a way of refiguring the
encounter between Thomas and the resurrected Jesus. This scene has
signaled the overcoming of doubt and the assent to the truth of Christian faith. It has been enfolded into a familiar plotline of death and
life, as expressed in the Christian tradition. It has been reinscribed in a
particular way, and has come to represent, in modernity, a performance
of faith over doubt, of belief over unbelief, and, perhaps most unique to
the times, of faith over reason, as Thomas stands as the modern skeptic
who is won over by the truth of the gospel. And yet, there is much more

to this story. This familiar reading has eclipsed other possible readings, particularly one centered on reenvisioning the significance of wounds.

While the familiar trajectory of interpretation presents the wounds as confirmation or proof of the crucifixion, their appearance within the sphere of life marks a different relationship to death, by transfiguring it without negating it. One of the concerns that underlies this book is the operative erasure of wounds in theologies of resurrection; while the wounds return in the biblical narrative and feature centrally there, they are folded into interpretations that continually cover over the wounds. These dynamics of covering over and exposing wounds, presented within discourses of trauma, are also operative within histories of interpretation. This means that a theology of resurrecting involves acknowledging an ingredient in each of the gospel accounts of resurrection—moments of misrecognition that convey the challenges of witnessing life; these moments map the demands of witnessing resurrection that is critical to both attesting to trauma and to transfiguring it.

As the field of trauma studies theorizes life in its *continuer*, the challenges articulated there provide a unique lens through which to view the resurrection texts. Life is not expressed in terms of a clean break, or as an overcoming of death. And yet there are expressions of life that extend beyond expressions of survival and aftermath. Caruth's opening question reaches for these new expressions. The resurrection narratives provide testimonies to life beyond trauma. The figure of returning wounds can serve as figures for this new expression of life. Several aspects of the appearance to Thomas come to the fore: the bodily markings, an awareness of multiple witnesses present, and the status of death within this precarious sphere of life. Highlighting these features of the narrative, as they correspond with insights from trauma, opens into a theology of resurrection that addresses returning wounds.

Surfacing Wounds

Is it for the good?

——*Thomas,* Les Revenants

In *Les Revenants* the contemporary Thomas reaches for the religious symbols to make sense of what is taking place. In approaching the priest, Thomas says that Chloe, Adele's daughter, had learned this story in church. If this is what the church teaches, why is it that the priest refuses to explain it? Didn't something like this happen before? Isn't this the story that the church keeps telling? Thomas is perplexed by the priest's refusal to answer. While the religious purport belief in the resurrection of the body, this belief cannot account for the present phenomenon.

And yet as the living witness something more than a ghosting, the *priest* is cast as the "unbeliever" here. He insists that the resurrection of bodies cannot be taken literally; rather, it must be accepted on faith. The pithy question and answer at the end of their exchange suggest an impasse. Whatever is taking place should not be brought into the realm of the religious, the priest insists, because the religious should be considered on its own terms. This encounter reflects a failure of the religious to frame what is taking place and, in fact, the insistence on its own irrelevance. The religious espouse a belief in resurrection but cannot, or will not, account for these appearances. It remains untouched and, interestingly, encased within the glass windows of the church. Thomas barges through the glass doors, confronting the priest, insisting that the returns must, in some way, connect to the story of resurrection that the church teaches to its followers. The priest metaphorically shuts the doors, containing the story within, as if to keep it secure.

Familiar Christian interpretations of resurrection unravel here, exposed as empty and irrelevant. This unraveling is most evident when wounds surface. When the dead return, wounds start manifesting on the living.[16] Lena, Camille's twin sister, had not been on the bus that day. She survived her twin, and is four years older when Camille returns. Not long after the return, Lena develops a wound on her upper back, and it grows larger the longer that Camille is present. This phenomenon is unusual in many respects. The dead, contrary to many supernatural thrillers, return without any signs of death. They are unmarked. Wounds begin to surface on the living *after* their encounters with the dead. The effect is striking, because the encounters begin to expose the impact of loss on those who survived the deaths. It is not the wounds of death that mark the bodies of those who return; it is the *wounds of life* that surface on the skin of those who remain. Although time has progressed, the wounds are fresh. The surfacing reveals that they have been untended.

This surfacing of wounds is also imaged in the natural world, as the village reservoir starts draining and dead animals, submerged underwater for what appears to have been a very long time, are gradually exposed— coming to the surface. Nature is off kilter. One of the opening scenes (and the opening credits) features a butterfly preserved in glass casing on the wall, breaking through and shattering the glass as if coming back to life. The image of taxidermy—of preserving the dead *as if* alive—is evoked throughout. The cinematography continually directs viewers to the water's surface and to what is submerged. In the opening credits, even the title words "Les Revenants" appear half above the surface and half below. Focusing attention on the surface of water and the surface of skin, viewers are aware that a lot has been submerged, hidden from view, yet lurking beneath.

And yet the longer that the returned remain, wounds start crossing, surfacing not only on the living but also transferring to the bodies of the dead. While Camille's return activates Lena's wound, Camille starts to develop marks on her skin at a later point. There is a symbiosis between the living and the dead, perhaps underscored by the fact that Lena and Camille are twins. This vision of sharing and crossing *is* unique, as it binds together the dead and the living, past and present, in a curious configuration.[17]

This cinematic depiction of the dead returning points to a phenomenology of wounds crossing and surfacing within a posttraumatic landscape.[18] Throughout the series, depictions of the living and the dead reveal the fine line between them. And the encounters between them peel back layers of what is hidden, only to cover them up again. What is hidden is exposed, and what is exposed is hidden again. What is revealed is covered over, and what is covered over begins to break the surface, becoming visible, ever so slightly. Breaking the surface, wounds also transmit, traveling across and between surfaces—skin and earth. The returns in *Les Revenants* tell us that wounds are not localized on any one body but, instead, curiously cross bodies. This seemingly woundless return shifts attention to the wounds of the living that are made manifest at a later point. This insight resonates therapeutically, as clinical work with trauma suggests that wounds must surface in order for them to be addressed.

While the "quasiresurrected" figures at first are not marked, their returns surface wounds, thus bringing unattended losses to the surface of the skin. Recalling the exchange between Sandrine and Jerome in the grief group, this phenomenon of wounds surfacing and receding speaks to life in its *continuer*.[19] The term *continuer* attests to unintegrated loss and its continuing impact in the present. A companion term is "ongoingness," which acknowledges that the impact of violence carries into the present. Instead of appearing as marks on the dead, wounds surface *in* life to reveal dimensions of life that may not have been accounted for—dimensions that we could identify in terms of the afterlife of trauma. These "invisible wounds" are active, although not recognized as such; they remain below the surface of life. When the dead return, the wounds rise to the surface, manifesting pain, loss, and grief. The returns foreground possibilities for healing; they surface wounds instead of repressing or erasing them.

Resurrection appears as an invitation to weave a new kind of body, less pure, pristine, and perfected than the resurrected body often presented in the tradition. It appears as an invitation to multilayered witness, involving senses beyond seeing, which in the tradition became the dominant sense to convey truth, faith, and knowledge of God. As the wounds of history return, reappearing in the present, Christian theology might offer a vision of resurrection that addresses these wounds, precisely because the wounds return. In each of the gospel accounts, the wounds reappear. Jesus stands before the disciples, returning with the marks of death still visible. "Touch them," he says.

This invitation, while inscribed in the biblical narrative in the Gospel of John, has been repeatedly erased in the interpretive tradition. This erasure is enacted precisely through the claims that Christians make about resurrection. Unless these dynamics of erasure are exposed and countered, claims about resurrection will be enacted apart from the bodily realities of suffering. What we witness with the priest in *Les Revenants* is an erasure of wounds enacted through claims about resurrection. There is an opportunity to speak about wounds that remain in life and yet a missed opportunity, as enacted through this encounter.

The priest cannot, or will not, account for these returns. And in his refusal, he fails to speak to this dimension of life. Thomas exposes the church's teachings, rendering them much like the butterfly behind the glass casing; it is made to look alive when, in fact, it has been dead for an immeasurable period of time. And yet the biblical presentation of the resurrected Jesus looks curiously like what is taking place in the village. Presenting the returns within the framework of Christianity (as is evident by the frequent visits to the church), the series does not reject the framework outright; instead, it highlights the insufficiency of its straightforward transmission and reception. While the biblical story has been deployed in the direction of truth (and the transmission of truth), this series presses the meaning of the story in another direction—toward questions of goodness.

At the heart of the Thomas scene in *Les Revenants* is a question that is not included in the biblical account. In the quick banter between the two, when Thomas asks about Jesus' resurrection, he follows with this: "Is it for good or not?" The priest responds, "The question is irrelevant." Thomas' concern is not a matter of belief but about whether the biblical story of resurrection is good. He is not interested in the truth of the Christian message but in whether it can speak meaningfully to what is taking place. The question of goodness precedes the question of belief. Will it bring about goodness? The fact that this question is deemed irrelevant is at the root of the failure of the narrative to speak. Thomas reaches for the narrative, but the priest is unable to see past truth in order to address the question of goodness. In fact, it is this dismissal that confirms the irrelevance of religion to what is taking place. Instead, the question of goodness presses for a different reading of resurrection, one that accounts for the phenomenon of surfacing wounds.

The surfacing of wounds evokes a posttraumatic landscape, bringing to the forefront the challenges of wounds remaining in life. Thomas wants to know whether the promise of resurrection can speak in the present: Is the story for good? Will it bring about goodness? The meaning of the return of the dead is opened up and turned toward what it may say about life in its *continuer*. Perhaps the dead return to surface wounds, as a way of insisting that wounds are not healed. They surface wounds not to harm but to provide the possibility for healing. Whatever resurrection is, it must take account of this manifestation. This insistence on the part of *Les Revenants* repositions persons in respect to wounds. Situating us at these points of crossing between the living and the dead, the animate and the inanimate, what do the returns reveal?

The image of invisible wounds rising to the surface is a visual image for the work of trauma healing. Wounds surfacing in life are foreboding images, but they are also productive ones. The same is true, I argue, for resurrection wounds. The return of wounds *in life* figured on the body of Christ can be a site of surfacing. The question is whether this surfacing is for good. This book reapproaches a familiar story in the Christian tradition and asks whether it can speak to the phenomenon of the *continuer*, of the afterlife within life. The show narrates a critical departure from a particular theistic conception of resurrection, and yet it also provides a route to return to it. This vision is not a return to supernaturalism, and neither is it a rejection of it. Instead, it maintains interest in the story for the sake of something else. Can this story, Thomas asks, make sense of wounds surfacing and crossing in life? It extends an invitation to reconceive of resurrection.

John 20:19-28

¹⁹*When it was evening on that day, the first day of the week, and the doors of the house where the disciples had met were locked for fear of the Jews, Jesus came and stood among them and said, "Peace be with you."* ²⁰*After he said this, he showed them his hands and his side. Then the disciples rejoiced when they saw the Lord.* ²¹*Jesus said to them again, "Peace be with you. As the Father has sent me, so I send you."* ²²*When he had said this, he breathed on them and said to them, "Receive the Holy Spirit.* ²³*If you forgive the sins of any, they are forgiven them; if you retain the sins of any, they are retained."*

²⁴*But Thomas (who was called the Twin), one of the twelve, was not with them when Jesus came.* ²⁵*So the other disciples told him, "We have seen the Lord." But he said to them, "Unless I see the mark of the nails in his hands, and put my finger in the mark of the nails and my hand in his side, I will not believe."*

²⁶*A week later his disciples were again in the house, and Thomas was with them. Although the doors were shut, Jesus came and stood among them and said, "Peace be with you."* ²⁷*Then he said to Thomas, "Put your finger here and see my hands. Reach out your hand and put it in my side. Do not doubt but believe."* ²⁸*Thomas answered him, "My Lord and my God!"* ²⁹*Jesus said to him, "Have you believed because you have seen me? Blessed are those who have not seen and yet have come to believe."*

The Incredulity of Saint Thomas by Caravaggio, ca. 1601–1602.
Oil on canvas, 107 cm × 146 cm. Sanssouci, Potsdam, Germany.

1

Erasing Wounds
John Calvin and the Problem of the Resurrected Body

Introduction

The wounds appear within a context of uncertainty, fear, and doubt. Crucified just days earlier by the Roman officials, his body was wrapped in burial linens and placed in the tomb. His followers, filled with grief, were not only uncertain about their future; they were now questioning the past. His ministry had been powerful, but short. Instead of ushering in a new reality, the present seemed to be closing in on them. These are curious wounds. Marks appear on a body that has just passed through a wall. Still shaken by the events and filled with grief, they locked the doors to make sure that no one would find them. And yet he appears from out of nowhere, standing in front of them. He greets them with words of peace. And before they can say anything in return, he shows them his wounds. The display is followed with celebration and then with instructions, as if he is guiding them again, extending an earlier time with them into another time. He breathes on them—not an exhale released from the cross, but a holy exchange of air, as a spirit is released into the room. They watched him die. Now they witness his return.

They were not all together when he appeared for the first time. Thomas had been somewhere else. But when they told him what happened, he had more questions. It is hard to pass on a story like that. Not being there, he wanted to see for himself. It did not seem real—or even possible. When he returns a second time, eight days later, they are gathered in the room, doors locked. Thomas is with them, and this time the ghostly figure speaks to him directly. He tells him to come closer, to reach out his finger, and to touch his side. The wounds are not just for show. They must now be touched. Thomas responds, exclaiming, "My Lord and my God." The apparition is named.

The Gospel of John features wounds. Distinct from the apparition stories in the other gospels, the appearances to Mary, the disciples, and then more particularly to Thomas, each raises questions about the status of Jesus' body. Earlier, Mary was instructed not to touch him, and yet Thomas is invited to touch. Jesus moves through walls, and yet he cooks a meal for the disciples. He is there and yet somehow not there. The Johannine writings play with our senses, displacing seeing as a primary means of witnessing the events taking place.

Postdeath wounds are curious figures of encounter. They are marks of his past suffering, but in this gospel they seem to be oddly alive in the present. They produce a curious mixture of blood and water when the centurion pierces his side immediately following his death. Water, throughout the gospel accounts, has symbolized life, but together with the blood, there is a mixture of fluids coursing through his body. The wounds mark the place where the nails were positioned, but there is something odd taking place on the surface of skin. The wounds of death are now on display, but the Johannine gospel does not tell us whether they are open or closed, exposed or sutured.

Handed down in the Christian tradition, the encounter with Thomas became known as the doubting Thomas story.[1] When Thomas encounters the risen Christ, he is moved to faith by the miracle of the resurrection. His doubt is overcome. And it became a central story for conveying the truth of the resurrection. Thus, the apparition stories lose their mystery.

In the Christian tradition, the Thomas encounter is often treated as a capstone on a case of mistaken identity. Those who have been mistaken will be moved by the truth demonstrated in the display of wounds. The gospel writers emphasize that the moments leading to his death are filled with faulty assumptions about his identity. Though tried as a criminal, even Pontius Pilate struggles to identify him—"Where are you from?"—yet Jesus refuses to reply. And even those closest to him seem to mistake him for someone else. But Thomas will not be fooled. Truth breaks through in his testimony, and he recognizes the resurrected Christ as such. His exclamation has been interpreted as an overcoming of his doubt. Triumph. Truth. Certainty. Conclusion. It is a perfect ending to a case of mistaken identity. With Thomas' words, the case is closed.

But this is a ghost story, and the spirits do not seem to be contained in John's account; in fact, they seem to multiply. The paraclete (Greek, *parákletos*) and the Holy Ghost are in the air, in the breath. The gospel writers tell us that this story is not completed and, in fact, can never be. All the books cannot contain the stories of the events that took place.[2] This means that the ghosts may still be out there. And if so, are they for good?

In the account, it never tells us whether Thomas actually touches the wounds. The touch is implied. And yet interpreters place Thomas' finger in varying proximity to the body of the resurrected Jesus. A visual tradition grows out of this story, transporting this encounter from text to the imagination of viewers. Rembrandt depicts Jesus with beams of light encircling him and Thomas' body bending back, his palm up as if he had retracted his outstretched finger when shown the wound.[3] There are many present, but the light emanating from Jesus does not reach all of them. Rembrandt suggests that Thomas declines the invitation to touch. In Giorgio Vasari's sketch of the scene, Christ embraces Thomas, but in the later painting, Christ shows Thomas the wounds.[4] These paintings have interpretive power, taking the biblical story and transforming Thomas into a figure through whom our deepest curiosities and deepest confessions can be expressed. They have also been used to communicate ecclesial aims. Commissioned at the time of the Counter-Reformation, Vasari was instructed to emphasize the leap of faith that Thomas made from unbelief to belief, from ordinary disciple to saint.

In Caravaggio's famous rendering of this passage, Thomas and two others lean in, as his finger presses into Jesus' flesh.[5] Caravaggio depicts Thomas' finger inserted into the wound of the risen Jesus. Jesus grips his hand, as if guiding his entrance. While other visual representations emphasize the gap between the finger and the body, Caravaggio presents a simultaneously intrusive and intimate scene. Placing the biblical disciples—and viewers—at eye level with the wound, he paints an almost glassy-eyed Thomas who seems to be staring past the wound, as if not to see it.

Theologians writing within the Christian tradition have also strategically positioned Thomas' finger. The biblical commentary is a common genre for theological articulation, as the theologian works to

interpret the meaning of the biblical text. Preachers within this tradition reach for these commentaries, to assist them in presenting the
ancient text to their contemporary followers. The transmission of the
ancient story continues, moving between past and present, unearthing
meaning by returning to the resurrection stories. The space between
the finger and body is an interpretive space in Christian theology in
which the meaning of Jesus' return is forged.

The wounds are prominent in this encounter, and yet the wounds
are often erased in the history of Christian interpretation. The wounds
come to stand for something else. Through a close reading of John
Calvin's interpretation of resurrection wounds, I display how, through
a reading of one theologian, the wounds disappear. Calvin is clearly
nervous about the wounds. A close reading of Calvin's commentary
exposes a certain logic operating in Christian interpretations of resurrection: the wounds present a problem to accounts of resurrection,
which need to perform certain truths. By revealing what is at stake in
Calvin's interpretation of this passage, I show how the wounds recede.
I begin with a close reading of Calvin in order to set the stage for
exploring the significance of resurrection wounds in our contemporary
setting. It is the phenomenon of returning wounds in trauma that can
call us to a rereading and to rethink the meaning of this return when
the wounds remain and are engaged by the disciples.

Calvin's Thomas

Before he wrote his biblical commentaries, John Calvin spoke them. A
leading figure in the sixteenth-century Protestant Reformation, Calvin
preached his reflections on this passage and others to those gathered
in the churches and streets of Geneva.[6] Before he put his comments
into written form, he spoke them. His commentary, *Commentaire sur
L'Évangile selon Saint Jean*, was published in 1553, seventeen years after
the *Institutes of the Christian Religion* in 1536.[7] Calvin gave great primacy
to hearing as the sense through which truths are received. This mode
of interpretation is significant given the primacy that Calvin gives to
hearing in his reading of this particular scene in John 20. Calvin's reading of the Thomas scene reflects theological investments in reading this
account, as we witness him folding his insights into Christian teachings
about resurrection and the afterlife. Concerns, warnings, and polemics
operate within his reading. He wants to turn attention away from the
sensuality of touch and instead emphasize that the process of faith is

nurtured by way of hearing the word and responding to it. Hearing takes precedence over touching.

Calvin's interpretation is distinctive for his reading of the wounds, and his instructions to his hearers are vivid and clear: do not place your faith in the wounds. They do not yield truth. Wake up, slumbering disciples, Calvin implores his listeners. While modern readers are used to ascribing doubt to Thomas as his distinctive attribute, Calvin depicts Thomas as a lazy, reluctant, obstinate disciple, one who, contrary to the vision of him as the intellectual, is "dull of apprehension." Calvin assigns a range of negative attributes to Thomas, and he presents him as a cautionary tale to persons of faith. The implication is that some of them might be like Thomas, who was once sharp in his faith but, over time, had forgotten the teachings of the faith. All of the disciples suffer from "weak faith," as they struggle to recognize the resurrected Christ standing in their midst. Opening his analysis of the chapter, Calvin writes, "It may be strange, however, that he does not produce more competent witnesses," and he goes on to speak about Jesus' appearance to Mary.[8] The incompetence and weakness of the disciples is a persistent theme in his commentary; Mary, Peter, and the others may have had zeal, but they had little or no faith. They were in a state of confusion and were subject to "carnal stupidity."[9] Some are slower to believe than others, and Thomas is representative of the ones who need more convincing. Throughout the commentary, the disciples stand for Calvin's "Congregation" who, like Thomas, struggle to believe in the resurrection. Those whose faith is strong are able to believe with little sensory assistance. The exalted route to faith is to believe through verbal testimony, since, for Calvin, hearing is the sense most proper to faith. Blessed are those who believe on the basis of the "bare word," to those who do "not depend on carnal views or human reason."[10]

The disciples, he tells us, are satisfied with "half of his resurrection," as if settling for an earthly vision when the fullness of the resurrection was available to them. In his comments on John 20:17 (Jesus' reference to his ascension), Mary is one whose hand pulls him to the earth rather than allowing him to rise to his place at the right hand of the Father. Desiring to "enjoy his presence in the world," the women (and here Mary is the representative of all the women witnesses) deny themselves the glory of the resurrection. There is some hope in collective witness, as he displays in his reading of the events in the Upper Room. They are able to sharpen and encourage each other in faith.

The wounds are first mentioned when Jesus appears to the crowd gathered in an enclosed room. His entrance is mysterious—no doors were opened—and he greets them with a word of peace. He then shows them his wounds. Calvin explains this disclosure: "It was necessary to add this confirmation, that by all these methods they might be fully assured that Christ has risen."[11] Using juridical language, as is common to Calvin, he says that the witnesses to resurrection need more proof, more evidence, that Jesus is the one he has claimed to be. John's aim, according to Calvin, is to accumulate evidence so that even the most slumbering of disciples can come to belief. He repeats terms such as "confirm," "secure," and "certain" to describe the aim of the gospel writers.

Thomas is not present at the first appearance of the resurrected Christ. Commenting on Thomas' entrance in verse 24, Calvin immediately tells us that Thomas' unbelief serves to shore up the "faith of the godly."[12] The gospel writers emphasize Thomas' unbelief in order to highlight and confirm faithfulness. His depiction of Thomas serves, in many ways, to show us the characteristics of weak faith—"dullness of apprehension," "obstinacy," and pride.[13] Thomas asks to "see in his hands the print of the nails," and it is clear that this request is an affront that conveys that Thomas has poor judgment, judgment that relies on the senses rather than on faith.

According to Calvin, Thomas is not satisfied with hearing about the resurrection. He does not believe by hearing from the others that Jesus has risen. Instead, he asks to *see*. This is already a mark against Thomas, who in Calvin's estimation acts inappropriately, displaying both obstinacy and stupidity.[14] Calvin writes, "The stupidity of Thomas was astonishing and monstrous; for he was not satisfied with merely beholding Christ but wished to have his hands also as witnesses of Christ's resurrection."[15] Calvin says that Christ does not blame Thomas, although Calvin's description reflects his own judgment upon Thomas. Because of his slowness in coming to belief, the means by which Thomas is brought to belief are radical; Calvin says that he needed to be "violently drawn to faith by the experience of the senses."[16] The damning picture of Thomas pales in comparison to Calvin's depiction of the women disciples, but it is damning nonetheless.[17]

According to Calvin, the appearance to Thomas and the display of wounds is God's accommodation to those, like Thomas, who need assistance in order to restore belief. Consistent with Calvin's theology,

[handwritten marginal note: why is that serious? more proof of reality of wound than... having over ...]

God accommodates Godself to human knowledge using appropriate means to communicate with humanity. This accommodation is obviously operative in this reading: "That our faith may arrive at the eternal Divinity of Christ, we must begin with that knowledge which is nearer and more easily acquired."[18] Calvin uses the visual spacing between Thomas' body and the wounds to make the point that some need to be closer to his body to believe. Some cannot accept the fact of Divinity except through greater proximity to his humanity. For those, like Thomas, who are operating according to "sensual judgment,"[19] they will be accommodated. The farther away from the body when you recognize that Jesus is indeed God, the better. Thomas' finger, then, is the finger of disbelief, extended as a sign that he is lacking in faith.

This scene is presented as bound up in providing the disciples with what they really should have been able to obtain by other means. God provides the visual and the tactile when in fact the more ardent and faithful only need to rely on the word(s). The implication throughout his commentary is that the disciples should have been able to believe without relying on the senses. The display of wounds is the sensual means by which God moves people to believe. God really should not have to provide proof, confirmation, but we need it, as God caters to our weakness. Commenting on John 20:26, in which Jesus invites Thomas to touch him, Calvin writes, "When Christ so readily yields to the improper request of Thomas . . . and invites him to feel and touch," we learn about Christ's willingness to do all he can to lead us to faith.[20] While Thomas should have been ashamed to need this sensual assistance, Calvin reports that Thomas is shameless. Again, he is not a skeptic so much as an ingrate.

Commenting on verse 26 in which Christ invites Thomas to touch the wounds, Calvin proceeds with a rather scathing portrait of Thomas, who is contemptuous when he should be ridden with shame and guilt; he is irreverent and proud, when he should behold Christ in awe and humility. He likens Thomas to someone who is mentally deranged, who is not in his right mind. Yet the most common way that he speaks about Thomas' lack of faith is in reference to sleep. It is as if Thomas has been slumbering, and, during the course of his encounter with the risen Christ, he suddenly wakes up. "Thomas awakes at length, though late," Calvin tells us, and, as persons who have been mentally deranged commonly do when they come to themselves, they shout. Thomas exclaims, in astonishment, *"My Lord and my God!"*[21] It is an abrupt moment, signaled by the short exclamation. Faith has not been extinguished in him, but it had been buried so deep that he was unable to access it. It was as if faith were dormant within him. Many are like Thomas, Calvin notes, who "grow wanton for a time";[22] they lose their way. And here, within the description of Thomas' moment of recognition, Calvin speaks to those who have wandered away from God. Their return to faith is foreshadowed by Thomas, whose confession sets out a path to make things right again.

The wounds are merely instrumental in leading Thomas to believe. Most of Calvin's attention is focused on Thomas' proclamation, "My Lord and my God." The doctrinal investment in this narrative is evidenced here. Calvin transports Thomas to the fourth century, presenting his proclamation of belief within these earlier christological controversies, which were concerned with clarifying the nature of Christ as both human and divine. He writes, "This passage is abundantly sufficient for refuting the madness of Arius."[23] Arius is the chief articulator of the dissenting position, in claiming that the Son, although the highest of all creatures, is still distinct in nature from the Father—thus, not fully divine. The fact that Calvin reads this history into this gospel account says to his listeners that Thomas' recognition of the risen Christ is in line with a particular strand of church teachings—namely, that which has come to be understood as orthodox. Thus, Thomas is not only a model for belief; he is an exemplar of right belief. Thomas declares, according to Calvin, "the unity-of-person in Christ."[24]

But the nature or status of the wounds in Calvin's commentary is drawn into an extensive polemic that Calvin is waging against the papists. He is making a case against the material piety of Catholic faith and the doctrine of transubstantiation (Christ's real presence in the Eucharist). In his reading of resurrection wounds, Calvin is warding off both the spectrality and the materiality of this resurrected figure. When working on the passage about Jesus appearing to the disciples through the locked doors, Calvin does not want to acknowledge the ghostliness of this appearance. While he does not want to deny that the divine is capable of moving through doors, he cautions, "And yet I am far from admitting the truth of what the papists assert, that the body of Christ passed through the shut doors."[25] Calvin tells us that we should not place emphasis on the "measures" that Christ takes to confirm our belief. He does not deny the measures, but he thinks the papists lose sight of the truth by focusing on the measures themselves, by attributing significance to the sensory, the bodily, and the material.

As readers, we enter into ongoing conversations and concerns of Calvin's that inform his reading of resurrection wounds. And these are especially important to know about, because they help to make sense of why the wounds cannot remain on the body. His interpretation is shaped in two distinctive ways. First, Calvin is wary of depictions of the resurrection as a fantastical event. While not denying its miraculous nature, he is conscious of those who would interpret the events in imaginative and fantastical ways. We can see this in his interpretation of the ghostly entrance of Jesus to the Upper Room. He notes that the Evangelist "does not say that he entered through *the shut doors*,"[26] in order to make the point that implication that he passes *through* the doors is an improper reading. The papists, he says, want to emphasize that the body resembled a spirit and, more than this, that the body was infinite and "could not be confined to any one place."[27] Rhetorically, Calvin registers impatience, even annoyance, with the emphasis that the papists put on the spectral elements of the text.

He spends a good deal of time emphasizing that the only spirit present in the Upper Room is the Holy Spirit, hence his long description of Jesus breathing on the disciples (v. 20). This act should be interpreted in connection to the gift of the Spirit: "Christ *breathes on* the Apostles: they receive not only the *breathing*, but also *the Spirit*."[28] When Calvin comments on verse 25, he does not mention that the Johannine writers have, again, made reference to the shut doors and to Jesus' appearance before the disciples. Calvin merely comments on the statement, "Unless I see in his hands the prints of the nails."[29]

In the role of commentator, Calvin carefully selects the portions of the gospel text to gloss. He omits verses that draw the reader's attention to the status of Jesus' body. In the accounts of the appearances of Jesus, he emphasizes the verbal invitations and responses between Jesus and Thomas. Moving from the focus passages, "Unless I see," to "Reach hither thy finger," to "My Lord and my God," Calvin controls the reading, leaving little room for the reader to speculate about Jesus' spectral entrance or Thomas' physical response to the invitation to touch the body.[30]

He clearly wants to downplay the ghostly and to say that these more fantastical elements should be understood within the broader intent of Christ's act to secure belief in his resurrection. Others seem to make more of these than they should, and he likens this to "childish trifling."[31] The derogatory references to fables and to childlike mindsets are prevalent in his interpretations of the resurrection appearances. They register attempts both to usurp the doctrine of creation and to provide fodder for belief in transubstantiation. The sacraments are at the fore of his warnings: "If we must believe without reserve all that we do not see, then every monster which men may be pleased to form, every fable which they may contrive, will hold our faith in bondage."[32] A certain reading of this passage leaves Calvin's readers vulnerable to superstition. Emphasis on Jesus' mode of entrance leads people down the wrong path. The priests misguide believers. He writes, "Most absurdly do the papists, on the other hand, torture this passage, to support their magical absolutions."[33] Simply stating Calvin's eucharistic concerns, the belief that the bread and the wine *become* the body is, as presented here, an exercise of fantasy and fable. From this perspective, it is clear why Calvin does not want to make much of the unusual means of Jesus' appearance.

While steering away from the spectral, Calvin also wants to steer away from emphasis on the material body. The Gospel of John presents images of the resurrected body as ghostly and fleshly. The wounds signal marked flesh. While Calvin will attempt to dematerialize these marks, he is doing so, again, within a polemic against the papists. The papists are prey to superstition, but they are also driven, he says, by their carnal feelings. What is interesting here is that Calvin likens the papists to the women disciples who remain weeping at the tomb. They will not be consoled, he says, and "are not entitled to great accommodation," because they "torment themselves by idle and useless weeping."[34] Calvin diminishes their concerns about the absence or presence of Jesus' body. The women remain near the sepulchre, he says, while the male disciples "return to the city." There is no worse insult, apparently, than accusing the papists of being women: weak in mind, prone to magical thinking, and carnal. Thomas is in bad shape, prone to "sensual judgments," but the women are not even capable of judgments and are weighed down by their carnal feelings. Christ, he says has amazing patience with these women, and bears with their faults, but Calvin also says that God withholds accommodation from them. There seem to be limits to which God will use sensual means to bring them to faith. Lurking behind his reading is not only the Eucharist, but also the material piety that is centered on the wounds of Christ. He associates Roman Catholicism with what is carnal; they remain, it seems, attached to a dead body, focused on the wounds of his passion.

Second, Calvin is aware that wounds on the resurrected body could support Arian claims of Jesus as a lesser divinity. Here, he references the christological controversies in the fourth century to interpret this gospel passage. Interpreting Thomas' profession, "My Lord and my God," he spends time explaining the "two clauses in this confession." These two clauses affirm that the resurrected Christ is both fully human and fully divine. With the recognition of the resurrected Christ as *Lord*, Thomas acknowledges the Christ who descended to us and humbled himself, manifesting himself in the flesh. The resurrected is the ascending and exalted Lord. The other clause pertains to divinity. Thomas, in his proclamation, immediately obtains "knowledge of his Divinity."[35] While Christ does attribute honor to the Father, he does not deny that he is God. The resurrected Christ accepts Thomas' profession that he is God. And, in this acceptance, the claims of Chalcedon are affirmed. He writes,

> But [Christ] plainly ratifies what Thomas said: and, therefore, this passage is abundantly sufficient for refuting the madness of Arius; for it is not lawful to imagine two Gods. Here also is declared the unity of person in Christ; for the same Jesus Christ is called both God and Lord.[36]

Calvin imagines Arius arguing that although Christ is a glorified creature, he is still a creature, evidenced by the marks on this flesh. In response, he interprets Thomas' proclamation as an affirmation of Western creedal affirmations. Thomas' proclamation is not only an affirmation of the resurrection; it is a Chalcedonian affirmation. "My Lord and my God" is, according to Calvin, a refutation of Arius' position on the nature of Christ. Belief in the resurrection is belief in the full divinity of Christ. Thomas perceives Christ to be God; this accounts for the culminating aha moment of Thomas and, for Calvin, the whole purpose of the Johannine gospel, which is to bring people to belief.[37] The wounds could raise Arian-like speculations if they remain on the body.

It will be important for Calvin to say that the material does not matter in and of itself. The wounds are instruments, but his hearers should not make more of them. The truth lies elsewhere. The encounter between Thomas and Jesus circles around this demand and invitation to see and touch the marks (*tupos*) of the nails on his hands and his side (*pleura*). *Tupos* means marks, prints, and an impression made by a blow of some kind. *Pleura* refers to ribs on the side of the body. What is interesting is that Calvin focuses his discussion of faith on the *tupos*, and deemphasizes, if not altogether excludes, discussion of the *pleura*. In downplaying the *pleura* and associating faith with *tupos*, Calvin places emphasis on the prints and marks, thus turning attention away from the material and turning to speak about the body of the resurrected Jesus as a tablet upon which God's word is inscribed. When Thomas comes to recognize Jesus as fully divine and fully human, he recognizes Jesus as the Word of God. To acknowledge these prints, as words, is to read the word of God.

But Thomas obstinately asks to thrust his hand in the *pleura*, an action which shows contempt for God's word. In fact, Thomas' hand is positioned as a fist in Calvin's writings, its move to the side a gesture of defiant contempt for the word of God. The extension of the finger to touch is the ultimate in sensuous judgments, so much so that the touch is portrayed here as Thomas' hatred of Christ as the Word of God. Calvin comments on the translation of *tupos* from the Greek, indicating that it can mean either print or place; variance in transcription here does not matter. The reader is free to choose, he indicates. And yet what is important to Calvin is that *tupos* is not fleshly and material. What is not included in Calvin's commentary is very telling. He does not include either Thomas' request to put his finger in the marks or the invitation to reach his hand into the body. By leaving out this aspect of the request and invitation, the commentator minimizes the attention the listeners or readers would pay to these more intrusive dimensions of the encounter. He excludes commentary on the two verses in which Jesus invites Thomas to see the *tupos* and thrust his hand into the *pleura*. By removing the invitation to touch, Calvin can avoid attributing any significance to it. He skips from interpreting verse 26 to verse 29, from Thomas' insistent request to Thomas' proclamation, "My Lord and my God."

We can see Calvin constructing a notion of faith in his reading of this passage, outlining what it is and what it is not. He continually insists that it is nothing about the materiality of the wounds that leads Thomas to the truth. This is what he says: "For in the side or hands of Christ he [Thomas] does not handle Christ's Divinity, but from those signs he infers much more than they exhibited."[38] Senses signal need and weakness, but they do not carry any truth in and of themselves:

> for it was not by mere touching or seeing that Thomas was brought
> to believe that Christ is God. . . . Faith cannot flow from a merely

experimental knowledge of events but must draw its origin from the word of God.[39]

Those who rely on the senses are weaker. It is as if Calvin is saying, blessed are those who do not need any proof, who do not need this "demonstration."[40] Touch and sight are sidelined here, and hearing is given primacy. Faith, he says, "springs from hearing."[41] It is only be relying on God's Word, by reading it and hearing it, that one comes to faith. This is a distinctively Protestant formulation of faith: the highest route to faith is through the word of God, both preached and read.[42]

SHAME

Erasing Wounds

Whence comes this, but because, after forgetfulness and deep sleep, he suddenly comes to himself?

—*Calvin*[43]

Thomas awakens, Calvin tells us. It is as if the seed of faith that lay dormant within him suddenly breaks the surface. As God's accommodation, as confirmation of Christ's identity as the Word of God, the *tupos* have served their purpose. The marks are not associated with skin, with flesh, and with carnality. But Calvin goes a step farther, claiming that the wounds no longer remain on the body of Christ after Thomas comes to faith. This is made clear in an earlier passage, in John 20:20, when he comments on Jesus showing the marks of the wounds to the larger group of disciples. He wants to make clear to his hearers that it is fitting for Christ to appear risen with wounds, but it is unfitting to think of the wounds remaining on Jesus' body. He writes,

> If any person think it strange and inconsistent with the glory of Christ, that he should bear the marks of his wounds even after his resurrection, let him first consider that Christ rose not so much for himself as for us; and, secondly, that whatever contributes to our salvation is glorious to Christ; for when he humbled himself for a time, this took nothing away from his majesty, and now, since those wounds, of which we are speaking, serve to confirm the belief of his resurrection, they do not diminish his glory.[44]

The marks of the wounds are God's accommodation to human weakness, and they are important insofar as they ensure our salvation. And yet he goes on to say this:

> But if any person should infer from this, that Christ has still the wounded *side* and the pierced *hands*, that would be absurd; for it is certain that the *use of the wounds was temporary*, until the Apostles were fully convinced that he was risen from the dead.[45]

Thomas, being convinced of Jesus' resurrection, no longer needs the wounds. They have served their purpose. At this point in Calvin's commentary, *the wounds disappear.*

Calvin's Thomas approaches the resurrected Christ after resisting the word about his resurrection. He represents many believers whose faith has grown weak and who need to be radically awakened to the truth. God provides additional evidence of the resurrection for those like Thomas. For Thomas, the encounter with Christ was a full sensory overload, and this is precisely what those who are weak in faith need; God goes to great lengths to accommodate human weakness. Christ's invitation to Thomas to see and touch the prints is a sign of God's accommodation and compassion for those who need more evidence. Thomas awakens to faith *by hearing* this invitation.

The wounds disappear with his proclamation. The wounds are instrumental in bringing Thomas to faith, but they have served their purpose. And we have glimpses of Calvin's motivations for insisting on their disappearance. The wounds could be cause for misunderstanding, leading both to a denial of Christ's divinity or to "monstrous" speculations about the resurrected body.[46]

In his reading of Thomas, the wounds become signs of God's accommodation, of God's lowering Godself to human limitation, but wounds are only necessary to bring about faith for those most limited. Those who are strong in faith will hear the word and believe. Reliance on wounds is what the papists foster, we can hear Calvin say. Thomas' fingers and hands—suggesting touch—form the thrusting fist of defiance, displaying contempt for God's word. Seeing and touching are subsumed under the central sense of hearing. The encounter between Thomas and Jesus, as narrated by Calvin, is not about wounds; it is about words. Can Thomas hear the word and read the inscriptions on the skin that is not really skin but, in fact, a canvas upon which the word of God is inscribed? In Calvin's commentary, his theological move is to emphasize the marks as inscriptions, thus steering hearers away from the notion of touching the wounds. Faith and belief are not tied to the wounds; they are tied to the word of God. According to Calvin, it is the fact that Thomas hears (not sees nor touches) that secures faith.

SHAME

Ascending with(out) Wounds

Calvin adds a curious component to his reading of the encounter between Thomas and the resurrected Jesus. He inserts Christ's ascension to heaven into his reading of the Gospel of John. This also becomes critical for thinking about Calvin's erasure of wounds. Once Thomas proclaims, "My Lord and my God," Thomas ascends with Christ into glory. Calvin writes,

> But *Thomas*, having acknowledged him to be *Lord*, is immediately carried upwards to his eternal Divinity, and justly; for the reason why Christ descended to us, and first was humbled, and afterwards was placed at the Father's right hand, and obtained dominion over heaven and earth, was, that he might exalt us to his own Divine glory, and to the glory of the Father.[47]

Thomas ascends with Christ. It is a striking moment in the text, a kind of beatific vision in which Thomas is drawn up into God's glory. He continues, "by the Christ Man, we are conducted to the God Man."[48] And Thomas' proclamation signals the completion of Christ's journey, from the humility of the incarnation to the glorious display of God's majesty.

Thomas' assertion of belief, as Calvin presents it, results in a rather radical vision of the believer's connection to Christ. Thomas is ejected from his setting and is drawn into the ascension of Christ into heaven. It is a strange and unexpected mystical moment in Calvin. Once Thomas proclaims belief, he is "carried upward to his eternal Divinity," with Christ.[49] This participation in his "Divine Majesty," as Calvin describes it, is the fruit of the resurrection. Christ descends to humanity in order that believers might rise with him to the "glory of his resurrection."[50]

In the other gospels, the resurrection appearances are followed by Christ's ascension into heaven. In this gospel, Jesus speaks about a heavenly home with many rooms, and he tells Mary that she cannot touch him because he is ascending, and yet there is no explicit account of Christ ascending into heaven. In fact, after the Thomas encounter, Jesus appears again to the disciples on the shores of the Tiberian sea, and Thomas is one of the disciples present there. So Calvin has Thomas ascending into heaven, while the narrative features him with his feet squarely placed on the ground, walking along the beach with others. The fact that Calvin inserts it into the gospel account displays his commitments to reading resurrection in terms of a heavenly ascent, with its promises located somewhere else.[51]

The heavenly vision inserted here also tells us why Calvin is committed to keeping the body of the resurrected Christ unmarked. Acknowledged to be the Christ, his royal status comes to the fore, as he assumes his place in heaven. Christ's destiny is highlighted here; he rises from his lowly birth in a stable upward to the glorious display of his majesty in heaven. As opposed to Augustine, who makes a place for wounds in heaven, Calvin features an ascending body without wounds.

The resurrected body cannot carry the marks forward, because the vision of heaven that Calvin presents requires a glorious body unmarked by human limitation. It aligns with Christ's identity to bear the marks, as he states, but there is no reason to carry them forward, given they are a means to an end that has already been accomplished. If Thomas were stronger in his faith, his ears better attuned to hear the word, he would not need to see or touch the wounds. Serving their purpose, the wounds remain, we might say, on earth, as the carnal traces of God's accommodation to human limitation.

And yet this woundless ascension is puzzling, given Julie Canlis' assertions about the importance of Christ's physicality in Calvin's vision of ascent. She writes, "For Calvin, Jesus' true 'flesh' in heaven functions just as it did here on earth: as a way of securing our full human participation in God. Jesus represents a creature fully in the dimension of God: the resurrection did not change his physicality into a spiritualized reality, but it was transposed."[52] She appeals to Calvin's discussion in the *Institutes* (IV.17.14), and states that the physicality is not compromised in Calvin, but that a difference is enacted. As a creature, Christ draws creatures into the divine life, and this human participation in the life of God continues, even after death.

It is not clear what constitutes this transposition. She continues,

> Ascension is primarily Christ's, yet his mission was to include us in his ascending return to the Father. Union with God is only through his body, his humanity, his "weakness." Ascent is with him and is "up" to his physicality, where he lives and reigns with the Father.[53]

Calvin's reading of Thomas supports this view of the believer's destiny. Canlis emphasizes that he is not advocating an escape from physicality and the body. Instead, the ascension is still physical. She says that Calvin insists that "Jesus' ascent into heaven was in the flesh" and that he ascended into heaven "*in human form*."[54] Although Jesus maintained human form, Calvin acknowledges that it was altered. Canlis writes, "Even Christ's glorified body, changed as it was, still has the physical limitations of a human body, 'contained in space, [having] its own dimensions and its own shape' (4.17.29)."[55]

This strong assertion of the body's importance in heaven seems out of step with insistence that the wounds must be left on earth, so to speak. If the resurrected and ascending Christ still has the limitations of the body, then why does Calvin insist that the wounds would not ~~EXACTLY~~ remain on the body that ascends into heaven? The affirmation of physicality seems to stop short of wounds. Countering charges that Calvin is dualistic (depicting a soul that ascends while the body is rooted to the earth),[56] Canlis appeals to Calvin's statements about physicality, saying that Calvin "heads off these worst dangers."[57] She says that he places "an *enfleshed* Jesus at the right hand of the Father" rather than an ethereal one. Calvin is disparaging those who "make a spirit out of Christ's flesh" (4.17.29).[58]

Why, then, would wounds not be the ultimate sign of limitation and humanity—marks of the human—that would affirm that the full range of humanity is, in the end, united with God? Two things are taking place in Calvin. He insists on Christ's physicality as part of the work of drawing believers into a new—and fuller—understanding of what it means to be human. Thomas is conducted upward with Christ, ascending to the heavens to be united with him. Christ's destiny is his destiny. Canlis emphasizes the importance of ascension as providing a future *for Thomas*. The promise of the ascension is "the *telos* of our humanity fulfilled."[59] Christ does not become less human but, instead, provides an expansive vision of the human. According to Canlis, "For Calvin, the Christian sense of the self is forever bound up with another—Christ—and it is this reality that redefines our self-understanding."[60]

And yet, he insists that wounds are incongruous with that vision. The glorified body must be human and thus marked by human limitation—marked but yet somehow unmarked. The Calvin of Canlis' presentation insists on the physicality, but the removal of wounds is still left unexplained. If the "physical limitations of a human body" remain in the ascension, then it would make sense to say that his wounds would remain as well. As marks of limitation, they can, according to this logic, still appear. And they, like other "limitations," would be transposed. The wounds would change. There is continuity of physicality, and yet it is marked by change through the work of the Spirit. But Calvin does not include them as markings in that way, as we see from his reading of the scene. Calvin removes the wounds instead of reconceiving them, because he does not consider them as marking humanity in any significant way.

The concept of transposed physicality—of change that occurs without shedding the physical—provides an opening to conceiving of wounds returning on the body of the risen Jesus. Canlis points to an opening within Calvin's thought that would make it possible for him to conceive of wounds as constitutive of the resurrection, as not merely instruments to secure belief but as marks of change that convey something important about resurrecting. This opening comes by way of Calvin's discussion of the role of the Spirit in the ascension. For Calvin, "the Spirit brings humanity to participate in *Christ's* ascent."[61]

The vision of the ascension, read in terms of the Spirit, is a vision of a creature transformed by being bound up with another. Calvin does not mention the Spirit in his vision of Thomas' ascension, but Canlis notes that the Spirit draws believers into a different reality. Calvin's vision of the ascension is thoroughly Trinitarian, which means that that the Spirit is actively at work, drawing the believer into a new life. Entering into heaven, the Son takes his place at the right hand of the Father, and he enjoys communion with both the Father and the Spirit. Ascending with Christ, the believer now participates in this communion, made possible by the Spirit. She writes, "It is the Spirit who brings us into a God-saturated life through his *engrafting us into the human, ascended Christ,* who is in the presence of the Father."[62] The ascension, in Calvin, also involves the Spirit's work of recreation.

We can no longer think in terms of a singular body ascending into heaven. The one who proclaims "My Lord and my God" is being transported—and transposed—and the process is one in which the person is now bound to Christ in a new way. Carried up with Christ, the believer is uniquely bound to him through the process of engrafting.[63] The Spirit attaches the believer to Christ, as if to stitch bodies together. The metaphor of engrafting conveys a process by which one thing is brought into another in order to draw its life from it. Horticulturally, engrafting is a process in which a scion is grafted onto a stronger, "better," strain of stock in order to sustain its life. The weaker plant draws energy and life from the stronger plant through this attachment, through its union with the other. The weaker not only is attached to the root; in time, it becomes part of the life of the other. The two become united through this incision. While the graft is wholly transformed, the source is not altogether what it was before the graft. Although Calvin uses this metaphor extensively, he gets into trouble with it because it implies that the believer not only becomes something different by attachment to Christ's body but also that Christ's body may be changed as well.[64]

Interestingly, the image of wounding and incision returns in this metaphor of engrafting, as if to counter Calvin's insistence that the wounds are no longer necessary. Yet reading this engrafting in terms of the Spirit, the wounds, as marks of human limitation, may be recreated as vehicles for continued participation in the life of God. According to Canlis, "Calvin saw the Spirit's work as that of transposition: taking what was in the realm of physicality and moving it into the Trinity's domain."[65] Transposed through the Spirit, the wounds could figure a new aspect of resurrection. If the work of the Spirit is to engraft believers into the life of God, then the wounds of resurrection could function meaningfully in Calvin's thought, without erasure. Wounds could be carried forward and drawn into a new moment. The wounds could have an afterlife.

To speculate about wounds remaining is beyond what Calvin offers. And yet to think of them as such might be to carry forward Calvin's theology of the Spirit. It might provide a way of giving significance to wounds. This depicts the Spirit's transposing work as moving the physical upward, as if out of the earthly realm and into the heavenly realm. The challenge and tensions of Calvin's writings at this point reflect how difficult it is to think in multiple directions. Thomas, for Calvin, ascends with Christ into an afterlife that is unfettered by human limitation. And yet he insists that the humanity of Christ is not shed but still functions to draw believers into fuller communion with God. To be engrafted into the life of God is a positive image of wounds for Calvin, and it describes a process by which believers are drawn into a different kind of living. They draw directly from Christ as their life source, because their identity is now bound to his. For Calvin, this graft forms a new identity *within* life and not simply beyond this life.

A theological space could open up for those gathered on the streets of Geneva. Listening to Calvin, they could begin to conceive of their lives differently. Calvin's inclusion of the ascension into this passage could offer a vision of inspirited flesh in the after-living. Like thread weaving together skin, the Spirit weaves a different configuration of humanity. These wounds feature connection and can foster a vision of interdependence—not out of this world, but within it. The domain of the Spirit may be rethought within life, and not simply beyond it. And while Calvin wants to relegate wounds to the earthly, carnal, and sensory, the wounds may come to life in a different way, even within Calvin's own writing.

While some of Calvin's reasons for removing wounds are contextually specific, his logic of locating the meaning of resurrection beyond, in another place, is consistent with the most familiar strains of the Christian tradition.[66] Resurrection wounds are temporary, reaching back to the crucifixion or forward to the afterlife. His insertion of the ascension in this text ties the resurrection appearances to a vision of the afterlife. Thus, resurrection is about another world and not this one. In turn, teachings about bodily resurrection throughout the Christian tradition have also pitted the natural against the supernatural, the earthly against the heavenly. The hope linked to the resurrection is the promise of bodies after physical death. It brings comfort to some to know that insofar as their destiny is attached to this resurrected body, they will share in the promised future with him. They will, like him, shed the wounds of this life and receive a perfected body in the afterlife. This shedding is also consistent with common perceptions of Christian interpretations of the body and the denial of the material world. It is consistent with a redemptive narrative that pulses through the Christian story and that permeates cultural scripts. Life, if it is to triumph over death, must not retain the marks of death. Wounds must be erased.

The space between the finger and the flesh, in Calvin's reading, is a space of enmity and disbelief. When Thomas reaches to touch, we imagine, in Calvin's best scenario, that it is the auditory that awakens him and not the touch. It is the voiced invitation and not the feel of skin that secures his belief. What is lost in this reading is the possibility that resurrection could speak in the meantime, in the in-between spaces of human life. This is underplayed in Calvin's commentary. Calvin thought that the wounds countered the promise of resurrection. And yet we can begin to glimpse a different trajectory for wounds via a theology of the Spirit's engrafting.

Ghosts

The biblical account is rich with significance for a vision of after-living. Life is being radically repositioned in the aftermath of death, without triumph but not without purpose. In Calvin's reading, Thomas ascends with Christ out of this world. He leaves the earthly and ascends to the heavenly. But the status of spirits and bodies in the resurrection accounts is not so tidy, neither in the Gospel of John nor in Calvin's own theology. Such clear-cut lines are hard to maintain.

In her reading of this passage, Mayra Rivera notes that the term "postresurrection" already positions the body of Jesus somewhere else. It places "this body beyond, rather than in-between life and death."[67] Positioning the body *beyond* the earth, she says, "occludes the spectrality" of the Johannine passage. In short, it fails to acknowledge the spirit(s) moving between. She asserts, "The Fourth Gospel's 'postresurrection' narratives are irresistible sites for a reading of ghostly encounters."[68] Calvin rejects the eeriness of the entrance into the Upper Room, because he is concerned that speculations about ghosts will lead to flights of fancy rather than to faith. Calvin will make sure to designate that the only Spirit in the room is the Holy Spirit, the Spirit in Trinitarian formulation. There is nothing haunting this room, according to Calvin. Rivera's critique about the occlusion of the spectral certainly applies to Calvin, and embedded in her statement is an awareness of theological investments in ways of reading. She notes that the Christian tradition, while it has the Holy Ghost at its center, is surprisingly bad at dealing with ghosts. It is the "ungraspable and uncontrollable character of haunting" that unnerves Christian theology, resulting in a Holy Ghost that is "now seen simply as the third *person* of a wholly divine trinity."[69]

The Fourth Gospel attests to movements that are stranger than they appear in Christian interpretations of them. The Johannine text is not a place of simple seeing but a site of complex and layered remembering. Rivera invites the ghosts into her reading of John. To welcome ghosts into our reading is to mark this passage for its capacity to witness to complex histories. Ghosts signal unsettled memories coming forward. According to Rivera, to linger with ghosts provides a more robust understanding of the power of memory, and of the Spirit as the "facilitator of memory."[70] Through her reading, she unearths the potential for the Christian narrative to attest to the problem of suppressed pasts, and of those whose pasts are often erased in the dominant narrative of history. These "apparition" accounts can speak to the complexities of memory by taking seriously the arrival of the Holy Spirit as a memory bearer. Guided by the writings of Gayatri Spivak, Rivera wants to think the haunting of the past (including the invisible wounds) together with the inspiration of a witness to "new possibilities."[71] Haunting is not simply negative. Ghosts do important work of resurrecting pasts in order to heal them.

Contemporary reflections on hauntology and spectrality offer a way of thinking about an ethical relationship with history that is figured by ghosts.[72] This ethical dimension also appears in the trauma literatures, suggesting that the phenomenon of reliving the past versus remembering it, and of awakening to a past that is not fully known, requires the presence of witnesses. Ghosts "presence" the past in this way. Avery Gordon's references to ghosts and haunting are similar, in that she speaks about haunting as instances of repetition when what is familiar becomes unfamiliar, when there is an alteration in the familiar that causes us to lose our bearings.[73] When something haunts, what was considered to be over is suddenly present again—when the "over-and-done-with comes alive, when what's been in our blind spot comes into view."[74] It signals a different orientation to the present, and even demands it. She writes, "The ghost, as I understand it, is not the invisible or some ineffable excess. The whole essence, if you use that word, of a ghost is that it has real presence and demands its due, your attention."[75]

Haunting, then, is not mere repetition of the past but a return of it that is purposeful. Gordon distinguishes haunting from trauma: "But haunting, unlike trauma, is distinctive for producing a something-to-be-done."[76] According to Gordon, the ghosts return to demand justice in the present. Thinking of this return not as a repetition of the past but as marking a change without the erasure of wounds may contribute to Canlis' vision of the work of the Spirit. The Spirit marks a change (transposition) in physicality rather than a departure from it. This process may provide a way of interpreting the Fourth Gospel in which the one whom the disciples had known (to be dead) returns—"comes alive"—in a form both familiar and not. The Holy Ghost of the Fourth Gospel may haunt in this way. This does not lead to superstition, as Calvin fears, but, instead, leads to rich reflections on how past memories, particularly marked by suffering, instantiate *in the present*. The Holy Ghost, summoned and breathed into the disciples, brings the past alive in the present in order to reconstitute life. The somatic dimension is so often dismissed, but the Johannine affirmation is clear: this Spirit, promised to the disciples, will not operate from outside of them but rather from within them.[77]

Flesh

The material and the spiritual are often read in opposition to each other. But the resurrection scene in the Gospel of John positions them together. Rivera insists that this gospel repeatedly interlaces the material and the spiritual by featuring a dynamism between spirit, flesh, and word. This is often covered over by the negative history of flesh common to Christian interpretation. She retrieves the concept of flesh, affirming the very aspects of flesh that have worried Christian interpreters such as Calvin. Flesh is changeable and impermanent. It is earthy and elemental. The wounds, for Calvin, signal each of these things, which adds to his concerns about giving them theological weight in his reading of the resurrection account. But Rivera would say that Calvin's concerns are not necessarily biblical, at least not according to her reading of the Johannine gospel. Evoking images of travel, transport, and malleability in her reading of the Gospel of John, Rivera presents flesh in positive and productive terms.

Flesh is distinct from body. "Body," she writes, "commonly denotes an entity complete in itself and visible to those around it. In contrast, flesh is conceived as formless and impermanent, crossing the boundaries between the individual body and the world."[78] Flesh is what flows between bodies and the world and also what links the two. Developing the vision of flesh, both in the Johannine gospel and in a variety of literatures, Rivera builds a case for flesh as profoundly receptive and yet ungraspable at some level: "Flesh is dynamically constituted through all of these processes of exchange and transformation—between bodies, between a body and the physical structures it inhabits, by the elements in which all bodies move and have their being."[79]

Contrary to the notion that flesh is reduced to a materiality that must be shed and escaped (i.e., Thomas must ascend out of it), Rivera draws out a notion of flesh as an affirmation of the connection between bodies and the world. It is to be embraced. Flesh binds individual bodies to a world. Flesh is marked by the world and by its various processes of life and death. Flesh attests to a way of being constituted in relationship with everything that is around us. As Rivera writes, "Flesh is a constitutive relation to the world—a condition for corporeal survival and flourishing as well as the source of its vulnerability."[80] It is precisely a Johannine (continuous) return to flesh that works against the temptation to abandon flesh.

Her reading of flesh underscores a basic insight of trauma, that violence, as experienced by persons and communities, renders us more vulnerable to each other. Perhaps trauma rolls back the curtain of our assumptions about autonomy, exposing this "fleshy" insight: that we are not immune from the processes of the world but, in fact, profoundly subject to them. In relation to trauma, this underscores the impact that violence has on us. Her descriptions of flesh thus bear a kind of traumatic sensibility. A retrieval of the notion of flesh does not just underscore the negative aspects of this; this vision of flesh offers a different route for engaging human life. If we pay attention to flesh, it can attune us to life as interdependent and interrelated. The stakes of this retrieval come through in her layered reading of flesh. Flesh positions us in relation to bodies, our own and others, with attention to attunement and care.

Thinking of Jesus' return in terms of a marked *body*, we see him as one subjected to the socio-material realities of his day. He was crucified under Roman imperial rule. This history is singular, in that he entered history and was subject to it. But this is not the whole account. The Johannine prologue also presents him in incarnational terms, as the eternal Word taking on flesh. If we read his return in terms of marked *flesh*, the history is not just singular but collective. His entrance into history affirms all that is fleshly, but also moves it toward its fullness. We can read his invitation to Thomas as an invitation to come into a different relationship to the world. Resurrection wounds are not simply marks of limitation. They are reminders to Thomas of an identity that is both responsive and responsible to something larger than himself. It is not an invitation for Thomas to escape the world but, instead, to come into a different relationship to it.

We can envision the surface of skin as a dynamic surface. Real histories of suffering surface in this body. But this body is never simply one. This is the truth of marked flesh. When he meets the disciples in the Upper Room and displays his wounds to them, he offers an invitation to glimpse and touch the flesh of the world.

Developing the figure of resurrection wounds with an eye to afterliving (expressed via Rivera as the exigencies of creaturely life) requires that we retain a connection between the ghostly and the material. Rivera's appeal to ghosts and flesh reflects her way of reading the interactions between spirit, flesh, and word in the Gospel of John. Just as Rivera listens to ghosts, she claims that the Gospel of John attests to a generative connection between spirit and flesh. Calvin is concerned that believers will be misguided by attention to the body of Jesus and to his wounds. Rivera instead allows us to read the Thomas encounter in a different direction. Thomas is not carried away from flesh but toward it. His recreation is a reorientation *to* the world.

Conclusion

Calvin presents this scene as a case of mistaken identity. He reads Thomas' proclamation as closure, as attesting to the truth. Case closed. And in so doing, Calvin forecloses the possibilities of interpreting this encounter in the midst of the ongoingness of life. Thus these apparition stories lose the capacity to testify to dimensions of experience that are much more about the between than the beyond. To prevent this loss, we must attend to these apparition stories without springing the body into the beyond. Lingering at the "seam of the past and the present," yields something distinctive.[81] And spirits are conjured up in this space. The challenge in this apparition story is not to think of spirits as opposed to flesh but to read both together.

What is unique about this apparition story is that spirits are not on the side of the dead and flesh is not on the side of the living. Instead, both are alive. The invitation to think with ghosts is an invitation to approach this familiar text in which the figure of return is on the side of both the dead and the living, both spirit and flesh. Calvin's concern about the fantastical and the fleshly represents an inability to see the wounds, the marks, in relationship to both. In a sense, Calvin is right. To think either of these exclusively is to miss the significance of what is taking place. And yet to think both together requires moving outside the logic that Calvin offers.

In Calvin's reading, we witness what happens to one appearance story when interpreted by one theologian. The spectrality and the materiality are a problem for Calvin, so they are minimized to the point where both the ghostliness and the fleshliness become matters of unfaithfulness. His treatment of wounds and his assertion that they are only temporary display concerns about what is passing away and the need to root faith in what is eternal, permanent, and lasting. In disparaging hearers from reflection on spirits returning through peculiar means, Calvin may fail to read this text on a level that matters to him— the pastoral level. In providing assurance of everlasting life, he does not provide his listeners a theological space to account for the continuation of life marked by death. And in this sense he may not provide room for grief, mourning, and loss. The women remain weeping outside the tomb, clinging to what is not there.

There is an invitation to inhabit more precarious territory in our reading. And while the doctrine of resurrection has been largely focused *beyond*, it has offered important insights about grief, mourning, and about how suffering is and should be approached.[82] It has shaped the ways in which persons release those whom they love and has guided them in understanding the passing of time. It offers instructions about tending to bodies—about touch and tears. Texts such as Gregory of Nyssa's *On the Soul and Resurrection* teach us that the discourse of resurrection is as much about the living as about the dead. In fact, it is a model for displaying critical questions about how to approach death, as Gregory and Macrina embark on a conversation about resurrection within the immediate context of their brother Basil's death. It is not just his future that is at stake, but what it means to continue on without him—to live beyond his death. The importance of "preaching" resurrection, if we think about Calvin's audience, is as much an articulation of life as it is a meditation on death. The weight and feel of transitions is difficult to capture in writing, yet "the Holy Ghost bears the marks of its relations to death and loss," Rivera writes.[83]

Calvin, by locating the meaning of this appearance in the *beyond*, fails to give meaning to an important juncture in which things are shifting. There is a crossing of death and life that takes place here. And spirits are moving. The paraclete, the Spirit promised before the crucifixion, is arriving, but the time is not specified. Jesus, who identifies himself as the other paraclete, appears, available to the senses and yet not. He breathes the Holy Ghost into them. And the scene recalls another in which the prophet Ezekiel is called to summon the breath-spirit (*ruah*) in the valley of dry bones. When he calls out, life returns to the bones, and flesh reconstitutes. Breath, synonymous with spirit, animates the bones, as sinews and flesh cover the bones with skin.[84] This interanimation at the juncture of death and life is both spiritual and material.

The danger in erasing these wounds is that the erasure occludes a testimony to what is most difficult about traumatic histories, whether personal or collective: that the wounds remain. And yet to reorient the logic of wounds toward the after-living requires care and attention. To think about these wounds differently is to draw from Calvin's thought for what Calvin could not bring into view. Resurrection wounds provide a curious constellation for conceiving of life that is marked by wounds but recreated through them.

2

Touching Wounds
Macrina's Scar and the Balm of Resurrection Flesh

Introduction

Near the end of Gregory of Nyssa's fourth-century hagiography (*Vita*) of his holy sister, Macrina, Vetiana, an attendant to the burial preparations, admonishes Gregory to draw closer to observe a mark on his dead sister's body. Amid the sounds of mourning and the perfunctory tasks of burial preparations, she asks him not to "pass over it" because it is one of Macrina's greatest miracles.[1] It is a notable moment in an extended death scene. Referred to as the "scar scene," this ancient scar prompts questions about the sacred status of marked bodies, particularly marks on the bodies of women. Early Christian scholar Virginia Burrus drew attention to it in a short essay titled "Macrina's Tattoo."[2] Connecting the mark to the ancient practices of tattooing, Burrus noted that the fine, thin, and almost imperceptible mark conveyed the possibilities for a positive marking, initiating a new moment, a becoming. She writes, "The delicate searing of steel on skin melds with the sustaining rhythms of breath and heartbeat, and the soul sings silently with the *scarred joy* of life (of a Life)."[3] Macrina's scar exposes a mark that represented past suffering but also represented a departure from that suffering.

Moved by the testimony of Macrina, Burrus inscribes her own experience into her textual analysis of Macrina's scar. She recalls her own tattoos as a means of marking identity through a reclaiming of her body. Rather than a reinscription of past suffering, the tattoos marked suffering, but indirectly. Burrus reads the scar within the wider scope of life, bringing together the story of the ancient mother of faith as she looks to both the past and future, situating the scar at the pivot between past suffering and a future becoming. The tattoo is a site, a cipher, for the passages of life. Neither an open wound nor smooth skin, its texture testifies to the "scarred joy of life." Burrus turns us to think about marks on skin as holy. Given its positioning in Gregory's wider corpus, the scar is a mark of resurrecting.

Attributing positive status to wounds touches a nerve within feminist theology. The vision of sacred wounds raises the specter of atonement theologies and the significant critiques by feminist and womanist theologians of Christian theologies of the cross. Prominent critiques of the centrality of death and wounds in the patrilineal configuration of the crucifixion provided a necessary intervention in Christian theological interpretations of redemption. The iterations of the Father-Son tale and the violence that comes with it, from Dorothee Sölle, to Delores Williams, to Rosemary Radford Ruether, to Rita Nakashima Brock and Rebecca Parker, the cry from the cross of women's suffering sounded, as a refusal to ascribe redemptive significance to the suffering on the cross. And yet the questions of what theological significance to attribute to wounds and the meanings that women draw from them still remain. The atonement exposed two aspects of feminist and womanist concerns: the sacralizing of wounds and the patrilineal configuration of salvation. In its patrilineal structure, the binding love of the Father and Son depends on the sacrifice, the wounding. Ruether raised the jarring question about a male savior and women's flourishing "Can a male savior save women?"—which was quickly followed by the suspension of "by his wounds we are healed" (Isa 53:5). Feminists and womanists sought other ways to structure this relationship, providing models of relational power that countered the abuses of hierarchical ordering of relations.

I reapproach the "scar scene" with this question of women's (marked) becoming, working both with—and also against—the symbol of wounds of Christian thought. Georgia Frank notes that Macrina's life story is overtaken by the account of Macrina's death. She writes, "The entire *Life of Macrina* can be read as a primer on grief."[4] And yet there is no commentary on the vision of resurrection that it presents. By pointing to a second scar scene positioned at the end of Gregory's "treatise," I suggest that it offers a unique vision of resurrection. Macrina becomes like Christ, not only in the pattern of her life and death, but also in the illumination of her body following her death. Gregory's Johannine patterning of the Macrina account inscribes resurrection within the story of her life. If the scar becomes a site for a Christian theology of resurrection, what does it teach us? And how might it respond to feminist concerns about the transmission of wounds in the Christian tradition?

Scar Scene

After a gathering of church bishops, Gregory feels a pull to visit his sister. Immersed in the political life of the church, he tells us that it has been a long time since he last visited Macrina, somewhere close to eight years. She is living in a monastery and has, in fact, become the abbess, the highest position among the women. Word of his arrival precedes him, and the brothers in the adjoining order meet Gregory and guide him to the church where the women are waiting. Macrina is not with them. Instead, he is led to her residence, where it becomes clear that she is close to death. He gives us an account of his final moments with her and the conversations and prayers between them.

Gregory draws us to her bedside. It is evening and the lamp is brought in, as Macrina says her nocturnal prayers while breathing her last. Hearing the news of her death, the cries of the women weeping sound just outside the door: "The lamp of our life has been extinguished," they cry. "The light that directed the path of our souls has been taken away."[5] Inside, the women begin to prepare Macrina's body for burial. Two women are in charge of the preparations—Vetiana (a widow) and Lampadium (a deaconess). It is clear that they are not only maidservants; they are disciples of Macrina. Macrina had insisted that Gregory assist in the burial preparations.[6] Vetiana reinforces the earlier request by speaking to him, asking him to pay attention to what is taking place.[7] This places Gregory in the midst of the women. It also places him in contact with her body, a body that throughout the *Vita* he has praised for its covering—the ideal ascetic. It is unclear why Gregory's presence is so necessary. This would certainly have been considered to be women's work. It is also clear that Gregory is not comfortable there, and that he is disturbed by what he sees and hears: "My soul was disquieted for two reasons, because of what I saw and because I heard the weeping of the virgins."[8]

They begin preparing her body—"the great assignment"—by discussing the type of linens that should be used.[9] As Macrina had eschewed adornment during her life, the maids discuss whether it is appropriate to clothe her in fine linens, so as to prepare her, like a bride, to meet her divine bridegroom. It is important to note how much of this scene is dominated by two objects: lamps and clothing. Gregory emphasizes how difficult it is to see; the lamps are brought in, but it is still difficult to find a way in the dark. Robes, garments, and clothing also play a critical role. This is fitting for a burial preparation scene, but Gregory is also playing in this account with the covering over and concealment of the body, which ties not only to the asceticism of Macrina but to his notion of "garments of skin" prominent in his reading of human nature and sin. There is a continual play in this account between seeing and not seeing, between concealing and revealing; any unveiling is coupled with a veiling.

But then Vetiana pulls the lamp close to Macrina's body and pulls back part of Macrina's robe: she "laid bare part (μέρος) of the breast."[10] "Do not pass over the greatest of the miracles of the saint,"she says.[11] She reveals a mark on Macrina's skin. She asks Gregory, "Do you see this faint mark below the skin?[12] It resembles a scar (στίγματι) left by a small (λεπτον) needle."[13] The problem of seeing is front and center here. Do you see what is faint, small, hidden, covered?

Vetiana proceeds to tell Gregory the story of the scar. Macrina developed a mass or growth (τὸν ὄγκον) that was spreading and moving toward her heart.[14] If left unattended, it would threaten her life. Her mother, Emmelia, pleaded with her to go to the doctors, but Macrina resisted—not wanting to lay bare part of her body to another's eyes.[15] Instead, she went to the sanctuary and prayed all night; with tears flowing, she cried out to God for healing. The tears poured to the ground. Tears mixed with soil, producing mud that Macrina used as a *pharmakon*, a medicine, rubbing it over the surface of the mass. When she returns home, Emmelia implores her again to seek help, but Macrina invites her mother to reach inside her robe and to make the sign of the cross over the site. Immediately, the mass disappeared. The mother's fingers trace skin, as if to *work* in the mud—the balm—created through prayer-filled tears.

The mass disappears, but a mark remains. Vetiana assigns meaning to it; she indicates that it remains as a reminder of "divine consideration."[16] The memory is marked on her skin. God was here.

Macrina's scar is unique in that it is not the direct product of an earlier wound. Since it is not subject to the diagnostic gaze, we know little about the nature of her "wound." Given its location, some scholars believe that it was breast cancer. Translated as sore, disease, and tumor, it is not clear whether the growth was visible on her skin. Georgia Frank implies that the sore was *not* a visible wound on the body; instead, the sore was internal. She writes, "Untouched by scalpel or nails, she bears a scar where none belongs."[17] She also notes that the location on the breast, recalls Christ's chest wound, as it is identified in John 20.[18] Thus, the mark was not inscribed on a previous sore but marked healing of an internal sore that was never visible. We tend to think of a scar as a product of a wound, as evidence of its closure.

Yet Macrina's scar is different. In one reading, the invisible wound is made visible in the scar. This is a wound brought to the surface of the skin. Macrina's and her mother's actions are emphasized here—as the text reveals more about the production of the pharmakon than the nature of the disease. The mark remains on the body as a sign of healing; it is a mark produced not by an internal wound but by its exterior witness.

Touch (the work of Macrina's fingers and her mother's touch) highlights the work of healing and points to the possibility of marking life differently. The mark is a multisensory production, featuring touch. The touch does not simply bring a wound to light—to the eye; it writes on skin that which is not readily available to the eye.[19]

This gap between Macrina's disease (what we could think of as an originary wound) and the scar is significant. The scar does not turn us back into the wound but, instead, focuses the work of healing on the surface of skin. The gaze is disrupted, and the scene is focused on other senses; here, on the touch between daughter and mother. The scar is hidden and witnessed only by way of moving through layers of misrecognition. A crisis of witness is also represented here. This is emphasized by Gregory's consternation—Why was I not aware, did not know about this great miracle? Something revealed after life was already operating within the life of Macrina. The secret revealed *after death* pertained to a miracle enacted *within life*. While the healing took place much earlier, the mark was only disclosed to Gregory at this point.

After the revelation of the scar, the discussions of adornment resume. Following Lampadium's instructions, they decide to cover Macrina with Emmelia's dark robe. Lampadium's words usher in light. The lamps reappear.[20] The robe is pulled over the body—the compounding of darkness—the dark night and the dark robe. But light begins to shine through the covering; Macrina's body begins to glow through the robes. Gregory returns in first person here: "But even in the dark, the body glowed, the divine power adding such grace to her body that, as in the vision of my dream, rays seemed to be shining forth from her loveliness."[21] The luminous transfigured body reminds Gregory of a vision he had right before entering the monastery of women. This is a vision at the threshold between his busy political activities (the world of men, we can presume—accompanied by his brother Basel) and the religious community of women. In that vision, he was holding the relics of the martyrs in his hands; the relics (the parts) glowed. The implication is that Macrina's part (μέρος) glows, and thus she had joined the ranks of the martyrs.[22]

The scene closes with the sounds of women outside the door, weeping, singing, and mourning the loss of their leader.

Note on Resurrection Garments

In Gregory's vision of creation, human beings were created with radiant bodies. He uses the image of clothing to narrate the journey of creation, fall, and redemption. While naked, and thus blameless, when they were created in the Garden of Eden, humans must robe after they have violated God's command. They lose their radiance. They are given "garments of skin" as signs of their creaturely, and fallen, nature. The progression of a holy life involves a shedding of the sinful nature—the garments of skin—and eventually the putting on of a new garment, a glorious garment in which one stands before God, righteous in God's sight. Born with radiant bodies, the promise is that they will return to this radiance. In Gregory's broader theology, resurrection flesh is figured as a newly woven garment, placed over the believer when the garment of skin was shed. Cameron Partridge writes, "So fond is Gregory of clothing imagery that it serves as one of the chief metaphors through which he envisions resurrection embodiment. Clothing imagery was uniquely able to reflect both radical change and continuity of identity."[23] The scar is the sign of resurrection skin, the first fruits of that restoration of the *imago Dei*. He makes this link between Gregory's resurrection theology and Macrina's body, noting, "What he can say is that humans will be transfigured, their bodies rewoven like new cloaks. Macrina's body is emblematic of this change, the subtlety of her scar like the first thread of her heavenly garment."[24]

Building on Partridge's insights, the Macrina scene could be envisioned as a burial sewing or dressing room in which new garments are being woven.[25] It is obvious that burial preparations will involve dressing her body. And yet the scar testifies to the threading of a new garment, not to be placed on the body but that uses the material—matter—of the body to construct a new garment. The distinction between bare skin and clothing blurs here. The scar shines through the robes, because the mother's and daughter's flesh are already curiously woven together. The pharmakon has worked its way into skin. Emmelia's touch on the surface of the skin may be likened to the puncture of a needle that begins to weave new cloth. As the women gather around Macrina, the scar signals a new garment being sewn.[26]

But the curious weaving of the glorious garment has *already* happened, and this challenges us to think about the timing of resurrection. This is not a moment in the afterlife, as we might think. Macrina's mark is a visible sign *of what was already present*—the eschatological dimension. It is a moment in this life in which Macrina is not trading in garments of skin for a glorious garment; instead, there is a simultaneity that is brought about by what we might consider ordinary practices of care. What is important to remember is that this "miracle" did not happen after she died; the resurrection flesh was already threading. The smallest needle thread just below the surface and circles over, providing a vision of skin that diverges, in many respects, from Gregory's familiar presentation of body, soul, and resurrection.

And yet the scar scene extends further into the closing pages of the *Vita*. It is this second scene that points to Gregory's account as patterned after the Gospel of John. The stories of Macrina's other healings begin to be shared, as Gregory closes out his account of her life.[27]

The Soldier's (Wife's) Story

In the aftermath of Macrina's death, Gregory provides an account of a story narrated to him. Just pages after the luminous garments, we meet him outside the tomb. He is in the throes of grief: "I fell upon the tomb and kissed the dust and retraced my steps, downcast and tearful, thinking of the good of which my life had been deprived."[28] In this condition he is approached by a soldier, who, upon hearing the news about Macrina's death, shares a story about a previous encounter he had with her. Positioning himself to hear the soldier's story, Gregory inserts a brief narrative commentary about how this is the last thing that he will insert before concluding his account.[29]

The soldier and his wife set out to visit the community of women, the order of which Macrina is the head, and they do so with the intent of seeking a cure for their young daughter's eye illness. Approaching the monastery, the couple separates into men's and women's quarters, respectively. The wife and child are able to meet with Macrina, and this visit is extended when, as the young mother prepares to leave, Macrina urges her to stay and eat dinner: "The blessed one would not let my wife go, and said she would not give up my daughter, whom she was holding in her arms, until she had given them a meal and offered them the wealth of philosophy."[30] Macrina kisses the child on the eye, as she offers the dinner invitation, and indicates that the family will be given something in return for accepting the invitation. The mother inquires further about the gift offered in return, and Macrina tells them that she has a pharmakon for healing the diseased eye. The soldier is not present for this invitation but, once his wife accepts, he receives word from within the men's quarters that they will be staying for dinner. Macrina had insisted that they remain, and they agree: "We gladly remained and disregarded the urgent necessity of starting on our way."[31]

One point of emphasis contributes to reflections about Gregory's writing and the nature of the account that he offers. The soldier notes that his wife told him everything that happened—in detail, systematically, in order—"as in a history."[32] This suggests a contrast to the soldier's report (he was not privy to most of what took place) and also a reflection by Gregory on the way his *vita* has unfolded. She tells the story thoroughly and orderly, as if "going through a treatise."[33] The soldier is struck by the precision of her account. Earlier Gregory notes, "If my treatise were not becoming too long, I would put down everything in order."[34] He acknowledges the disordered nature of his account of Macrina. But Macrina, guided by the Holy Spirit, "explained it all clearly and logically."[35] He attributes a certain way of telling the account to the guidance of the Holy Spirit. When the Spirit is present, the chaos and disorder subside. The wife is likened to Macrina, as both are able to provide a "full" account, guided by the divine Spirit. And yet Gregory's account or treatise is less secure, less credible.

The soldier continues. His wife's story is interrupted at the point when she is recalling Macrina's promise of the medicine (the pharmakon). Suddenly, they both realize that they left the monastery without it. "How did we forget?" she cries out. The soldier takes control and orders his men to go back to retrieve it. But attention turns to the mother, the nurse, and the child. Looking at the child in the nurse's arms, she discovers that the disease is gone. She makes a statement about how everything that Macrina promised occurred, but that the "true pharmakon"—of prayer—"has already worked." The healing has already occurred without the pharmakon. He transfers the child from the arms of the nurse to the arms of his wife. The placement of the child close to the wife's breast mirrors that of Macrina, who cradled the child in proximity to the scar. Georgia Frank connects the first scar account to John 20 and the side wound of Christ, by locating the scar on the breast.[36] This mark at the breast replaces the image of the nursing mother and, instead, provides a scar that is not linked to birthing but to rebirthing, to regeneration.

This miracle prompts the soldier to believe in the miracles contained in the Gospel of John. He reports that he is moved from doubt to faith by the events taking place. It is the faith of the handmaiden, Macrina, who has become the vehicle for his belief. Here, the soldier is likened to Thomas, who believes in the Christ because of witnessing the miracle of healing touch. But he is not the dispassionate skeptic, as in familiar renderings. The soldier weeps with joy, overcome with emotion, and then his story ends. Returning to the first account, the narrative of Thomas is also implicit. Gregory takes his place in the midst of the group of disciples witnessing the miracle and the revelation of the scar. If we reflect back to the earlier scar scene, Emmelia is figured as Thomas, who approaches the wounds of Macrina with doubt—pleading with Macrina to consult with the experts in order to be healed. Macrina's refusal leads to a Gethsemane-like experience, as she pleads for healing. She then invites her mother to reach inside the robe and touch.

We have something very different here from the plunging finger of Thomas who is invited by the risen Christ to reach into the pleural cavity. Instead, we have a mother-daughter healing scene; the mother touches the skin, as if to smooth the pharmakon into her daughter's skin. She touches rather than penetrates—a counterpoint to the plunging finger of the traditional Thomas.

And here Gregory offers a different way of reading this text, emphasizing not the play between belief and doubt but, instead, between healing and suffering.

Recasting the resurrection encounter with Thomas, Macrina becomes the risen Christ who appears to her disciples with wounds. Emmelia, reinscribed as Thomas, worries—concern reframes doubt—about Macrina's wound and yet participates in Macrina's healing, transfiguring wound into scar. Emmelia's lack of trust or faith is directed very differently than the traditional readings of Thomas. The wounds that Emmelia approaches are not external, but are externalized after mother and daughter apply the pharmakon. Gregory takes his place amid the other disciples, as they later witness a divinely inscribed scar, a mark of both suffering and healing. The doubt is tied to the first scene and is that of a concerned mother. The soldier's doubt is centered around his inability to believe in the miracles attested to in the gospels; it is Macrina's healing that prompts him to believe in the healing Christ. The focus of his faith is not on the crucifixion but on the ministry of Jesus. As the disciples gather around the scar, they witness the divine inscription on skin. A healing balm is generated via touch. The scar marks suffering and healing but does so not by inscribing the memory of suffering but by leaving a mark. It is remembered (a memorial of divine visitation), and yet the memory is of a healing, of a *transfiguration*. The testimony of the soldier suggests that a pharmakon is not needed, because a "true" pharmakon has already been at work. The prayer, the tears, and the touch have, again, created an alternative pharmakon.

The radiant glow of Macrina's skin resonates with images of the transfiguration, although the Johannine account does not include a separate transfiguration account. Transfiguration suggests an epiphany, a disclosure or revelation of something that was not previously known. What is the "truth" revealed here? This gospel account is often presented as representing the triumph of Christian faith; Jesus' invitation to Thomas prompts this profession—"My Lord and my God." Could the mother-daughter interaction point us to a different interpretation of this passage, interpreting resurrection not as a triumphing claim that garners the unique truth of Christianity but that links those within this tradition to the vision of healing so central to the narrative of Jesus' life? The plunging finger of Thomas that seeks to secure belief is transfigured into the healing fingers—changing the "truth" that emerges from a reading of this scene.

Gregory presents Macrina as modeling an exemplary life, a life of service in imitation of Christ. In Gregory's account, he highlights her Christlikeness. But this stops shy of what the scar scene in its Johannine postresurrection format displays: Macrina is transfigured as the Christ and the community of witnesses gathers around her. If this is a resurrection account, then we have to ask: What is the significance of resurrection if narrated in this way?

Recent scholars, even with the attention to gender and genre, have focused their analysis on the relationship between Gregory and Macrina. However, the scar sequence sidelines Gregory as a major actor, and the focus shifts to the women: Emmelia, Macrina, her disciples, and the soldier's wife and daughter. It is Gregory who struggles as a witness. Gregory acknowledges at several points in these scenes that he is not a credible witness to what is taking place; the soldier's account also reflects this. Both men are not privy to the whole story (the soldier reliant on his wife's account since he was staying in the men's quarters), and Gregory points to the women as the ones who have the capacity to narrate what is taking place.

We have, in this second scar (and healing) scene, a more extensive vision of the community that Macrina had constituted. The soldier, like Gregory, is outside the account. He is reporting what his wife had conveyed, given her proximity to Macrina. She shares a detailed and ordered account with her husband, which contrasts with the chaos of grief and questionable status of Gregory's own account. This is a counternarrative to the resurrection accounts in the Gospel of John in which the women's witness is discredited, and the male disciples are the central actors. In that Gospel Mary Magdalene is forbidden to touch the resurrected Christ, and yet the woman's touch is featured here. This also provides a way of rethinking the denial of touch to Mary Magdalene. As witness, she is denied touch, but here, in these scar scenes, the woman's touch *is* the miracle, the healing balm.

Paired with this second account, the scar takes on a Johannine figuration. In the postresurrection account, the risen Christ invites his disciples to eat breakfast together; here, the encounter between Macrina and the ill child takes place within the context of a meal. Also, the soldier's testimony of belief parallels the encounter between Thomas and the risen Christ. The guidance of the Holy Spirit is folded into the woman's account. And yet this second account again rewrites resurrection wounds in terms of healing and touch, while in the Johannine account the wounds figure in terms of faith and belief. The soldier and Vetiana both identify the miracle of healing, enacted through Macrina.

Her marks (and being marked) are not sacrificial, requiring loss, negation, or submission but, instead, requiring agency and connection. These marks of "divine consideration" are positive inscriptions.[37] But the "consideration," what we might think of as divine blessing, comes via the touch of the mother and daughter. This second account begins with the portrait of Gregory's grief. He kisses the dust of her tomb, and he is crying. But the dust and tears do not constitute the pharmakon, as they did for Macrina. Her prayerful tears had created a pharmakon, and, with the assistance of her mother, the pharmakon was smoothed over skin. And yet the soldier's story implies that Macrina's skin *became* a pharmakon. She holds the child, cradling her as a nurse or mother, perhaps close to her breast. But the food that she gives the child is not that of a mother (breast milk) but the pharmakon coproduced from the earth, the mother, and the daughter. This triad continues in the soldier's story.

Taking seriously the centrality of women, it is important to note that this is not simply the association of women with maternal care. As with Macrina and the soldier's wife, they are able to tell the tale, to give an account. This ability is not incidental to Gregory, since rhetorical training is important to him. With respect to Macrina and the soldier's wife, their speech flowed, and their accounts were clearly rendered. He indicates that, guided by the Spirit, they were able to tell of the events, while Gregory and the solder were overcome by emotion. The scene of weeping women grieving Macrina's loss parallels the experience of women at the tomb after the death of Jesus; these women were not taken seriously as witnesses. In the Gospel of John, the male disciples take over the position as credible witnesses. This is not the case with the Macrina postdeath scene. In the moments following Macrina's death, Gregory is aggravated by the sounds and noises of the women's grieving, and yet he suggests that the tables have turned—he and the soldier are filled with emotion. Gregory is outside the tomb, weeping. And the solder becomes Thomas, who cannot "see" the truth of the miracles in the gospels on his own but needs to be guided into this vision. He does not encounter the wounds of the resurrected Christ, but, instead, gathers around the miraculous healing skin of Macrina. He does not gather around the wounds but, instead, the scar.

While Jesus was known for his healing ministry, the wounds that he tended are rarely linked to the resurrection wounds that he bears on his body following the crucifixion. Macrina's scar returns us to this question of healing and to a unique vision of bodies resurrecting, of the blessing of life at its most threatened points. Through this account of Macrina, the ministry of healing and meaning of resurrection are intertwined.

To witness a mark challenges Gregory to rethink his depiction of Macrina, and thus his characterization of the holy and sainted life. The bodies of the ascetic women are of great interest to Gregory.[38] His treatise on virginity reflects how central the concept of a pure life reflected in the disciplines of the body is to Gregory.[39] In his writings on the Beatitudes, he presents Macrina's body as the "uncut meadow," the "untouched earth" that, in Peter Brown's description, "bore within itself the promise of abundance";[40] the virgin earth of paradise, Macrina's body would also be able to provide a means back to that pure paradise. It was the untouched and thus, unmarked, nature of her body that was able to mirror perfection and paradise: "The woman's untouched flesh was both the mirror of the purity of her soul and a physical image of the virgin earth of the garden of Eden."[41] It makes sense, then, why Gregory would be "disquieted" by her marked body, by this inscription on her body. While identified as a miracle by Vetiana, Gregory would not immediately have been able to interpret this marking positively. Why, we can imagine Gregory questioning, would the divine mark bodies? Gregory is interested in their unmarked bodies. And yet Macrina's revelation marks bodies in a way that takes Gregory off guard. Her teaching disrupts his depiction of the holy women.

Gregory attributed a unique status to the community of women. While outside the gates of the paradisal garden, their purity in life positions them in relation to the restoration of the human condition—at a threshold.[42] If they become pure vessels—vessels of the resurrection of the flesh—their pure wombs are a channel back to paradise. The Macrina account, however, provides a different vision of the community of women, who through their cobearing provide a vision of illuminated flesh, of resurrecting as healing *in life*. This highlights the second meaning of wombs, as vessels of "bearing" but not biological life. As they stand at the threshold, it is their healing touch and care that weaves together the shared flesh of resurrection. They produce a woven garment, radiating and thus lighting a path out of the depths of grief. They provide a portal for the movement out of grief—a passage of rebirth. The power shared between mother and daughter (or daughters) provides a vision of wombing, of bearing, of standing at the threshold. It is the work that they do there, the practices that they enact there, that constitutes "bearing." This is bearing as blessing. This is a companion narrative to the annunciation; as the womb brought the divine into the world, the wombs would also carry the world back to its paradisal origins, so to speak. The womb of the holy mother became a vessel; the vessel would provide a passage, a return. The vision of mother and daughter is one of accompanying and companioning.

The first scar story is a story of a past healing, marked on the flesh. It is revealed to Gregory just moments after Macrina's death. But then there is another revelation—a second scar story—that is conveyed after her burial but again refers to an event that happened in life. The second departs from the first in that touch proliferates and marks the flesh of another. This is not a healing *of* Macrina (the first, enacted between mother and daughter) but *by* Macrina (the second, in the community of women). The tears of Macrina made a medicinal balm, mixed with the dirt of the earth. Thus, her skin becomes a pharmakon; the scar is a mark created by faith, dust, tears, skin, and blessing of the mother-daughter. Their bond created a unique medicine. And yet the pharmakon spreads, extending into the miracle beyond Macrina and her mother.

Scholars intrigued by Macrina's gender focus on the relationship between Gregory and Macrina, and yet the scar scenes have very little to do with Gregory. Instead, the focus is on multiple configurations of women: Macrina, the maidservants, Emmelia, the soldier's wife, and the girl child. The community of women would identify Macrina as a holy mother, acknowledging their role as faithful disciples. Macrina's relationship with her own mother is narrated in a unique way. When the relationship between Macrina and her mother is described at several points, Gregory depicts it as a relationship of comradeship or companionship. Their roles shift throughout Macrina's life. Who is mothering whom? Who is bearing whom? The account notes that Macrina cared for her mother's body, and the mother guided her daughter into a blameless life.[43] Just sentences later, the daughter is presented as Emmelia's philosopher-guide to the immaterial.[44] Gregory tells us that Macrina was engaged to a man who died before they were married. She bartered with her father, making the case that she should "keep faith with an absent husband,"[45] thus not remarrying. Instead, as part of the case presented before her father (interestingly, her fiancé was a defense lawyer), Macrina resolved to stay with her mother. Emmelia often used to say to her that the rest of her children she had carried in her womb *tri angulation?*

for the fixed time, but this daughter "she *always bore*, encompassing her in her womb at all times."[46]

As the exception to that of Emmelia's other children, Macrina's birthing takes on a nonbiological dimension; the womb is presented as more than a vehicle for bringing life into the world; it is a means of bearing life in all its ambiguities. Here we have a different vision of the function of the womb, not to bear children but to *continually* bear them. The "bearing" is not merely physical, although it maintains its material dimension. The bringing forth of life continues and has a connection with bodies, skin, hands, and physicality but also brings attention to an aspect of divine care—embodied and sacred. This *enwombing*, as we might call it, is especially meaningful when envisioned from the point of death, since the power of bearing that is conveyed in Macrina's scar is situated in the context of death and loss. The status of the womb was certainly important at that time, especially for thinking about the status of Christian women in the fourth-century society.[47] Certainly, we have women represented here in varying states, but many would not have been virgins or mothers. If we think in terms of this double sense of bearing, birthing is actually subordinated here to healing (and consoling)—at the points of illness and death.[48]

Emmelia continually bears Macrina, and Macrina does not want to "lay bare" her skin before the doctors. These are obviously two different terms, but the rhetoric, in translation, places the two together. One vision is of the covered body, unmarked, untouched, and therefore a vehicle for the divine to mirror, to inhabit. The other vision is a marked, touched body that signals God's visitation but not entrance. The enwombing between mother and daughter provides a new surface, one aligned with rebirth. We might think of this in terms of Macrina's last great teaching, reorienting Gregory to truths that will only be grasped at a later point. This point of uncovering, of laying bare, enacted before Gregory, is an invitation for him to reassess the source of the radiance. His vision is altered by the scar sequence, and the sense that he makes of his vision is that Macrina has "joined the ranks of the martyrs"—her body glows like the saints—pure, untethered. And yet a source of her radiance is revealed to him in the scar, as her body is "laid bare" before him. What Gregory cannot "see" is that the illuminated body of Macrina is not radiant because it has been abnegated but because it has been blessed.

The bare earth and the bare skin are all marked *in time*, but the mother continually enwombs, implying a continuation of relation. The divine visitation is the work of hands, and we come to see that it is not the grand work of redemption that saves but the touch on wounds that is rarely accounted for but marked nonetheless—the divine was here.

If we read this as a resurrection story, and the scars as marks of resurrection, then we witness a distinction that is not often made—between sacred wounds and sacred scars. What would it mean if the latter is not a *direct* product of the first? The elements of the Johannine gospel are refigured here through Macrina's resurrecting scar. The story of the scar does not stop with the first account; the scar has an afterlife. But the afterlife is evidenced *in life*. Gregory calls us back to the scar a few pages later, this time more indirectly. With this pairing, the Johannine patterning to the scar scenes becomes more pronounced—Thomas, seeing and believing, and witnessing. A postresurrection account, this scar sequence tells us that while resurrecting is already occurring, it is rarely conceived or grasped as such.[49]

While the death is difficult to comprehend and witness, the resurrecting is equally difficult. And yet the constancy of enwombing, always bearing, seems to be the good news. "Laying bare" is a euphemism for truth telling. Macrina did not want to lay bare her body, expose it to the gaze; instead, the fuel of rebirth will come through other means—of bearing and blessing.

With the emphasis on Macrina's death, it is more difficult to see that Gregory is not only presenting her life and death as a parallel to the story of Christ but also is providing an account of her resurrecting (and inviting us to rethink the meaning of resurrection). As represented in Gregory's other writings, Macrina has been a primary guide in his theological vision of resurrection. While it is noted that Macrina is transfigured as the Christ in Gregory's account, scholarship stops short of acknowledging Macrina as the resurrected Christ and the community of women as witnesses to resurrection. It becomes clearer, via the scar sequence, that Gregory provides a retelling of the postresurrection account in the Gospel of John. In this Johannine reformulation, Gregory offers, perhaps without full awareness or intention, a vision of resurrection in a mother-daughter configuration. This raises questions for feminist theology but also Christian theology more broadly.[50]

Genre

One of the curious aspects of these scenes, and the *Vita* as a whole, is the degree to which Gregory makes the reader conscious of his writing process. While Gregory is the author of the account, there is a question as to what extent he is in control of his pen. Throughout the *Vita*, Gregory conducts a running conversation about the nature of the account that he is writing. The play of genre persists throughout his text, and Gregory calls attention at several points to his own writing. It is as if he is perplexed about its undefined form. He begins by writing a letter, which turns into a treatise, which is too unwieldy and does not end. Gregory notes that the account has either gone on too long or that it is not ordered, as he thinks it ought to be. There are four internal references to length. He is aware that it has run on too long, but he is also aware that it cannot contain everything that needs to be said. Gregory's attunement to the nature of his writing turns the reader's attention to it. The type of inscription seems to be the same question that we bring to the scar: What kind of inscription is this?[51]

Scholars of late Christian antiquity have raised questions about the representation of women in texts such as this. Francine Cardman raises the question: "Is she [Macrina] ever available to the reader apart from Gregory's representations of her?" Is Macrina perpetually pinned under the pen of her theological brother? Cardman turns to this scar scene, suggesting that it signals some resistance to Gregory's authorial control.[52] It is, in fact, this scar scene that reveals Gregory's lack of control as an author and as a witness to her life. Gregory indicates that the account has gotten away from him, that he set out to do something and ended up doing something else. He questions the genre of what he is writing within the work itself. Gregory is also only learning about the scar at this point, whereas the women were privy to this incident much earlier. The use of lamps and clothing alone could convey that Gregory, as narrator, is "in the dark" as well as slightly disturbed by the "laying bare" of his sister's body to the human eye. We witness the author questioning the credibility of his testimony to her life and death in the *Vita*.

One of the earliest articulators of Christian orthodoxy, Gregory defers to his sister Macrina on matters of the afterlife. In *On the Soul and Resurrection*, Macrina guides Gregory in Christian teachings about death and resurrection.[53] Macrina is aligned with the heroes, the martyrs, the philosophers (Socrates, Diotima, Thekla, Odysseus), as she tutors Gregory in the critical passage between death and life.[54] But Macrina was always drawing Gregory back to the Christian scriptures for guidance, and this direction should be heeded in our reading of Gregory's presentation of her life. It is important, then, to think about Gregory as providing an account of Macrina's life that parallels the gospels primarily, that does not display her as Plato or Homer, Socrates or Odysseus, but presents her in relationship with the Jesus of the gospels. While scholars have pointed to the multiple influences and connections—philosophy and literature—the most striking parallel is to the Gospel of John. What has not been considered is whether Gregory is providing, perhaps unawares, a gospel account, a narrative told about the life, death, and resurrection of Christ *via* Macrina. *This* genre—a gospel accounting—would have been most pleasing and honorable to Macrina, who was concerned about her brother's constant appeals to Greek literature. The account is understood to tell the story of Macrina's life. And yet, read in parallel with the gospel, it tells the story of death and resurrection.

The *Vita* is much hailed as one of the first instances of Christian hagiography. But this "life writing" is suspended throughout. It has been noted that Gregory's account of her life is, as he presents it, more of an account of her death. Given the large amount of space that Gregory apportions to her death, this could raise the question of whether this is an elegy to Macrina. We could imagine that the writing of her death might challenge an author, a brother, and a mourner. But Gregory attributes to Macrina an even greater status, and the question becomes how to write the life and death of Christ. Thus, Gregory takes on the responsibility of a gospel writer, attempting to put in words the meaning of the life, death, and resurrection of Jesus to those who survive him.

He sets out to tell her story, but this scene points more to what he does not know about her story, and to aspects of her life that are revealed to him that he cannot account for. Jesus forecasts in his farewell discourse to the disciples that they will come to understand what is occurring to them only at a later point (implicit in the farewell discourse in John). Their way through the death will be marked by the inability to grasp it in the moment. Certainly, Gregory's presentation suggests something of these challenges, perhaps reflecting why he has such a difficult time identifying the nature of his account. At the point of the scar, and the point of the pen, there is a destabilization—a struggle to give an account, which reflects something of the nature of resurrection witness.

Gregory presents Macrina as exemplary, in her life and in her death. But the scar scene opens up another dimension: she is exemplary of a

Christian vision of resurrection. She has served as a guide to Gregory in matters of faith, and in *On the Soul and Resurrection* she guides him into his reflections about the promise of life after death for Christians. Gregory's vision of resurrection is heavily indebted to Macrina. But her teachings about resurrection continue here, and, received after death, they craft a vision of resurrection that parallels the Johannine account. Noting the expanse of the death account may occlude a subtle shift that takes place within that account—a shift to resurrection and the after-life. The scar scene in the text occurs after Macrina has died. There is no doubt that Gregory reads her not only as one who has lived a life in imitation of the Christ; she is one who becomes, by the end of the *Vita*, the Christ. She is transfigured as the Christ. Thus, her postdeath burial scene gives way to resurrection.

Interpreting the Scar via the Feminist Critiques

The Christ handed down to women in the Christian tradition "reveres the wound in the side of the crucified one," according to French feminist philosopher Luce Irigaray.[55] The transmission of this story is toxic for women; as soon as a woman ascribes to the will of the Father, according to Irigaray, "she also is 'crucified.' "[56] The call to turn away from wounds in feminist thought is represented well in Irigaray's writings, and the alternative that she offers is one in which women's becoming does not depend on wounds. If women are to be reborn—resurrected—it will not be a resurrection patterned upon a prior crucifixion. Instead, it will constitute a vision of a collective, bodily resurrection—a vision of shared flesh. Irigaray's critique has been influential, identifying a central problem within Christianity but also within Western thought more broadly.

In *Marine Lover of Friedrich Nietzsche*, she explicitly challenges the crucifixion wounds as the primary means by which Western Christianity has described the salvation. The chapter of her most strident critique is titled "The Crucified One: Epistle to the Last Christians." In heralding the wounds as the channel through which salvation is envisioned in Western Christianity, Christianity continually dismisses its core affirmation—incarnation. The message of the sacrifice enacted between Father and Son also renders the woman the "instrument of conception," or a "receptacle that, faithfully, welcomes and reproduces only the will of the Father."[57] Here, she implores her readers (congregants!?): "Search for the traces of the divine in anything that does not preach, doesn't command, but enacts the work of incarnation."[58] Irigaray implores believers to depart from the wounds as a central symbol of their salvation. Addressing those still held captive under the patrilineal message, Irigaray, the bearer of good news, begins to imagine incarnation without wounds.

There is no Thomas scene following Irigaray's resurrection. This vision is of shared flesh without marks, without wounds. Her vision is encapsulated here: "The deepest depths of the flesh, touched, birthed, and without a wound."[59] Irigaray imagines the coming of flesh in contrast to the dominant Christian story in which incarnation is always supplanted by crucifixion. Resurrection after—and through—death is the paradigmatic Father-Son story of salvation; new life emerges from the crucifixion wounds. They are necessary to bringing about new life. In fact, the patrilineal message of Christianity continually draws believers to the wounds, inviting them, like the Christ in the gospels, to find new life by plunging themselves back into wounds. This resonates with Irigaray's other readings of Western texts, most notably her rereading of Plato's cave, in which she attempts to undo the logic of the passage into knowledge as one of continually eclipsing birth, flesh, pleasure, and the maternal (and material). Like Irigaray, other feminist and womanist theologians question the centrality of the death account and refocus attention on other moments in the Christian narrative, turning to life for the promise of resurrecting.[60]

And yet Irigaray's vision of women's becoming raises concerns from within feminist thought, in that, in the process of rejecting death-dealing wounds as the channel of women's becoming, she presents unmarked and woundless flesh as an ideal. This woundless vision is problematic, in its presentation of a utopic vision of women's becoming. In its affirmation of embodiment, it provides little room for thinking about varieties of bodies and marks of suffering. Both Amy Hollywood and Catherine Keller, feminist thinkers deeply influenced by Irigaray's thought, contest her vision of flesh without wounds. Catherine Keller responds to Luce Irigaray's erasure of wounds on the body of the resurrected woman and vision of the pure flesh of becoming. She speculates, "I wonder, though, if we need to think this body as quite so pure, so new-born as Irigaray's woundless utopia of the flesh. I suspect rather than the deep flesh, even in its resurrection, will carry the scars."[61] Working within the Christian textual tradition, she can trace the problematic inheritance of glorified wounds for women. To attribute significance to wounds has been problematic, because it so easily feeds the logic of redemptive suffering.

And yet to erase them is to promote an ideal that is equally damning for women. Is there a way to "work through" wounds without reinscribing them as negative marks of identity? Amy Hollywood wonders if there is a way of aligning Irigaray's vision with the "realities of loss and limitation."[62] While celebrating the joys of existence, Irigaray fails to acknowledge the ambiguities of embodied existence, the ways in which life is marked by experiences, both positively and negatively.

Sharon Betcher extends this concern about unmarked bodies by noting that a divine vision of newborn flesh could easily reinforce late-market capitalistic obsessions with ideal, perfect bodies.[63] She has noted that the vision of healing and miracles set out in the Christian gospels often treats marked bodies as objects to be healed. The vision of healing and miracles set out in the Christian gospels can be "bad news" for those whose bodies do not conform to societal norms. Betcher notes the problematic partnership between Western cultural notions of bodily perfection and the Christian message of healed bodies. If the aim of Jesus' ministry and the sign of God's blessing is the whole and healed body, then Christian theology aids in denigrating bodies that do not heal, that do not figure the ideal whole body. The good news of Christian theology would be to figure healing differently, and to detach it from the compulsions of cultural perfection and perfect Christian bodies. Transforming the gaze is challenging work since it requires moving against some of the most familiar readings of the work of Jesus. "Do you want to be healed?" Jesus asks the blind, the lame. The implicit answer is "Yes, yes, we want to be healed." The problem, Betcher notes, is that Christian theology needs to alter its vision of healing to affirm variation and change, to recognize that life processes affect all of us, instead of reinforcing the shame (or guilt) placed on those whose do not fit the norm. Healing, then, cannot be aligned with perfection, wholeness. If Christian theology prizes or praises those who come away "unmarked," then it builds within the Christian temperament a disgust for "morphological variation."[64]

What, then, does a reading of Macrina's scar contribute to this set of concerns? What's at stake for feminist theology in returning to the scar as a symbol that envisions women's becoming? If we think about Macrina's scar as a retelling of the Johannine story of resurrection, what difference does this make? Macrina's scar offers an alternative vision of resurrection, departing in significant ways from a repetition or imitation of crucifixion wounds. Resurrection—the promise of women's becoming—does not prescribe the erasure of marks but instead offers an altered vision of the marks that disrupts the transmission of the patrilineal story. The disruption occurs from *within* the patrilineal telling. The challenge lies here to attribute theological meaning to wounds, because they mark identity in significant ways, but to not reinscribe the suffering as definitive for women. Thus, the challenge is not *whether* to regard wounds, but *how* to regard them theologically. What is continually missed, as evidenced in the positioning of Gregory, is that *resurrection rewrites healing*.

The "seeing and believing" statement in John 20 is most often linked or extracted to an abstracted and spiritual commentary on faith. In this text, the "seeing and believing" statement links to the ministry of Jesus, to the John 9 story of Jesus healing the blind man. When Vetiana pulls away the garment, she discloses a truth of the relationship between suffering and healing.

Altered Vision

A reading of Macrina's scar suggests that the "good news" about scars does not reside in either reinscribing suffering or in erasing it. The resurrection scar stories present marks of women's becoming in an *altered form* by offering a rewriting of the Johannine gospel known for its emphasis on the relationship between the Father and Son. One of the chief concerns of feminist theologians is that Christian theologies of crucifixion and resurrection transmit a toxic logic of redemptive suffering that does not alleviate women's suffering but rather perpetuates it. Thus, ascribing sacred status to wounds inevitably ends in sanctifying the suffering rather than healing it. This retelling provides a critical *redirection*—away from redemptive suffering to a different relationship between suffering and healing.

I want to illustrate this by returning to the significance attributed to the scar, first by Vetiana, and then by Gregory. It is important to note that there are two interpretations. First, there is Gregory's. Outside the gates of the monastery, before entering to visit Macrina for the last time, Gregory has a vision of glowing relics of the martyrs cupped in his hand. The vision repeats three times, and the dazzling glow from the relics overwhelms him: "I was not able to interpret its meaning clearly, but I foresaw some grief for my soul and I was waiting for the outcome to clarify the dream."[65] Gregory notes that the dazzling brightness did not bring him comfort but, rather, foreshadowed something

more difficult and disturbing to come. At this point, he arrives at the
"outskirts" of the community of women, and he encounters a workman
there who tells him that Macrina (known as the Superior) is ill. He
is situated at the threshold of the intentional, enclosed community of
women. His query into the meaning of the three visions of the relics is
suspended as he enters the property. This entrance marks the beginning
of the death narrative.

The memory of this earlier vision returns to him as he witnesses
Macrina's body glowing through her burial garments, which belonged
to her mother. Despite the fact that her body, although dead, is still
intact, Gregory suggests that he can now make sense of the earlier vision
after seeing Macrina's parts glow. The vision of the radiant light stream-
ing through the dark garments seems to provide Gregory with clarity
about his earlier vision. He interprets her radiant, postdeath body, as
confirmation of Macrina's ascension to the rank of a martyr. Their parts
glowed, and thus her glowing body represents the glory of a martyr,
who undergoes suffering in imitation of Christ and will be recognized
and rewarded for that suffering. The radiance speaks to God's favor
upon Macrina's life and ascribes to her an esteemed position.

However, Vetiana, the one directing the burial scene, offers another
way of interpreting Gregory's earlier vision.[66] Drawing back the robes
to display Macrina's mark, she says that this is a mark of divine visitation, and it should be "cause and reason for unceasing thanksgiving to
God."[67] What is the divine marking? The mark acknowledges a suffering, but it manifests as a sign of blessing, marking the cooperation
between mother, daughter, and the earth. The dust of the earth held and
becomes a healing salve, and it is a site of "locational memory."[68] When
Macrina prayed her final prayers, she offered thanksgiving to Christ
who made possible the passage from this life into the next. The images
that she uses there are of God whose hands fashioned humanity and
who gives us back to the "dust of the earth for safekeeping." This Christ
"breaks down the gates of hell" and conquers death. But the passage
back to paradise is curiously linked to the mother's womb:

> O God everlasting, towards whom I have directed myself from my
> mother's womb, whom my soul has loved with all its strength, to whom
> I have dedicated my body and my soul from my infancy up to now,
> prepare for me a shining angel to lead me to the place of refreshment
> where the water of relaxation near the bosom of the holy Fathers.[69]

Entrance back into paradise is made possible, Macrina prays. But what she forecasts here is that the passage is forged by the care and companionship of women. From dust, humanity was created, but it is the creation of mud, the medicine, that leads to paradise. It is the water, the tears, of Macrina that will constitute the waters of refreshment through which humanity returns to God. God visited and marked flesh, through the touch of mother and daughter. Macrina's prayer is laced with references to the cross and to the crucifixion, and the destination of the bosom of the Father seems to reinscribe the patrilineal story of redemption. And yet Macrina's scar signals the miracle of resurrection through other means.

When Macrina's body begins to glow under the garments, Gregory does not directly link the radiance to the miraculous mark he has just witnessed. "Even in the dark, the divine power added grace to her body," he remarks, and then he immediately appeals to his earlier vision of the glowing relics that was received *outside* the gates of the community. He connects back, interpreting the events, in line with his vision, emphasizing vision, seeing, and eyes. Gregory seems to defer to Vetiana's opinion about robing ("her opinion prevailed"), but he seems not to have heeded her exhortation to witness the miracle. Vetiana cautions him from the start, perhaps forecasting that Gregory will fail to witness this miracle, even before she reveals it to him. Instead of acknowledging that something is conveyed there, he folds it back into what he knows. In turn, he does not give her power to interpret what is taking place. Despite her warnings not to "pass by" the miracle, it seems that he may have done just that.

But the disclosure of the mark within the enclosed space of the community of women may not be so easily missed—or dismissed. Vetiana's account points to an alternative vision of what it means to "bear the marks."[70] The inscription bears witness to a dynamic set of relationships, reframed in terms of Emmelia and Macrina's comradeship and companionship. *This* is the cause for ceaseless thanksgiving. Emmelia traces the sign of the cross on Macrina's skin, seeming to inscribe the sufferings of Christ on her skin, but the mark that appears and that remains is not the inscription of the suffering crucifixion but a sign of God's touch upon skin. It is a mark of care, protection, and caress. If we carry over this over into the next scene in which Macrina's body illuminates, we can begin to think of the illumination of the garment differently, as the daughter's skin is lined with the mother's garments. Could the glow be coming from the scar, from the work of mother and daughter?

The repetition and imitation of the crucifixion wounds undergirds Gregory's interpretation. And yet Vetiana inserts a story about a different mark that reframes resurrection in relation to past suffering but not patterned upon it. If we follow Gregory as sole interpreter, we can miss this interruption. If we heed his warnings, we can begin to turn attention elsewhere. However, we do not need to dismiss Gregory's return to his earlier vision of the relics; we can think instead about how the vision of radiance is reinscribed by Vetiana and the company of women. If we imagine the glowing parts in Gregory's hand, we can think about the sewing of the resurrection garment as a weaving together of parts, as if the boundaries between persons are also transfigured in the stitching together of a new body.[71]

Implications for Becoming

The scar scenes move us into the territory of resurrection. A retelling of resurrection via the scar yields an altered vision of becoming, one that does not reinscribe wounds into a vision of resurrection. Both Burrus and Hollywood are interested in the power of feminist thought to speak to the ambiguities of life, to speak in the midst of the spectrum of joy and pain, ecstasy and despair. Hollywood says, "Although I embrace Irigaray's (and many of her most astute readers') desire to bring pleasure, possibility, and natality into philosophy and psychoanalysis, I think there is a danger in refusing to think, *at the same time*, the realities of loss and limitation."[72] Can women's writing bear traces of the divine and thus mark lives as holy across this spectrum? "The question of how women might symbolize and so mediate their own losses," according to Hollywood, is unanswered in Irigaray's vision of becoming. Could Macrina's scar symbolize and mediate loss? Women need resources for countering the losses, the trauma, Hollywood writes.[73] Burrus traces the "secret of the mother's transformative touch" back to a vision of the Eucharist. While women's desire gives way to an "erotic communion,"[74] I can hear Irigaray admonishing her listeners to imagine shared flesh without reconstituting wounds.

The "truth" of the resurrection, conveyed through the symbol of the scar, is that these textures (grief and joy, pain and pleasure) will always be present in a life, often simultaneously. Interlaced with joy and pain, a life can be marked as holy in all its ambiguities. Yet the scar sequence presents something even more radical. The symbol suggests that *lives* are layered, because life is not singular. The suffering and healing cannot be separated, because the lines between persons are newly woven. Emmelia and Macrina, the mother and daughter, continually bear and enwomb, and in so doing they enact a truth about resurrection: soil, tears, and touch remake humanity into a new creation. The truth lies in the weaving of a new body. The scar provides a different ending to Gregory's vision of the glowing parts: "I was unable to interpret its meaning clearly, but I foresaw some grief for my soul and I was waiting for the outcome to clarify the dream."[75]

But perhaps this "truth" can only be felt in the midst of grief.

As Macrina cradles the infant in her arms, her part (*meros*), now a healing agent, touches other parts. As such, she enjoins others to gather, linking the disciples together and reorienting them from gazing at wounds to assembling them through the power of touch. And herein lies the miracle—that the parts are linked, interconnected. Thus, the pharmakon yields a new constitution of relationships, a new identity. The truth that this lays bare is that the texture of the scar is not simply a layering of one's life experiences—both pleasure and pain—but a *layering of lives*—in an affective and sensory interweaving of persons in a new community. The stitching, the careful work of hands, is not a working over of pure flesh, nor does it have that as its end; instead, it surfaces a collective. The lump of clay is reconstituted and blessed, and in this process of touch, suffering is expressed under a different cover(ing);[76] resurrection is the weaving of community.

Irigaray displayed, throughout her writings, the problem of the womb in Western thought. She was countering Freud's vision of the destiny of the young girl: the womb is the tomb. The history of Western thought was a flight from the origins of the womb, an erasure of primary origins in the mother. So it seems like bad news to reclaim the womb, but here we can reimagine enwombing between Macrina and Emmelia as the stitching together of a garment, a continuous accompaniment in life. Thus, Gregory's vision, incomplete when he enters the community of women, is redirected; holding the parts does not refer elsewhere. The truth lies in the holding.

The scar sequence unveils layers of witness. There is Gregory's account of Macrina's life and death—his telling of the story. And then Gregory is witness to another telling, the narration of the women, as they interpret what is taking place. What happens, between these layers of witness, is a different reading of the Gospel of John, turning readers to ask different questions about the meaning of resurrection presented there. It pulls the healing texts into the resurrection appearances but raises questions about how the two are linked. Macrina's tears mix with the earth as she reaches down, cups the moist earth in her hands, and creates a pharmakon. In John 9, Jesus creates a healing balm, moistening the dirt with his saliva; he wipes it on the eyes of a blind man, and the man's sight is restored. In this retelling, Gregory raises the question of who is the healer and who is being healed; the mother cups the pharmakon as well, rubbing it into her daughter's body. And yet we do not know if the pharmakon directly produces the marking. There is something very ordinary and non-miraculous about this story—a worrying mother, and a daughter who seeks other routes to address her suffering. She pleads with God to make the disease go away. But it is Macrina's unusual relationship with her mother that catches our attention, as Gregory has marked their relationship in an unusual way. Macrina is enwombed continually in the midst of joy and pain.

What *is* unusual and not ordinary is to interpret this touch as sacred. This touch is undergirded by a vision of shared flesh, sewn together, to create not only a garment of one but a collective garment. There is never a pure and unmarked body, because as others are marked by the extremities of life, so, too, is the one. Irigaray's vision is of *new-born* flesh, pure, unmarked. And yet it is important to locate the promise of becoming in *rebirthing flesh in the midst of life*. If feminist theology flees from wounds, refusing to attribute significance to them, then it cedes this space to the endless repetition of the patrilineal wounding narrative. The movement through death, through pain, is not problematic in itself, but it needs to be reinscribed in Christian understanding. The reinscription via the scar envisions shared flesh with marks. In its marking, it is also transfigured. This simultaneity exposes the "dense site" of the scar, and the tensions that it can hold. The "tattoo," Burrus notes, is a "deep surface—of complex and layered meaning, fusing (without quite confusing) rebellion and surrender, nobility and degradation, flesh and spirit, worldly and holy power."[77] The memory of suffering is not there naked and exposed; it is protected, covered, and witnessed.

Conclusion

Augustine offers a curious moment at the end of *City of God* in which he speaks about scars on the resurrected bodies of the martyrs. It is a strange point in his text, but the wording emphasizes those who will gaze upon those bodies—the way that we regard them is vitally important. He writes, "But the love we bear to the blessed martyrs causes us, I know not how, to desire to see in the heavenly kingdom the marks of the wounds which they received for the name of Christ, and possibly we shall see them."[78] Gregory's vision of Macrina's scar can be interpreted in this way, patterned on the wounds of the crucified and of those who imitate him in his sufferings. But Macrina's scar alters the gaze and turns, instead, to the touch of blessing on life, a mark of a shared flesh, marked by the joy and suffering of life. The image of Thomas' hand, reaching out in disbelief, becomes the mother's hands caressing skin. The texture of a new creation radiates.

3

Surfacing Wounds
Christian Theology and Resurrecting Histories in the Age of Ferguson

They are on lockdown in the aftermath of his death. It is unclear how long they have been there, but he appears in their midst, as if out of nowhere. He offers no explanation for the display of the wounds. Some say it was to confirm his identity, to prove that he was the one that he claimed to be. But the wounds bring back memories. They remind them of what they wanted to forget. The events in the Upper Room tell a story about wounds that surface, testifying to wounds that "have never passed away." Histories of suffering return in this space, both perilous and promissory. His body tells truths about the past, but it also signals a future. It speaks something more, not beyond history but across it. The past is alive, but they hold its difficult truths in tension. He sends them out, with life-giving breath. Stepping out, a new collective life takes shape.

Hidden Wound

The wounds of racism live under the surface of our collective skin. While many refer to them as wounds of the past, author Wendell Berry narrates racism within the United States by employing the image of a hidden wound. "The wound is in me, as complex and deep in my flesh as blood and nerves," he writes.[1] He reaches to the stories of his childhood, convinced that the mechanisms of a racist system are present in the stories of individuals. Growing up white in the American South, Berry ponders the ways in which his childhood shaped him to see, or more curiously, *not to see*, the racism that permeated every part of life. Instead of a grand issue that was openly discussed, racism was woven into the everyday and lodged within the stories passed down through generations. The reality of racism was manifest in its operations, forming and shaping each facet of life. But it was not acknowledged for what it was. Berry identifies racism as a historical wound that lives just below the surface of collective life, occupying a space within each inhabitant. Titling his reflections *The Hidden Wound*, Berry presents the problem of race as a wound that is there but not visible, active, and accessible. It is a historical wound that remains hidden but nonetheless powerfully shapes the present. Hiddenness has a dual sense: wounds are out of sight, and they are intentionally covered over. It is handed down from one generation to the next, but "its pain has never been openly admitted."[2]

Berry's narration is a soul-searching reflection on what it means to bring to consciousness one's participation and culpability in a history that precedes one and yet somehow imprints itself deeply, individually. As a white man, Berry says that he had always known this wound, but it was at another level, unknown. Racism is an inescapable evil lodged inside that may or may not be registered and brought into conscious life. The wound is composed of events and nurtured, thickened, and woven tightly by the stories that support ways of life. Experiences, narrated through time, combine with explanation, and a logic builds over time to account for the racist structures of society. This is "just the way things are"; and, layer upon layer, the wound is covered over. To acknowledge dissonance between the experiential and the explanatory is to "register" the wound. Because the question of race is lodged within him, he insists that the wound must be surfaced and worked through. There is a necessary process of coming to terms as a white man in the United States with a "complex and deep" history of race.

Berry names its effects as a moral crisis, but even morality does not capture what he identifies as a severing of one's affections. As a young boy, he began to encounter a system that belied his own affinities and required him to mistrust his strongest human connections. Artificial boundaries were reinforced and fortified with the logic of superiority and hate, and as a grown man he began to reflect on how formative those teachings of his childhood were. The wound that grew in him cut him off from a certainty of the heart that he experienced in childhood.[3]

Racism was not a betrayal of a moral order, although he would certainly say that was operative, but a breaking of bonds of affection and trust. Racial divisions, and the appointed roles assigned to each race—white and black—severed his affections, his capacity to love.[4]

Although Berry introduces this wound as part of his personal history, he also employs the image of wounds to speak about a collective condition of how race lives on in the present. Berry names it as a collective wound, but he insists that the suffering is not equal, the consequences not the same for white and black Americans.

Willie Jennings retrieves Berry's image of the wound to respond to situations of racialized violence in the Age of Ferguson.[5] These incidents touch a nerve and remind us of this wound and how easily it can be reactivated. He conveys, along with Berry, the sense that the wound is shared: "The deep wound of our racial history has never passed—no one in America lives without it."[6] He also underscores the insight that the wound, while linked to a historical past, is present; it remains in and with us. Unhealed wounds of the past persist and surface in the present, appearing in unrecognizable ways, in forms that confound. These symptoms of an untended wound manifest in life but are not integrated. They appear as figures of what was never fully reckoned with. Examining the wounds of race within the United States in relation to the story of Thomas positions the story of resurrection within the context of the aftermath of historical violence. It is a powerful contemporary example of what happens when these histories surface in public and when Christian theology reckons with the past.

Sacred Bandages

A wound remains, untended, below the surface of the collective skin. Coming to terms with history involves a spiritual reckoning and a process of unraveling the stories that were told about why things are the way that they are. Berry explores the spiritual toll of these long histories and implicates Christianity in covering over the unsurfaced wound. Berry writes, "Far from curing the wound of racism, the white man's Christianity has been its soothing bandage—a bandage masquerading as Sunday clothes, for the wearing of which one expects a certain moral credit."[7] This image of bandaging what has not come to the surface highlights the insidious role of Christianity in this history. Christianity claims to offer healing, but in fact it is implicated in covering up and covering over wounds that lie beneath the surface. If and when they are surfaced, Christianity does not allow them to be exposed to the light.

"White man's Christianity" renders the Christian story in a particular way, offering a justification of white superiority. The story, as it transmits, divorces the Christ of faith from the Jesus of history.[8] The particularities of the history drop out as the eternal story hovers above the soil of everyday life. The Band-Aid narrative spiritualizes, interiorizes, or privatizes the wounds. Wounds become symbols for sin or human limitation, but they are unable to speak about the wounds of race. There is a disconnect between the violence at the heart of the Christian story and racialized violence.

Christian accounts of resurrection often include visions of healing and newness, visions of light overcoming the darkness. Visually, it is not difficult to see how these theologies of resurrection function. They can actually block healing from taking place. Such theologies promise resurrection as a miracle cure for the wounds of history. But in doing this they can cover over the surface without tending to the wounds beneath the surface. They are sacred bandages on untended wounds.

The image of the hidden wound speaks to the challenge of coming to terms with one's history and what it would take to register the wound when approaching it from a position of privilege. Berry turns to the wound, pointing to a process of awakening to the long stretch of our histories and to the ways that they have formed us, both individually and collectively. The insidious nature of racism is such that it can live within us for a long time and become part of how we come to understand ourselves. Berry notes that he registered the wound at some level. But what stirred him to reengage that history, to bring its truths to the surface? While he knew that it was working on him, the move to surface and tend to it required more than awareness.

Berry approaches the wounds through recalling the stories of his youth. Staying with the stories is important because those visceral memories are instrumental to registering the wound. The stories also point to some of the hidden dynamics at play in how racism operates more broadly. The concreteness of stories evokes the particulars of place and our attachments to them. They bring up feelings, desires, without losing the sense of place. Stories capture something of the weight and texture of racism. Stories keep us close to the skin. From the earliest age, Berry had an awareness that certain lines should not be crossed; these lines required him to betray the natural allegiances he felt as a young boy. The somatic and affective experiences of early childhood—his affections—are reflected in his stories, and they present readers with the dissonance between the filial bonds formed in childhood and the logic of division that dominated the larger social space.

Given Berry's indictment of Christianity, the question is whether the Christian story can be read otherwise. Black theologians are attuned to the dynamics of covering over and surfacing wounds that have been operative in Christian narrations of the story of life emerging from death, of cross and resurrection. They are aware that a Christian narration of wounds can cut multiple ways. Rather than covering over wounds, the Upper Room provides narrative components to speak to the return of wounds in the present. It attests to the haunting of history and to the work of inscribing that history otherwise. Approaching the Thomas story with an eye to the dissonance and to its affective dimensions, this ancient story might open to alternative ways of theologically narrating the wounds of race.

Ongoing Crosses

Black theologians brought the narrative of the Christian cross together with the history of slavery in the United States, linking those histories and insisting that the Christian story must contend with the violence of slavery and segregation. They differ in their assessment of whether the symbol of the cross is redemptive, but they agree that the cross cannot hover above the soil of human histories. It must be read in relation to the subjugation of peoples, the collective dynamics of power and privilege. The cross is something that Christians must contend with; it is the symbol that insists that white and black Christians confront the shame and humiliation of that event, and the cruelty that they can enact. The cross turns them to do the work of confronting histories of harm. Black theologians raised important questions about how to interpret the violence at the center of the Christian story, but they differ in terms of how they position black communities of faith in relation to it. The cross speaks of suffering and violence. But can the cross be a liberative symbol for multiple communities?

Theologian James Cone offered one of the most recognizable affirmations of the power of the Christian cross to speak to the wounds of race within the United States. He reinforced the centrality of the cross, presenting it as a solution to the suffering inflicted on black peoples. The cross offers both judgment and healing, and, in Cone's thought, the

symbol of the cross represented the paradox of God's work of redemption. Both terror and beauty are held together in the "God of Jesus
revealed in the cross and the lynching tree," Cone writes.[9] The black
church, through its use of spirituals and testimonies, has been able to
hold that paradox. Cone insists that it takes a certain way of viewing the
cross to see redemption enacted there. It takes a certain way of reading
that event not only to surface wounds but also to transform them.

Cone insists that gazing at the cross is necessary, as a confrontation
with the violence of that history. The problem, Cone says, is that both
white Christians and black Christians want to turn away from the hor-
ror of the event. By linking the cross and the lynching tree, Cone makes
it impossible for them to turn away. The gaze, as Cone presents it, is a
way of seeing double, of being able to connect crosses across time. He
brought the ancient cross of Christianity into the present, insisting that
Christians could not read that event apart from the crosses of history.
The cross is not just a past event but a kind of represencing and restaging
of that horrifying event, jolting white Christianity out of its compla-
cency. The shame of crucifixions for blacks and the denial of harm done
by whites must be confronted by a theology of the cross.

Whereas Cone says that white America must turn to the cross to
see the suffering that they have enacted there, Willie Jennings questions the ability of white America to do so. The problem with white
Americans is not that they cannot turn to see the cross; they can stare
up at the cross, but they are looking through a lens that reflects their
own image—of whiteness. Insofar as this gaze has become normative,
it produces christologies in its own image. When black Christians look
through this lens, they are asked to witness the continual erasure of their
bodies from redemptive reach. Jennings wants to expose the dynamics
on the ground, so that we can see the production of this lens from the
ground up.[10]

Instead of Cone's vision upward, Jennings' attention turns down-
ward to the ground and soil in which the Christian cross is placed. The
problem of modern Christian theology is that it is wedded to colonial
practices that it attempts to continually erase: "A Christianity born of
the colonial wound" forgets its origins.[11] To remember these origins is
to expose the insidious use of Christian teachings to justify the enslavement of black peoples. This history indicts white Christians. Jennings'
critique leads to this stunning truth: Christian theology is produced
by erasing wounds. It sanitizes and purifies. Theology birthed from

this wound is dependent on ongoing practices of erasing these origins. It insists on pure beginnings that hover above the soil. And if and when theology hovers above the soil, it denies harm done to bodies on the ground.

The soil is diseased at its very roots. Jennings asks us to think about how the disease might be confronted and cured through the cultivation of a different engagement with the crucifying tree. He turns attention to the cultivation of practices over time that erase the wounds of history, and to the Band-Aid of Christian thought to which Berry refers. Modern theologians presume that they could interpret the ancient story apart from the soil. Jennings' image of the soil turns the concept of imagination away from a soaring activity, directed from viewer onto the cross, to a more grounded one. Jennings roots Cone's cross in the soil.

The recent surge of racialized violence in the United States underscores the need for this continued theological work. The crucifixions are still taking place. While the frequency of incidents is apparent, there are growing questions about how these incidents are linked—to each other and also to the history of slavery. Additionally, the examination of that history comes at a time when the term "post" is invoked, such as "a post-racial" America. But assertions that America is "beyond race" correspond with the uptick in racialized violence, suggesting that there is something wrong with the narrative that America is "beyond" race.

As analysis of the state of race in the United States emerges in public discourse, it exposes the notion that history is not a record of events in the past. History, for those attuned to race, is the unaddressed harm that lives on. To register this history as over and past is the privilege of those who write history. And yet the record of the past and how it is registered in bodily life are not the same. The notion of an afterlife captures something of the way that the events of slavery remain alive in the present. This requires a shift in how we think about history. The first way to view history is as a record of past events, and the second way is as a more complex interplay of past events that were pushed below the surface of collective life by those who maintain positions of privilege and dominance. Instead of thinking of slavery as a series of events in the past, this notion of history requires thinking about the ongoing effects of racism that extend beyond recorded history. Referring to this as the afterlife insists on taking the second notion of history seriously. It requires thinking less in terms of something being "over" and more in terms of levels of visibility and presence. The events live on, but to varying degrees of visibility.

Trauma theories provide a way of interpreting the past as "alive" in the present, via the phenomenon of traumatic repetition, but they are not able to account for the lived experiences of ongoing racism. The concept of "insidious trauma" emerged within trauma studies to distinguish how the dynamics of race constitute trauma. Viewing racism through the lens of trauma, although not uncontested and without critique, highlights the limitations of thinking of trauma as determined by an event and its aftermath. Writers such as Geoffrey Canada were contesting the concept of PTSD, arguing that communities like his did not experience an "after" or end to the harm but, instead, lived with ongoing violence.[12] The harm was also linked to broader systems that benefit from keeping certain populations in more vulnerable positions. Insidious trauma was not trauma isolated to an event but a continuing series of events that comprised the conditions of ongoing life. Traumatic symptoms can be identified, but the diagnosis seemed to miss critical dimensions. The image of "invisible wounds," often used to represent trauma, must extend beyond the clinical framework to speak about the processes involved in rendering suffering invisible and of keeping those truths from coming to the surface. We can think of this in terms of the wider politics of trauma.

But trauma studies also underscore certain truths about how histories of unaddressed violence function. This is perhaps best expressed through the fiction of Toni Morrison: history haunts the present, precisely because the events were not addressed and justice was not done. In terms of the history of racism in the United States, the notion that slavery is "over" misses the ways in which that history cannot be bounded by a particular date or piece of legislation. In the experience of trauma, what is not integrated returns. The ghost in Morrison's *Beloved* is the figure of a history of wounds returning. And while this return speaks about the wounds of race experienced by black America, it conveys a much broader message about the hidden wounds of race that live on under the surface. Wounds and ghosts mark the landscape of "post-racial" America. The identification of a *hidden* wound expresses that well; wounds live on below the surface of conscious life. And the surge of racialized violence *is* a manifestation of what exists below the surface.

While the centrality of the cross has been called into question in twentieth-century theology because of the horrors of history, it is the notion of ongoing crosses that comes to the fore, as wounds surface, as if to resurrect and enact long histories of suffering. This calls for theological accounts of the "afterlife" of the crosses of history. This draws on the Christian conception of the afterlife, reading it not in terms of an event in the future but as a condition of living amid ongoing violence. The afterlife speaks to a constellation of dynamics that operate when histories of harm remain untended. It suggests that there is not just a refusal of white America to see the cross, as Cone adeptly names, but dynamics of not-seeing that persist and weave into logics that imbed deep within persons and groups. Berry's image of the hidden wound captures the more unconscious dimensions of how racism lives on, and the dangers of viewing racism in solely active and visible terms—as prompted by conscious intention and action. Its persistence below the surface of skin points to what is more difficult to access and acknowledge.

To make sense of the "living on" of racial wounds (as inhabiting the skin of both black and white America but also perpetuated through systems), it is crucial to read the wounds of cross and resurrection together. The wounds of crucifixion return, not to be relived but to surface the ongoing wounds that lie just beneath the surface. Turning to the cross alone is not sufficient, because the challenge is to surface the wounds made invisible in the ongoingness of the crosses of history. The dynamics operative in surfacing wounds are complex, and they involve working through denial, fear, and the insidious operations of privilege.

The Johannine account of resurrection in the Christian gospels uniquely situates the return of the risen Jesus within a context of wounds. The display of wounds is at the center of the story, first in the appearance to the group and then more particularly to Thomas. Those appearances link resurrection to the memory of an event that "never passed away." The cross, the event, does not end. Instead, the event lives on. But it does not do so without interruption, and the encounters in the Upper Room suggest a confrontation with wounds and new configurations of life on the other side of death. By linking the crucifixion and the Upper Room, it may be possible to address wounds of history surfacing in the present, countering the forms of Christian discourse that falsely bandage them.

This, we could say, is where the Gospel of John distinctively points. Jesus says to the disciples that they will come to terms with that event only after it has happened.[13] The history returns but does so accompanied by a spirit that not only insists that this particular history matters and that wounds must be surfaced but also offers a different way forward. His return is not simply a confirmation of what has happened, but it restores a critical dimension of the life that he lived—featuring a reconfiguration of relationships, given the ongoingness of the histories.

This makes the site of the Upper Room even more important; the wounds that return are figures of traumatic after-living. Can these wounds speak to the insidious dynamics of historical wounds?

The Upper Room

Jesus came and stood among them and said, "Peace be with you." After he said this he showed them his hands and his side. Then the disciples rejoiced when they saw the Lord. Jesus said to them again, "Peace be with you. As the Father has sent me, so I send you."

—*John 20:20-21*

In each of the gospels, the resurrection appearances feature encounters with the risen Jesus. Those whom he meets struggle to identify him, even amid familiar surroundings. The Gospel of John, in particular, highlights the problem of seeing. When he returns, the disciples are not able to recognize him by merely looking at him. The sequence of appearances to Mary, to the group of disciples, and to Thomas provides a commentary on sight, which culminates in a final statement about the relationship between seeing and believing. His encounters require some other means of recognition. The gospel account places a wedge between seeing and recognition.

And here, when he returns in the Upper Room, there is something wrong with their sight. When he appears, the first thing he says is "Peace be with you." After he offers these words, he displays his hands and side. He shows them his wounds. The verse following indicates, rather simply, that the disciples rejoiced when they saw him. They appear to have no problem recognizing him, but it is their ease of recognition that prompts Jesus to repeat himself, addressing them a second time, "Peace be with you." The repetition of the statement is unusual, if read as a mere greeting. It causes us to think that they may *not* have heard it the first time. They claim to see. But his repetition may be an indication that he is not so certain that they comprehend what is taking place. Their ease suggests that their seeing is misguided. The lens through which they are looking offers them a vision of his appearance;

yet this vision is subsequently called into question by Jesus, who repeats himself, even after they have celebrated his return.

Jesus, by repeating his words, calls into question their seeing. Their ease suggests that they might be placing this encounter within a framework that is familiar to them. Perhaps they quickly incorporate this encounter into what they know or expect. While they "see" him within a particular framework, his return cannot be so easily grasped. His body cannot be so easily identified. He stops them from reinscribing this appearance within the framework of what they have known.

Multiple misrecognitions have already taken place in this gospel. Just before this scene, Mary, the first to witness his resurrection, mistakes him for the gardener and only comes to recognize him by the altered sounds of her name. The compilation of the gospel stories does not disparage the failure of the disciples to see; instead, it expands the role of witness to engage multiple senses. Seeing—a privileged sense in the Western tradition—is being displaced here. Their misrecognition is not that they fail to look or even look away. The problem is that their sight needs to be called into question. Looking through their familiar optics, the disciples could be operating with what Jennings identifies as a faulty optics, a symptom of the broader problem of a "diseased social imagination."[14]

He registers the conditions in which they are operating. Gripped by fear of the world outside, they are in danger of becoming entrenched. They are afraid of losing control. Sight is displaced because the ease through which they claim to see suggests, instead, a failure to see. The other senses come into play here, as a means of calling into question not just their ability to see (as traditionally rendered) but the broader problem of the optics. John Calvin's analysis, as representative of a whole strain of Christian thought, returns: to believe is not to be dependent on sight. Instead, faith is about believing in what cannot be seen. But belief, read this way, is lifted off the soil. It is, in Jennings' terms, interpreted from the "commanding heights."[15] The problem of sight lies in an un-interrogated optic.

He follows this with three directives. He tells them that he is sending them out, that they will need to leave the room. It is a commissioning: "As the Father has sent me, so I send you." Then he breathes on them, instructing them to receive a holy spirit. This breath links to words about forgiveness. He speaks to an aspect of their life together, about how they are to hold on to the past. Retaining the past in a certain way will affect you, he tells them.

Jesus follows the display of wounds and the words of peace with breath. He returns to give them breath again. "When he had said this, he breathed on them and said to them, 'Receive *a* holy spirit.'"[16] While this is often extrapolated as the gift of the Holy Spirit, there is a strong link etymologically to literal breath. A link between this spirit and the breath of life in Genesis 2:7 has been noted by commentators;[17] there is a statement here about life at its most fundamental level. The particular word for breath used here emphasizes the natural and embodied dimension of breath. Receive breath back again. It is as if they had been deprived of it. Within the context of fear and lockdown, the breath becomes short. The living Jesus stands in front of them, but what he reveals is that they, as the living, are not taking in life. On lockdown, there is no air. And if they are to be sent out, they will need to be sourced at this most basic level. They need breath in order to go out, to be sent. This gift of breath turns us back to the question of whether the disciples were themselves in a half-dead state—cut off from their life force. His breath, released as spirit, becomes a life source for them.

John 20:23 names very specifically the need for breath in relation to the practice of forgiveness. Retaining the sins of others who have harmed you literally drains the life from you. It takes away breath. Holding those sins is like having that animosity reside within you, thus denying the air needed for basic life function. To have those sins live in you is like being out of breath. Forgiveness, as he speaks about it here, is directly tied to a somatic experience of breathing.

Breath, spirit, and wounds are bound together in this Johannine gospel, and they function to tell truths. Jesus promises that a spirit will carry his memory forward, but the memories are difficult, and the wounds mark their return. The introduction of a spirit into this space is significant. The spirit is both familiar and not, just as Jesus is. The Johannine spirit mixes elementally—blood and water, skin and air. Spirit stirs senses, as memories return via the wound. The spirit is the memory of the past that haunts; and yet released into this space, exhaled into the collective space, it takes new shape.

Hearing news of this appearance, Thomas insists on seeing the risen Jesus for himself: "Unless I see and touch, I will not believe." Jesus appears again, a week after his first appearance, and he enters the same way—coming through the walls. While the means of his appearance

SURFACING WOUNDS   83

arrests our attention, it can take away from the status of the disciples. They are *still* inside the room. Thomas is with them the second time, and Jesus repeats the words of peace before addressing Thomas directly. Thomas' earlier request is forceful, even violent, as he declares the terms of his believing. He must repenetrate the wounds of the crucified. The physicality of this request suggests that Jesus' wounds will be reopened with the thrust of Thomas' finger. He does not want to just see—he wants to put his finger into the side. He insists on access to the body and, at some level, to command what is taking place. He wants the encounter on his own terms. It is how he knows to approach what is unfamiliar to him.

Jesus returns to the disciples and invites Thomas to come closer and to plunge his hand in the wounds: "Put your finger here and see my hands."[18] Jesus appears to satisfy Thomas' demands by inviting him not just to touch the wounds but to reach his hand into them. Jesus takes Thomas' request even further. Do not just put your finger into my side. Plunge your hand into it.

And Jesus repeats Thomas' request, as if to confront Thomas with his own words. Instead of fulfilling Thomas' request, his invitation reveals Thomas' insidious logic. In John Calvin's reading, the wounds are simply a vehicle to lead Thomas to belief. But here, the wounds of history are returning on this marked body, and that history is brought forward in such a way that believing is inextricably linked to engaging those wounds. The force of Thomas' request is not affirmed. Instead, it is opened up to him. He is confronted with what he is capable of, what harms he has done.

The earlier appearance suggests that the disciples glossed over the wounds. They see them, but they do not register them. Celebrations ensue. Jesus' appearance to Thomas directs us to the possibility that wounds can be reopened; the wounded body returns, as if vulnerable to re-wounding. Thomas' request is often interpreted as a bold affront to the truth of Jesus' return. But it is rarely interpreted as violent or coercive. Thomas sets his terms when he is outside the Upper Room— "Unless I see and put my finger in the marks, I will not believe." He brings those demands into the room. Now facing the marked body, the request is repeated—aired out in the open.

When Thomas enters the Upper Room, the air is different. Jesus has already been there, and a spirit has been released. The Jesus whom Thomas insists on grasping does not simply match his request, because the risen Jesus is not altogether the same. This body is continually changing throughout this scene. What kind of body is this? It is not a body that can be grasped or possessed. It is fleshy and spirited. It is here and not here. In his return, Jesus rejects the grasp. He is familiar and yet not. Thomas is invited to plunge his whole hand in. Bodies awaken, as the memories flood in. The materiality of the scene is difficult to deny. This new spirit bears the memory of violence enacted upon bodies. He is the crucified one. He is the shamed and humiliated one.

With the gift of a spirit in the form of breath, truths surface. Jesus stands in front of Thomas, and he brings history forward to be healed. But the room needs to change. And truths need to be told. Thomas stares into the wounds, and he is confronted with his past and the force of his own demand. And it is as if Jesus, in matching Thomas' words, insists now on different terms: It is not enough to see the marks. He will have to touch them.

Wounds surface pasts, and the two appearances suggest that when Jesus returns, displaying those wounds, it is met with two responses. First, the disciples do not register the wounds, but they celebrate his return nonetheless. This is like a soothing bandage, a gloss over what is taking place. Thomas' response represents a logic that potentially reinscribes suffering. It is a response that imposes control. Both of these responses to Jesus' return make sense, especially within an environment on lockdown. But Jesus' display of wounds surfaces truths that the disciples are not prepared to see. He begins to reorient them to life there. And if transformation is going to take place, it will require registering and surfacing wounds. Surfacing wounds is not a smoothing over; it involves confrontation and engagement.

The Upper Room is often depicted as a space of transformation in which the disciples come to terms with their lives following his death. They are concerned with their future, and the room depicts a meeting of past and present that will determine how they move forward. And yet this room is under the grip of an old logic that has a hold on the disciples; if wounds surface, there will be conflict. When we first meet the disciples, there is no possibility of encounter there, unless new air is breathed into the space. When it is, new terms are set, and the force of an old logic is exposed.

a meeting of past & present

Crooked Room

Melissa Harris-Perry invokes the image of a crooked room to speak about the experience of black women in America. They are continually subjected to distorted images of who they are. The structures of society serve as the walls that define their movements. And yet the problem lies with the architecture. The crooked room names their predicament. The image comes from a psychology experiment in which research subjects were placed in a crooked room and were asked to describe their orientation. The studies reveal that when people sit on crooked chairs in the crooked room, in time, they perceive that they are oriented correctly. And yet that perception is a distortion of reality. According to Harris-Perry, the crooked room is the product of the construction of white America, with structural racism written into the blueprint. Black women suffer the effects of living amid the stereotypes that culture places on them.[19]

Black women, she says, are "attempt(ing) to stand upright in a room made crooked by the stereotypes about black women as a group."[20] It is difficult to balance oneself and to define one's own ground when you live long enough in a space that continues to view you negatively. The challenges are not simply external; there is psychic impact in living with these distortions. How is it possible to be recognized otherwise—either internally or externally? Those who do not fit into the idyllic vision must nonetheless be perceived according to its measurements. While the room *is* crooked, those standing within it are subject to its rules.

Harris-Perry points to testimonies of black women who model upright posture in a crooked room. Just as some in the cognitive psychology research tests were able to stand upright despite the tilt, there are some black women who have been able to find their way, while recognizing the distortions. These women register, at some level, that something is fundamentally wrong with the architecture. The analogy of the crooked room points to the ways in which seeing can be distorted by the structures that govern everyday life. The construction of the room is rarely questioned, and it requires individuals to conform, to move in particular ways within its walls.

Harris-Perry identifies the predicament as a problem of recognition.[21] The struggle of the room is a more fundamental struggle than one of goods and resources; it is a struggle to find "meaningful recognition of [one's] humanity and uniqueness."[22] She underscores this point. She employs a phrase from Charles Taylor to echo the problem of the crooked room: "A person or group of people can suffer real damage, real distortion, if the people or society around them mirror back to them a confining or demeaning or contemptible picture of themselves."[23] These mirrors distort the reality of the situation and have, Harris-Perry emphasizes, great negative psychic impact.[24] In the crooked room, structured according to the logic of the white gaze, occupants cannot see straight.

Harris-Perry's invocation of the crooked room provides a way of thinking about the long-term effects of systemic racism. While speaking about the effects for black women, the distorted logic misshapes life for all who inhabit the room, requiring both internal and external work. The room offers a commentary about the effects of the collective suppression of historical wounds. The room is constructed over time and by the stories and practices that sustain certain ways of living. Habits of mind and body form the walls, such that the walls are not recognized as boundaries of thought, as limitations placed on those who move in the space. The walls fortify the logic of racism.

In that room, wounds cannot surface, truths cannot be told. The result is that the logic suffocates and distorts. Berry's image of the hidden wound returns. The hidden wound images the effects of living under these conditions and how harms, left unaddressed, become part of the architecture. He says that registering and bringing the wounds to the surface will not be easy, especially given that the logic is smooth, facilitating a certain way of life for some. The logic constructed over time is protective for some, and when the collective wound is exposed, fear can take over, and occupants can react in often-surprising ways. Those most powerful can perceive themselves as under attack.

While there is a logic to racism, the somatic and affective dimensions of living within these systems has a different kind of hold over us. Although it does not make sense that those who are in power feel under attack, the stories told over time construct and sustain a narrative that seeps into skin. Describing the ways that stories were handed down to him, Berry writes, "This repetition of what was known in common, I think, was a sort of ritualization of the family's awareness of itself as a unit holding together through time."[25] Those stories were casually told and retold. But they form bonds of identity and allegiance. They work on the affective level. Berry's attempt to trace the fragmentation that gradually took place within him suggests that the power of systemic racism lies in an intricate weaving of word and body.

Jesus confronts Thomas with the force of his own request. The logic with which he has been operating is exposed. It is turned back at him, as if to reveal parts of himself that he does not want to see. Berry opens his book with an epigraph from William Carlos Williams, "I am—the brutal thing itself."[26] It is the jagged tooth upon which his fuller reflections are cut. While he does not return to it, it expresses the position of Thomas. This "I am" statement points to a stark and individual task—to confront the brutality made possible by the day-to-day stories that we pass on to subsequent generations. While the transformation in the Upper Room points to the cultivation of a collective imagination, not everyone is positioned equally in respect to these wounds. There is individual work to be done.

In the crooked room, wounds remain below the surface. But when Jesus appears to the disciples, he presents them with wounds. He displays them in the open. Reading the Upper Room as a crooked room recasts this biblical scene as a surfacing of wounds that live just below the surface. Until its distorted logic is exposed, it cannot yield life. When the wounds surface, the disciples fail to register their impact. They see and yet don't see. Misrecognition is at the root of racism, Harris-Perry says. "Misrecognition has been a central theme in African American intellectual traditions. . . . Racism keeps others from seeing."[27] The memory comes forward in order to surface wounds, but it also brings the possibility that wounds, once surfaced, may yield something new. The walls begin to take different shape as new air is breathed into this space. Suddenly, what they think they see is altered by the presencing of wounds. Believing entails alterations in how they "see" the world. Through dismantling sight, Jesus opens the disciples to a kind of witness that involves affective work, signaled through his invocation of breath and touch. He turns them to the wounds and to the surface of skin. He invites them to come closer and touch.

If we think of the three "Peace" statements as unfolding moments in a surfacing of historical wounds, it is important to acknowledge the fear under which they are operating. And when Jesus returns and displays his wounds, they will be difficult to see. Remaining in the room distorts perception.

Jesus acknowledges that releasing familiar logic may involve resistance; he confronts Thomas with dimensions of who he is. The nearer you get to the wounds, things will begin to stir within. Jesus' words name the fear. The encounter with the risen Jesus confronts Thomas on the affective level. He is awakened, in Berry's words, to his "complicity in history and in the events of [his] own life."[28]

Facing the wounds of the risen Jesus, Thomas experiences something that prompts him to exclaim, "My Lord and my God." It is not clear exactly what takes place. But the space between his finger and the wounds involves an unraveling of the logic most familiar to him and a surfacing of past truths that are difficult to register. How Thomas finds a way forward is uncertain (we do not know if he responds to the invitation to touch the wounds), but the communal nature of the scene expands beyond Thomas. His encounter points to one aspect of the work of surfacing memories of wounds. The overall sequence turns to the work of the community in working through this history.

If the turn in the narrative comes when Thomas approaches the wounds, it is important to reflect on the identity of the risen Jesus and who Christians profess him to be. As a sacred narrative, this encounter yields a vision of God. Christians claim that this body is not just any body but God's body. And, as such, it is a body that bears the marks of suffering across time. This has been narrated via theologies of the cross, but crucifixion marks only tell part of the story. The resurrection marks insist on a surfacing of the histories of forgetting and erasing of wounds that sustain the crooked room. The crosses of history are able to stay disconnected, because those who witness them enact dynamics of erasure and denial; no reflective and interrogative mechanisms are in place to question the lens through which the event is narrated. As Jennings notes, there must be attention to the practices that cultivate particular ways of seeing and not-seeing. The Jesus who returns cuts through fear and exposes his wounds. And he makes the wounds visible on his body, marking the impossibility of erasure. For Jesus to return with these marks is another facet of God's work of bearing the suffering; this body holds the memory of all sufferings and marks them bodily.

While theologies of the cross diverge in meaning, Christianity is distinctive in its claim that God suffers. These wounds are a means by which people interpret God's relationship with their own suffering. The interpretations range from viewing the crucifixion wounds as God's solidarity with them to viewing them as God's sacrifice enacted in their behalf. And yet this image of a resurrected God with wounds alters the meaning.

Wounds are spirited, and breath is enfleshed. Divinity and humanity cross in a curious configuration. Memory is brought forward, awakening and inhabiting bodies. This gospel places wounds before the disciples to insist that memory-work constitutes their lives going forward.[29] They are commissioned, sent out, to continue what he started. Before his death, he tells them that he is giving them a spirit that will remind them of what has come before and that will link past, present, and future. This spirit will not do so in any linear way but, instead, will inhabit them, bearing with them in the after-living.

But this is not a spirit hovering above the soil.[30] The return of wounds indicates that this memory-work will take place on the ground and on the surface of skin. This return of wounds does not just resurface past trauma but provides a site of encounter in which wounds, surfaced, can be tended. The fact that this wound-work is rooted in God's body, in the wounds of the divine crossing death and life, means that this witness is placed within a broader cosmology. This body bears wounds across time. And thus this symbol holds promise. It is a body that holds the suffering and makes possible a way other than one of animosity and hatred. The promise held in these marks does not come to fruition by gazing at the marks but by registering in them one's connection to historical wounds.

He exhales these words, "Receive a holy spirit." The presence of spirit in the accounts of death and resurrection are unique in the Gospel of John. In his final talk to the disciples before his death, Jesus promises another spirit (*parakletos*) to them, implying that he is spirit, that they have known something of this spirit, because they have been with him. He then breathes his final breath on the cross; the exhale is connected to spirit (*ruah*), which is the term in Hebrew for wind and breath. And then when he returns, he exhales a new spirit (*pneuma*), which is to be inhaled by the community gathered in the Upper Room. This spirit will guide the community in the after-living. The importance of spirit in this gospel is clear, and its connection to literal breath, memory, and the cycles of death and birth are expressed throughout.

When Jesus promises the paraclete, the spirit who arrives in the wake of his departure, he says that the spirit will guide them into truth. But this involves remembering distinctively (not as the world does).[31] There is a way of registering wounds, a way of holding those memories, that does not allow the discourse of wounds to hover above the surface, to be abstracted. Instead, the particular textures of life are carried forward. This is what makes hauntings so powerful. They bring back the memory, both in a way that is familiar and not. It is the interplay of familiarity and distance that is important. Truths cannot just skirt the surface.

This spirit is often identified in Christian history as *the* Holy Spirit. Early Christian apologists turned to this gospel to support the developing concept of what we now refer to as the Trinity. In so doing, they defined the Spirit in connection to the Father and the Son. Its nature and function presented within a Trinitarian figuration, commentators gave definition to the Spirit by determining its origins and linking the work of the Spirit to the other two. There was a growing need to tie the Spirit to Christ, warding against claims to independent spirits. The Trinitarian development reflected the early Christian community's search for, and securing of, identity. huh

There is something powerful, however, about an undetermined spirit here. It captures a moment in which recipients are attuned to the past coming forward and to practices of discerning and shaping how the past will be received and made new. The undesignated nature of spirit—*a* holy spirit—may foster attentiveness to particular memories, particular histories. Rather than a general call to accept the gift of *the* Holy Spirit, it may be helpful to think of memories carried forward from a particular time and place, pasts carried forward that bear histories singularly. Receiving a spirit requires attuned responses to where memories come from, which requires knowledge of the soil from which they arose. Spirit *as memory bearer* carries forward the spirit of a place, a situation. When Berry speaks about how stories transmit, they are not abstracted; rather, they are textured. He instructs: The nature of that spirit comes through the shape that you provide for it. Your body, your breath. As my breath meets yours, it will take shape in your midst. This cooperative work is interpreted as holiness work in some traditions, as a participation in the ongoing work of God in the power of the Spirit.

The lack of designation also cautions against the spirit of demand and command that Thomas displays. If *the* Spirit is claimed, it can retain the lockdown logic. Having received *the* Spirit, he can retain the posture of drawing things into what is familiar to him. The difference between *the* Spirit and *a* spirit lies in an ungraspable quality conveyed through the Johannine iteration. It requires both an attentiveness to the location of histories and emphasis on practices of discerning spirits, which will mark their common life together.

This body returns with the memory of a history that insists on being held and brought forward. And as Christians turn and return to this story, they confront this particular history (the Jesus of history) and also claim its power to speak to the ongoing crosses of history (the Christ of faith).[32] His spirit, although distinct (another paraclete), persists in the after-living. He gives form to that spirit, displaying that it is tied to his marked body, but the forms it will take upon release are yet to be determined.

However, instead of drawing attention away from their fear and vulnerability, he invites them to stay close to the surface of skin. The communal work of remembering operates on a visceral level. Breath is singular, yet it is released into a space, recycled to sustain ongoing life. Jesus speaks about how to give life shape, and the contours of a life shaped by the ways communities attend to wounds. Hold them, but do not hold on to them. The capacities for doing this work, identified through the term forgiveness, will come through memory-work. The capacity to acknowledge and reckon with particular histories, but also to encounter these wounds to discover points of crossing. A story of God rooted in history but nonetheless to be lived multiply, in different spirations.

This biblical story is often lifted off the soil and is complicit in a logic that fortifies the walls of privilege. This Band-Aid covers over the account of wounds, sweeping them into a narrative of salvation, offered to some who stand securely within the walls of the Upper Room. And yet there is a way of claiming the significance of this body and this event without falling into the exclusivist ways in which resurrection texts are often employed—claiming resurrection in order to secure the promise of a life for a few. When the disciples approach the wound, they are implicated in the particularity of history and also drawn into the collective work of carrying memories differently—not in the same way that the world carries them, but in a spirit that holds the memories and touches wounds.[33]

Theologies of wounds can often get entangled in logics of glorifying wounds. But this gospel account does not support that. The disciples are not called into greater suffering but invited to discover in the wound a crossing. The wounds can alter their perception and draw them outside their own suffering not in order to abandon and deny it but to reorient them to it. The body that they encounter holds memories of suffering across time. When they come closer, they will find, together, ways of remembering that do not reinforce the erasures of memory. The wounds can be a productive site in which difficult memories are held (and not erased); they can also be the site of potential transformation, in which the crossing of memories might bring about healing.

Telling the Story

In the four resurrection accounts in the gospels, the risen Jesus appears before his disciples, and they do not recognize him. Seeing is impaired. In line with trauma theory, wounds returning in the present bear the marks of past suffering that was not integrated. This surfacing of past wounds holds both peril and promise. Memories return to haunt the present as a way of reckoning with the past. It is a "good haunting" in that it calls forward a past that has been unacknowledged and unreconciled.[34] The goodness lies in the promise that the past comes forward to be addressed. The surfacing of wounds opens up possibilities for breaking the cycles of traumatic violence. But it is also vulnerable to misunderstanding, since the appearances take place in the present, removed from that history. The "past" must be met by a particular kind of witnessing that can account for the complex dynamics of after-living.

By placing black-lynched bodies as the object of the gaze for the witnesses at the foot of the cross, Cone insisted that Christian witness is intricately tied to the suffering of black peoples. In turn, if the good news of resurrection is to be proclaimed by Christians, the witnesses positioned at the site of wounds returning must think in terms of the ongoingness of crosses. How might this ancient resurrection story connect with the contemporary situation of wounds resurrecting—coming to life again—in public spaces? This resurrection of wounds is a traumatic image in which the harms of the past come to light in the present, displaced from that history and thus subject to multiple distortions of memory. Part of what constitutes the trauma are the dynamics of forgetting and denial that are enacted. The disciples represent, in this telling, responses that reflect postures of white privilege, that insist on seeing according to a logic that denies recognition to persons of color. The bandage of Christianity serves some interests at the expense of others. Thus, resurrection involves the return of the wounds that white America does not want to see. Wound-work, then, has to take place according to a different register, targeting the affections.

One of the observations that James Cone makes of Reinhold Niebuhr is that while his theo-logic of the cross is compelling, his failure to account for black suffering reflects a failure to *feel* the cross. This is why the African American spirituals are so important to Cone, because they nurture an affective connection to suffering, drawing participants into a meditation on the cross that cultivates a sensorium of piety. Niebuhr sees, but he does not "feel" the wounds of enslaved peoples. He lacked a "heart to feel it on its own."[35] This latter "seeing" ties to the broader sensorium of experience, ways in which we come to know our world. His inability to link the ancient cross to present-day crosses was the consequences of a formation process that interpreted the Christian message apart from the soil of lived existence. Seeing is a dominant sense in Western thought. But it also operates according to the logic of aligning sight with knowledge, light with truth.

This disconnection between the logic and the affections is what Berry is describing in his analysis of the hidden wound. It was a betrayal of affections, of stunted development of one's affective capacities, that obstructs whites from not only seeing black suffering but from accessing the hidden wound that is also lodged inside of them. Registering these wounds would require the ability to link experiences, feelings, and histories.

Jennings diagnoses this problem by saying that there is a problem in the transmission, or traditioning, of the Christian story, precisely in that the formation processes of the discipline of theology remain unexamined. Speaking of the "soothing bandage" of Christianity that Berry identified, Jennings says that Christian theology has been operating with a "diseased social imagination."[36] It is not just a logic that is transmitted, but ongoing processes that fortify that logic. There is a dissociation, or unwillingness to see, that resides under the skin of Christian theology. It is a wound that involves forgetting the "imperial matrix within which orthodox Christian tradition continues to exist."[37] For Jennings, Niebuhr's failure is a manifestation of broader systems in which persons are trained "not to see" some things. The problem is not just a failure to enact the logic or to supplement it with emotion. The problem lies in the *formation processes* that constitute the discipline of theology. The failure to surface historical wounds is a problem of the larger social imagination. The fact that Niebuhr could not "feel" black suffering is symptomatic of a larger problem with Christian theology and its formation process. Blocked vision is the product of (theological) socialization.

The question facing Thomas and the disciples is whether they will leave the room. This requires individual work, but the shaping forces of the room are such that it cannot just be solo work. Thomas' exclamation

is often read as the climax of the resurrection appearances: Thomas
comes to belief, and his doubt is overcome. But we are not sure if
Thomas engages the wounds or if he falls back into a logic of power and
control with his statement, "My Lord and my God." How do we know
if Thomas confronts his own complicity in the history of wounding?
The capacities to heal a diseased social imagination is the work ahead of
them—the work of truth telling, memory bearing. Is this a cautionary
tale, with the warning that if the reader holds on to the past in the same
way, he or she will not come to life again? The interpretive lens through
which we read this gospel account may determine whether it offers a
bandage or a healing balm.

Reading the Gospel of John with attention to wounds rooted in a
particular history means that truth cannot be accessed unless one con-
tends with one's own past. In this body, the past comes forward, refusing
the superficial bandaging of familiar versions of Christianity. Reading
close to the soil and the surface of skin, a countertheological vision can
be glimpsed. But its future, its expressions, have yet to be given shape.

Crossings

The question of whether resurrection wounds can address the insidious dynamics of historical wounds cannot be answered by stopping
with the vision of the risen Jesus surfacing wounds. The realities of the
ongoing crosses of history, where wounds return and surface, could
lead to a belief that ongoing violence is inevitable. While it is important
to acknowledge that declared endings and conclusions should be held
more tentatively in light of what we know of trauma, there is a danger
of accepting the surge of racialized violence as the new societal norm.

This points to the need to extend a reading of the Upper Room
to imagine the encounter as not just the surfacing of wounds but the
potential crossing of wounds. The story provides theological touch-
points for conceiving of what takes place when historical wounds are
surfaced. We meet Thomas, again, at the moment when he is invited to
plunge his hands into the side of the risen Jesus. The encounter exposes
the logic of the crooked room and confronts Thomas with the force of
what lies below the surface of his own skin.

Surfacing work counters the "soothing bandage work" of a Christianity "masquerading in Sunday clothes."[38] The encounter can ignite
responsibility and enable responsiveness. The commissioning of the disciples is envisioned as working with wounds, as modeling a way of

standing in the midst of the ongoing crosses of history. The communal work involves intercepting the logics that can surface with wounds. Just as Cone says it is difficult to turn one's gaze to see the suffering of the cross, there are equal difficulties in staying with wounds that, once surfaced, become subject to dynamics of resistance, renewed violence, and denial.

When histories of suffering surface in the crooked room, they are unlikely to be recognized. They are either not seen at all or they are viewed according to a logic of competition. Histories of suffering, when surfaced, often compete for attention within the public sphere. This competition model of memory is introduced in the work of Michael Rothberg, who presents an insightful diagnosis of how traumas are represented and remembered. When the wounds of the past return, resurfacing in public, they are often jockeying for space in the marketplace of memory. In a crooked room, there is limited space. He says that memory often works according to a zero-sum game; only some histories can be recognized. Remembering Jewish suffering (represented in the Holocaust) means closing off one's view of other historical traumas, such as the history of slavery. There is only so much memorializing space in public, so historical traumas, ranging across times and places, are competing for this space and, strangely, must discount the gravity of other traumas in order to receive public attention.

Instead of opening up a rich field of dialogue between histories of oppression and legacies of violence, the competition model pits the suffering of victims against each other. While each experience of suffering is unique, it can lead, Rothberg warns, to the creation of a "hierarchy of suffering."[39] Suffering is *scaled*, as if measured on the atrocity scale to discern whose trauma is worthy of being represented and remembered. Remembering one group's trauma entails diminishing, and forgetting, another group's trauma. Attention and resources are limited. While some wounds are lifted up, other wounds remain unacknowledged. This is determined by the social, political, and economic interests shaping remembrance.[40] Within the competition model, histories do not cross; they compete. Any resonance between histories of suffering is blocked.

And yet the reality is that they *are* connected. There are points of connection that are difficult to detect, given the powerful grip of the competition model. One way to discover those connections is to think about memory *multidirectionally*. Rothberg proposes, "I suggest that we consider memory as *multidirectional*: as subject to ongoing negotiation, cross-referencing, and borrowing; as productive and not privative."[41] He is attempting, in his analysis of memory, to move away from the exclusivism of cultural identities to a mode of remembrance that "cuts across and binds together diverse spatial, temporal, and cultural sites."[42]

Rothberg's proposed method of reading history insists that interpreting events singularly is an expression of the logic of privilege. He insists that events of suffering in history are never purely singular. Instead, the notion of singularity and purity is sustained by an "imperial matrix" which insists on keeping histories from touching one another. He is working with a keen understanding of how power works in crooked rooms, how the forms of sovereignty enacted by modern nation-states profit from disconnecting histories. This is one dimension of the competition model: the particularities of events can be insisted upon to such a degree that it obstructs resource sharing. One of the underlying intuitions in Rothberg's proposal is that there is a kind of fundamental connectivity possible in experiences of suffering. This is expressed similarly through Judith Butler's notion of precarity and shared vulnerability; she offers a vision of identity that resonates with the Johannine vision: "I in you and you in me."[43]

To read *across* histories is to intercept a logic that keeps these histories from touching. Rothberg crafts a way of reading history that draws attention to the posture necessary to stand in a crooked room. He aims to display a mode of reading history singularly *and* collectively, finding points of connection that do not place histories of suffering in competition for limited resources. To read singularly is to attend to the texture of each history. To read collectively is to situate it in respect to other histories, displaying what he calls a "generous act of memory."[44] He features a reading of W.E.B. Du Bois' visit to the Warsaw Ghetto following World War II.

Although the competition model requires abandoning the particular history of one people for another, Du Bois' experience suggests that he discovered a way of drawing connections between the suffering of Jewish people in Poland and Jim Crow America. When standing in the ruins of the Warsaw Ghetto, he began to see the "intimate links between race and space."[45] The "ghettos" were not the same, and yet the link between them was the operating logic of the modern nation-state. The problem of the color line stayed with him, but it was no longer in his mind, he says, as a "separate and unique thing."[46] Standing in this one place, it illuminated the suffering of another place, one in which

Du Bois was immersed. What emerged from his travels was a sense of "proximity" that moved the problem of race into a larger sphere, while deepening his analysis of its particular contours. The particulars were not sacrificed, contrary to the logic of the competition model. But standing in the soil of Warsaw, Du Bois discovered "a way of holding together commonality and difference."[47]

This image of Du Bois standing amid the ruins of the Warsaw Ghetto is powerful. His writings about the Warsaw experience reflect his challenge: to refuse the grip of the logic of crooked rooms. How does one cut across that logic? The capacity to rethink one history in relationship to another was made possible by being brought into relationship with another's history. There is a displacement that occurs "in the ruins" that became productive for Du Bois. It comes about, Rothberg claims, by recognizing that the logic of power destroys the passages by which wisdom and resources can be shared, by detecting how potential alliances are severed by the operations of the crooked room.[48] In the crooked room, histories are cordoned off.

And yet standing in the Warsaw Ghetto, Du Bois does not claim to "know" the other's suffering. In fact, he claims not to have a clearer understanding of it. But something is activated in him, making it possible for him to cut through the logic of domination, power, and control. This "point of contact between apparently separate histories" was not a straightforward identification with another history.[49] But Du Bois recognized that both histories were, at some level, "deeply implicated in each other."[50] His encounter exposed a way of holding one's history in proximity to another, touching without grasping.

This is what is made possible in the Upper Room. A kind of knowing that works with resonances and proximities is activated in order to register what is often invisible. The Upper Room narrative offers an invitation to hold suffering in this way, as it speaks to the conditions and capacities necessary for surfacing historical wounds. But it also provides a reckoning with those histories beyond what Rothberg offers. Du Bois is certainly exceptional in his capacity to hold suffering in this way, and yet the Johannine vision renders the exceptional as a way of after-living. A spiritual vision speaks to this activation (and capacity building) and sets before its readers a path toward a more collective vision of crossing wounds.

Conceiving of his wounds as potential sites of wounds crossing reveals the possibilities for dismantling the logic of the crooked room.

The wounds that return on the body of the risen Jesus attest to a singular history but also to a collective one. The encounter with the risen Jesus operates similarly, as the disciples encounter in this body both the singular suffering of one and a constellation of events across time. Spirit here, figured in terms of breath and memory, animates the space and potentially materializes, in and through them, counter movements to the logic of the crooked room. Their movements enact a new relationship to the crosses of history. They cannot simply envision a new reality; they need to feel this reality awakening within them.

When the risen Jesus appears, his wounds provide a site of crossing, not by erasing the memory of crosses, but by bringing the memories together, not to erase them by folding them into one, but by making room for distinctive histories to be held. The "Peace" sequence in the gospel circumscribes this space of memory-work. In these appearances, the memories of past suffering come forward. In a curious meeting of past and future, the disciples are instructed to receive a holy spirit, a spiration of holy breath, in whose power they will reconfigure rooms.

This body surfaces histories but also marks a crossing of those histories. If memory is the past made present, then the figure of wounds returning within the sphere of life is an evocative biblical symbol for the return and potential crossing of histories of suffering in our present time. This is a crossing in which pasts meet, traversing and potentially transfiguring each other. Histories of suffering can come together to cancel each other out, or they could meet, to discover that they are, at some level, touching.

Memories of suffering surface, as he displays his wounds. And yet he presents them *forward*, presenting them to the disciples not as a cross but as a potential crossing. When wounds surface in the Upper Room, the disciples confront the marks of suffering brought forward on the body of Jesus. The wounded-resurrected Jesus that Thomas and the witnesses approach invites them to witness in his return the potential crossing of multiple histories. Resurrection wounds feature a dynamic crossing of old and new and, in turn, the creation of a site from which crossings can be envisioned and enacted, propelled by the vision of tending and transfiguring wounds. Multiple histories meet there. The aim is to address the ongoingness, by forging passages across wounds.

The memory of crucifixion is still alive for those gathered in the Upper Room. The work that they will be sent out to do requires a transformation of heart and mind. The cross returns not as an object or event but as a site of crossings in which the disciples will reckon with these histories and will be asked to carry them forward in a different way. It will take a powerful imagination to conceive the world differently from the site of ruins.[51]

Attention turns to the capacities of those who position themselves there. What enables some to witness a crossing amid the ongoingness? To do this work from the site of ruins, from the wounds, requires the cultivation of new capacities for imagining life. To think of resurrection as a site of crossing wounds without canceling or erasing them positions the crosses of history within a space in which suffering can be engaged. While each wound is particular and must be engaged as such, there is a danger of *not* linking the wisdom and insights of each—of placing them, instead, within the competitive framework of public memory. In the symbol of wounds crossing, particulars meet and cut across, not to sever but to offer a "transnational" wisdom. This meaning of trans- points to a passage *across* wounds rather than a hovering above the surface.

This wound-work is spirited, and the Upper Room is a communal site of witness.[52] Cone insists that it takes a powerful religious imagination to witness the beauty and terror together in the cross event. We could think of Du Bois as an exemplary figure who exercises a powerful act of imagination from the site of ruins. And yet this ignores the communal vision put forward in this gospel account. The disciples stand together, walls closing them in. Whether they will engage the wounds is unclear, but the conditions are set for this work.

Touching Wounds

Few contemporary theologians have felt the backlash of telling the Christian story differently than womanist scholar Delores Williams. Her statement that "there is nothing divine in the blood of the cross" was a landmark moment in which she challenged the dominant logic of atonement in Christian theology.[53] She was motivated by the pursuit of a theological vision that could tell difficult truths about the ongoing wounding of black women.

She took issue with one way of narrating the story of the crucified Jesus. This telling emphasizes that the redemption of humanity comes about through the death of Jesus, who takes upon himself the weight of human sin by dying on the cross.[54] Though deserving of sin, humans are relieved of the punishment by the sacrifice of the God-Man. While this logic has been critiqued on several fronts, Williams was concerned about the image of Jesus as the "ultimate surrogate," which presented the position of surrogacy, known well to African American women, as not only acceptable but also one to be imitated. Her concern was that attributing redemptive power to crucifixion wounds set the stage for glorifying suffering and keeping those who suffer most in society in subordinate positions. This models a way of surrogacy that benefits white man's Christianity. Black women know that experience, occupying the crosses of America. And yet to valorize that experience through the figure of the crucified was to keep women on those crosses. Just as Christ's suffering was necessary to bring about redemption, so, too, black women's surrogacy can be sanctified by theo-logic. The good news of redemption was delivered to black women within a crooked room, thus contributing to their struggle for recognition.

Instead of countering the master logic of violence and domination, Christian theology, Williams says, capitulates to it. Whereas the whole of Jesus' life demonstrates love and healing, the tradition has placed emphasis on his death. The damage is lived out on—and in—the bodies of black women. Black women have been standing in this logic of the cross so long, we can hear Williams say, that it has done real damage. It has stopped them from seeing that the white gospel has had them on the cross all along. Williams believed that the story of Calvary was distorted, and to decry its sanctifying power was to lift the burden of the cross off black women. The good news for black women lies in rooting their faith in a God who, "through Jesus, [gives] humankind new vision to see the resources for positive, abundant relational life."[55]

The firestorm of response came from many angles. But her refusal to attribute divine work to crucifixion wounds overshadows the significance that she attributes to wounds in a womanist vision of life. Williams did not reject the redemptive power of the Christian story altogether. Instead, she shifted the site of that redemptive locus away from the cross to the life and ministry of Jesus.[56] Redemptive power can be found in his vision of righting relationships, which is displayed throughout his ministry. In rejecting a dominant reading of the Christian cross, Williams shifted the redemptive locus of the Christian story to the life of Jesus. The ministry of Jesus demonstrates a different way of living. His ethic provides guidance for women to "revalue life" and to transform the "social relations and arrangements sanctioned by the status quo."[57] The resurrection, for Williams, signals the return of Jesus' ministerial vision. He returns to show humankind that this way of life will not be defeated.

The crosses of history, according to Williams, are countered by the vision of righting relationships. But Christianity's continual identification of redemption with those crosses minimizes the redemptive work of Jesus' life. It is not the defilement of the body—his suffering—that should be given redemptive status. It is his power to bring life that must be emulated, not his sacrificial death: "Jesus came for life, to show humans a perfect vision of ministerial relation that humans had very little knowledge of."[58]

Outlining six ways that Jesus displayed his ministerial vision, Williams points to the importance of touching wounds. Jesus' ministry not only righted relationships between persons but also provided a vision of "righting relations between body, mind, and spirit."[59] It was a holistic ministry that did not divorce word from flesh, mind from body. One of the components of this ministry was healing. The healing ministry of Jesus demonstrated his care for life—a "ministry of touch and being touched."[60] She mentions the touch of lepers and the touch of the woman with the issue of blood. He displays to the disciples the wounds of those around him. He instructed them to do what most others did not want to do, which was to move in closer and touch the wounds. Jesus approached people who were deemed unworthy of recognition. Countering convention through his touch, he often named the logic of power as gripped by a spirit of fear.

But Williams' ministerial vision can also be imagined on the other side of death, in the after-living of the crosses of history. Jesus, who healed through touch throughout his life, returns, but now does so within the precarious territory of the after-living. The work of touching wounds resumes. He had taught his disciples this way, but they had lost sight of it. They have lost their capacity to feel. They must be reanimated and redirected to this work. They must now discover how to reanimate life "from the ruins."[61]

Whereas he turned the disciples to engage the wounds of those unrecognized by society, he now bears those wounds. Subject to the defilement of the cross, he surfaces wounds in order to teach them another dimension of the ministerial vision. God shows them how to live "peacefully, productively and abundantly in relationship."[62] But this "righting," this healing ministry, will confront them with the aftereffects of the defilement of the cross—with the shame, the denial, and the entrenching of logics that threaten to perpetuate violence.[63]

In this vision of resurrection, Jesus is inviting Thomas to participate in the ministerial vision. But Thomas will need, as well, to address his relationship to those wounds. It would be too easy to turn Thomas to the work of healing without considering the ways in which the cross event exposes the "hereditary evil" that lives within him.[64] To continue the ministry of Jesus must involve a reckoning with past harms. There is a confrontation with the cross that we can imagine taking place. The defilement, the cruelty, of one's actions does not disappear but, in fact, takes different form.

It would be easy to fold "a healing ministry of touched and being touched" into a domesticated vision of Jesus' life, providing not the surrogate picture but the servant model of discipleship that Jacqueline Grant warns about.[65] But this is not what Williams presents. The cross requires those who witness it to confront the destruction of the vision of life that Jesus offers. For Thomas, this must involve an examination of his relationship to that wounding.

Resurrection is tied to a process of revaluation. If the cross is the symbol that denies value to some lives, then the return of Jesus, the defiled one, reassigns value to those denied value. Williams continues to emphasize that the womanist task is to revalue "the life-world of African-American women."[66] She concludes her analysis of the cross and redemption by turning to the task of "revaluing value": "the task of revaluing value is absolutely essential for theological and ethical works dealing with black women's reality."[67] Distinct from the work of black male liberation theologians, she says that black women have had to "reconstruct and redeem from invisibility the life-world of African-American women."[68] These skills and capacities that black women have attained to survive and redefine life are vital to navigating the territory of the afterlife.

The invitation to Thomas has an element of confrontation, in that Thomas has to face his own complicity in a logic that devalues certain lives. But it also reorients Thomas to what Williams calls the work of revaluation. Touching wounds, then, can be an image of rein-scribing value—a vision of fierce care—in which an undomesticated vision of the fight to claim life under new terms is inaugurated. Jesus' return gathers the community around a new ethic. Touch symbolizes revaluation. This touch retraces the surface of skin, drawing new lines that allow persons to stand up straight and to be recognized. Refusing the dominant and distorted vision of power and control in the Upper Room, the ability to stand up straight is facilitated by touch. Fingers move across the surface of skin, and the walls of the Upper Room take different shape. It is possible to consider wounds as reminders of a way that he had taught them. Discipleship is work on the surface of skin. And the walls of fortifying logic dismantle, as the contours are redrawn through touch.

The power of Williams' insights is that she opens to a way of conceiving of the ongoingness of crosses by placing emphasis on the ongoing work and struggle of communities to enact an ethic that values life. If the cross is the ultimate sign of the devaluation of life, then resurrection wounds may be the sign of a new assemblage of life. Womanists, Williams claims, know this territory well. The good news is that the ministerial vision that put Jesus on the cross, that threatened the powers and principalities of his day, could not be crushed. Instead, the wounds return, both as a symbol of survival and a symbol of the definitional work facing the new community. It is as if her theological vision anticipates the analysis of trauma—a wisdom is already contained there. The problem of the Upper Room is that the forces of evil and hatred represented in the cross still have a grip on even his closest followers. The memory of crosses still lives on within them, but they carry these memories collectively while also developing ways of moving that construct new paths for response.

Williams provides a powerful way to think about wounds returning on the other side of the cross. Rejecting the sacralization of crucifixion wounds does not foreclose conceiving of resurrection wounds as productive for the after-living. The "ministry of healing the human body, mind and spirit"[69] continues, but in a new register. She writes, "God's gift to humans, through Jesus, was to invite them to participate in this *ministerial vision* ('whosoever will, let them come') of righting relations."[70]

Recalling the centrality of Jesus' ministry close to the surface of skin, it is fitting to think of Thomas' touch in these terms. Reviving the ministerial vision in the after-living, Jesus' invitation to Thomas demands a reorientation of his senses, signaling the need for Thomas to develop affective capacities for addressing wounds. It will not be enough to see. Instead, the womanist vision of righting relations between body, mind, and spirit, appeals to multiple senses for the work of revaluation.

Williams does not speak about the Upper Room in her writings. However, she develops the biblical landscape of wilderness as a territory to speak about the space of living for black women. Like the figure of Hagar, black women made a way in the wilderness, displaying the spirit of struggle and enacting a "communitarian survival ethic."[71] For this community of women, struggle was not a one-time event but an ongoing practice of giving value to what is devalued and made invisible. Williams imagines the terrain of the wilderness in two ways, influenced by moments in the history of slavery. She identifies the first with the antebellum period. Here, the wilderness is a physical space that is embodied and sensuous. It is a territory in which women encounter the divine. This wilderness has an earthiness to it, and it features a sensuous connection to the soil. The second, the postbellum wilderness, is a place of struggle under the hostile conditions of oppression. Her rhetoric is more abstract and metaphorical. The wilderness is more of a mental condition in which black women experience alienation and rejection.

In the course of her writings, Williams begins to speak more of the second—the postbellum wilderness. Emily Holmes notes that the more perilous dimensions of the wilderness can threaten to overwhelm Williams' depiction of the wilderness as a positive space of encounter.[72] Perhaps this reflects Williams' growing attunement to the pressures of the "crooked" structures and its effects. What can be lost in a greater emphasis on the postbellum wilderness, Holmes says, is the powerful depiction of the body as "primary medium of divine encounter."[73] Holmes points to the constructive possibilities that can grow from the "be-wildering and the powerful incarnation of God in women and men's own bodies" that Williams offers.[74] One aspect of the wilderness is more life affirming, and the other more death dealing. The latter, we could say, is a wilderness that becomes increasingly detached from the soil.

And yet both depictions of the wilderness may be operating simultaneously in the territory of after-living. Both express dynamics at play in the Upper Room. The disciples are confined within a logic that cuts off their resources, that frames the suffering around them in terms of a "zero-sum game."[75] And yet breath is released, signaling the possibility of animation and reconnection—a vision of powered bodies.[76] This power, located in the afterlife, is lost when the redemptive locus is solely attributed to the cross. The wilderness is struggle, but it is a struggle rooted in the elemental powers of life: bodies moving, struggling together, toward visions of life in the ongoingness of devaluation.

If we conceive of the resurrection appearances as rooted in wilderness soil, senses are activated and materiality affirmed and reengaged. When we meet the disciples, they are under the grip of death. The way ahead will involve struggle against the forces of the logic that binds them, but the rediscovery of the wilderness as natural space will be instrumental in the struggle. One of the important aspects of healing touch is its affirmation of bodies. But this touch can also point to a revaluation of life: affirming the goodness of the body, a reanimation of the senses, and a realignment of the affections.

While the wilderness metaphor speaks to the struggle of black women, Williams chose to identify it as a wilderness experience rather than a black experience because she believed that the metaphor "provided an avenue" for other works.[77] The touchpoint was the biblical metaphor. Others will find the metaphor of the wilderness conducive for their projects of liberation. She opened the way for this, without foreclosing the particularity of that metaphor for black women. The wilderness offers, for Williams, a metaphor of potential crossings. She notes that womanist theologians can claim this metaphor as foundational for their work, thus claiming its singular importance; but the biblical wilderness tradition opens up to questions of the nature of life amid ongoing struggle that is expansive. Womanists can invite others to gather around this question: "What is God's word about survival and quality of life formation for oppressed and quasi-free people struggling to build community in the wilderness?"[78] This is connective work for those gathered at the site of resurrection wounds.

Williams' insistence on returning to Jesus' life makes touching wounds one of the tenets of after-living. The crooked room gives way to another landscape. Is this a new wilderness that the disciples step into, a re-inauguration of the ministerial vision in the perilous territory of the afterlife? The doors to the Upper Room open, and senses are awakened. He directs them to leave the crooked room by way of the crossings that they will construct together.

The wilderness, narrated by Williams, is a place of peril and possibility. Jesus, the minister and teacher, returns. The promise of resurrecting wounds might take root in Williams' wilderness soil. It is not the landscape of solo witness but the soil of multiple witnesses. The brutality that lies within must be confronted. Just as stories woven through generations have educated us into fear and hate, there must be counter-narratives that loosen that hold, reattaching us to a common life. Forging paths across wounds will require the development and deepening of our affective capacities that are attuned to the ways that fear takes hold and our hearts can harden. Just as processes, habits, and ordinary practices of life created the conditions of slavery and the embedding of racial wounds within the collective body, so, too, ordinary practices of tenderness and empathy can be nurtured, recovered, revivified. To envision the Upper Room as a more perilous space is not to take away the good news of resurrection but, instead, to pull away the bandage of faith that has secured salvation for only a few. The habits and formation processes of Christian theology must be reexamined. The bandages can no longer hold.

Conclusion

If Christian theology is to have a future in the Age of Ferguson, the ongoing crosses must be met with a different vision of the afterlife. When histories of past harm surface in public, there are forces operating that threaten to push them away and to make them invisible once again. When they surface, there is anger, confusion, fear, and uncertainty. The politics operating at the surface of the collective skin suggest that there are few who are equipped to discern the dynamics taking place. Instead, anger is misread. Shame goes unaddressed. A certain way of narrating the Christian story does little to address these complexities. It administers a sacred bandage, turning attention away from the realities taking place on the ground.

The Thomas story, read through another lens, provides a glimpse of the formation of a community that can encounter these wounds. When we first glimpse the disciples in the aftermath of his death, they are operating with the logic most familiar to them. They are under the grip of the logic of power and privilege, susceptible to the forces that define life within death-dealing economies. But when he returns, Jesus confronts them with their own participation in the devaluing of life. He does so as one devalued, as one who was marked as a criminal and sentenced to death. His life was deemed to have no value. When he returns, he brings the memories of past harms forward, displaying them, insisting that the disciples come to terms with the past. This is difficult work that they are not equipped to do. Although they attempt the easy route, heralding the return of the Jesus whom they knew, he refuses this quick access. He registers the fear beneath their celebrations. While they try to grasp him on their own terms, he cuts through the logic of fear with his words and releases a spirit to them in order to prepare them to confront the wounds of the past. As the power of spirit inhabits them, they will face the past without being condemned to repeat it. Any future will require a reorientation of their senses, an awakening of mind, heart, and body. It is not enough to think their way out of this room. The logic that has them within its grasp can only be unraveled by releasing the hold of fear and hate; it must work with affects, moving between word and skin to unravel patterns of thinking and feeling. He invites them to feel their way into the world again.

Spirit, as memory bearer, also releases into this space, bringing truths to the surface. They need new breath, new air. The life that follows is not fully determined and has yet to be given shape. In this singular body, the disciples encounter the particularity of suffering. And yet insofar as he is received as the Christ, this body ties them to histories of suffering across time, calling them to touch across the logics that confine and divide. Breath awakens those who gather, and they reattach to their senses and to the soil. Instead of covering over wounds with sacred bandages, a different telling of the story turns the disciples to wounds, both to examine the hold of a certain logic on them and to invite them to touch wounds, to bring to life what the world deems of little value. Newly resourced in this space, they will embody new ways of gathering and develop new articulations of how to live. Amid the ruins, they enter the wilderness.

4

Discovering Wounds
Veteran Healing and Resurrection in the Upper Room

Introduction

He told them he would return. In a little while, he said. You cannot bear all that I will endure, but I will send you a spirit to sustain you.

When he appears, they celebrate and welcome him home. There is something different about him, something not quite visible but somehow altered. He singles out Thomas and asks him to touch the wounds. Thomas reaches, and his finger circles the perimeter of the wound, as if to expose it to the open air. It is a clearing. The others lean in, waiting, staring into that wound for what seems like a long time. And suddenly they know why they are there.

❁ ❁ ❁

The ancient stories—Homer's *Iliad*, Sophocles' *Ajax*—still speak in the present. Jonathan Shay, a psychologist working with veterans, uses the story of Achilles in the *Iliad* to interpret present-day wounds. Achilles' story, he says, is "also the story of many combat veterans."[1] While these epic narratives reflect the particular customs and codes of ancient Greece, their testimony to the war experience connects the ancient warrior to the contemporary soldier. The epics provide both distance and proximity, in that they speak of something that present soldiers experience, but do so indirectly, through the story of ancient warriors.

Shay insists that the ancient story has healing potential.[2] There is a resonance between the ancient and contemporary stories; it touches those who have experienced war, connecting them across time.

The stories of ancient warriors wrestling with the psychological and moral effects of combat can also provide containers in and through which current war stories might be owned more collectively. The staging of the Greek epics resists the treatment of war as a privatized and individual experience. In his restaging of these ancient epics via *Theater of War*, Bryan Doerries claims that the audience is an active part of the storying. He facilitates a process by which actors and audience come together to witness a dramatic portrayal of the afterlife of war. The citizens of ancient Greece, the audience, were written into the script. When the epics were performed, a public conversation was taking place. War is collective, both the waging of it and the aftereffects. The ancient story provides a container in which the war story can be held, in its complexities.

By bringing the ancient and contemporary stories together, Shay and Doerries do not intend to conflate the experiences or to "tame, appropriate, or co-opt them."[3] Instead, the proximity and performance of the texts awakens within readers and viewers an unsettledness that is a critical part of moral engagement. It raises questions not just about how veterans can heal from the wounds of war but about why the nation fights, and at what cost. The epics push against contemporary American visions of welcoming home service members, visions that can bypass the examination of war and its effects.[4] The performance calls for a broader response and responsibility.[5] It awakens the collective.

Veterans reengaging civilian life often struggle to tell truths about what they experienced during their military service. Returning home, they discover that the reintegration process is loaded with societal projections and expectations about their service and their experiences in combat. They are aware that their experiences must align with a role prescribed by the nation. Their service is idealized, and their experiences, both in theater and post-theater, often bear the extra weight of these ideals. The dynamics of the return involve navigating disparities between their private experiences and the public role that they are expected to embody.

The mundane and ordinary challenges of reintegrating back into family, community, and employment are not acknowledged, because these experiences do not fit the profile of the war hero or even the honorable service member. Instead, their experiences are swept up into narratives of service, sacrifice, brotherhood, and courage that they must continually embody. The arc of these narratives depends on a movement to rise above the pain and struggle in order to reach a positive end.

The rise of PTSD and suicide rates present a vision of the return from military duties as more complex than the arc of the transcendent narrative. Many service members struggle without an obvious good end coming into view. The narrative of the honorable soldier is incongruous with the lived experience. The tropes function to keep a certain depiction of the nation in place, but they can cover over the more complex struggles to acclimate to the ordinariness of everyday life. Zoë Wool calls the more inconclusive struggle of after-living, a "messy remainder."[6] This remainder attests to dissonance between the personal and the national story that is expressed in the varied experiences of the after-living—of returning to "normal" life after engaging in the extremities of war. It allows room for the service member to go off script, to acknowledge feelings of betrayal, apathy, anger, and shame. *We make others suffer for us and turn our eyes from them when they return*

The concept of the invisible wounds of war stems from contemporary analysis of the challenges of returning veterans. But there is often little analysis of the role that society plays in prohibiting these wounds from surfacing. To make these wounds visible, to surface them, requires examination from all members of society. At present, citizens have little engagement with American military practices. Through a recovery of the epics, Shay and Doerries attempt to challenge this disengagement and to position veterans' wounds within the collective body.

The national story requires the extraordinary; it needs heroes. Greek epics present tragic heroes rather than redemptive ones. Speaking more tragically than triumphantly about the war experience, they temper the hero stories and expose the texture of after-living.[7] The tragic hero finds himself in circumstances that do not yield either good or bad ends. Instead, war is a series of difficult moves with conflicting choices, often yielding no clear winners or losers. Much is lost, not to be regained. No one *really* wins. The complex moral terrain of tragedy may take some weight off the shoulders of the soldier, by providing a backdrop that can acknowledge suffering without sanctifying it.

The Christian story, in contrast to the tragic vision, is redemptive. It positions the contemporary warrior within a different kind of drama. The story does not end tragically but triumphantly. Warriors are not subject to chance, fortune, or fate. Instead, they operate within a world that works according to the will of an all-powerful God who, through battle, conquers the forces of evil and is, in the end, victorious over those forces.

In the Christian narrative, Jesus, the savior, offers up his life as a sacrifice for the redemption of humanity. His life is put on the line for the sake of the world. Jesus, as the Christ, is understood to be the incarnation of God on earth. The Johannine gospel opens with the pronouncement that the Word, the Logos, takes on flesh and enters into the world, dwelling in the midst of all living beings. And it is through the incarnation, this taking on of flesh, that the redemption of the world is enacted. Jesus is the incarnation of the eternal Word, and his life, death, and resurrection display the drama of how God saves the world. His death is often interpreted as a sacrifice offered to redeem humanity. Whether offered as a ransom, as expiation, death is the price paid, the cost for buying back humanity, freeing them from the powers of sin and death.

In *G.I. Messiahs: Soldiering, War, and American Civil Religion*, Jonathan Ebel says that American soldiering follows an incarnational logic. Ebel identifies the role of the soldier within the United States as a Christ figure—as "soldier-savior."[8] The soldier, in fighting for the nation, in his or her willingness to offer his or her life, becomes a savior. The recipient of this salvation must respond to this act of sacrifice with gratitude for the act performed on their behalf. The one takes the place of the many. The suffering of the soldier is not in vain. Instead, it is meaningful. The willingness to die for the nation mirrors the voluntary nature of Christ's relinquishing of his will in order to carry out the will of God, the Father.

The christo-logic also reveals an interplay between word and flesh. The flesh of the soldier is offered, but it is not simply a body. It is intricately connected to the word of the nation that attributes meaning to it. Ebel writes, "The trope explains soldiering, yes, but it also reveals soldiers, both living and fallen, to be the Word of the nation made flesh; America among us. And American civil religion seems to require this incarnation."[9] The acts performed by the soldier make the nation visible. At homecomings for service members, we can see the ritual of word and flesh performed and repeated. The soldier performs a service that carries significance beyond his concrete actions.

This narrative is deeply rooted in American soil. Dan McAdams says that Americans interpret their lives according to a redemptive logic, and they interpret their "deaths" and "resurrections" in light of the

Christian story.[10] This redemption story has both its sacred and secular versions, but it is nonetheless a core component of the idea of America. It is part of American civil religion. Christian assumptions undergird collective warring. In turn, Ebel says that the assumptions are increasingly detached from Christianity, but they remain as vestiges of a Christian logic of redemption. Christianity is increasingly "substructural," Ebel notes, meaning that the conceptions of "embodied virtue, supreme sacrifice, and atonement" originate from the Christian tradition and remain in some form. Ebel unearths this substructural logic. Both McAdams and Ebel believe it is important to keep the theological impulses in view, because they continue to exert a force; they are operationally potent, even if they operate less visibly.

The redemptive story comes under scrutiny when we confront the suffering of veterans. Attention turns to the place of suffering, of struggle, and even of death, within this story. They are not only overcome in the final moment of the redemptive drama; they are ascribed a positive function within it. In the redemptive plot, the negative moment is necessary to bring about the greater good. The sacrifice is required. The struggle is positively cast as strengthening character or as test or trial on the way to the culmination of the story.[11]

Suffering is not just inevitable but necessary to bring about that victory. This logic of suffering and sacrifice makes the suffering of Christ, and thus the "soldier-savior," a necessary component in bringing about redemption, and in the case of America, the redemption of the nation. While meaning is attributed to the idea of suffering, veterans often feel like the reality of their suffering is not welcomed. The nation does not really want to address the wounds. This structuring narrative of *necessary* wounds quickly discards the wounds that appear on the other side of death. For soldier-saviors, their return to life after war means that their wounds must be covered over. If the risen Jesus returns, displaying the wounds, they must be marks of victory that ensure salvation. For the returning service members, their wounds serve this function as well. But this does little to address the real harm that these wounds inflict.

While there has been significant scholarship exposing the problem of the alliance between the Christian story and the American war story, there have been few attempts to reclaim the Christian story from the perspective of those who have been touched by war most closely.[12] They tell truths about the afterlife of war and reapproach the story of life,

[handwritten margin note: What does this imply for Americans?]

death, and wounds in Christianity. This chapter pursues a vision of an afterlife enacted by a community committed to veteran healing.

Warriors Journey Home (WJH), a veterans' group in Ohio, offers a picture of wounding and healing, and of a collective process of gathering at the site of wounds to tell difficult truths. Members of WJH do not use the language of resurrection, yet their vocabulary and practices refigure the scene. They reframe resurrection and an interpretation of the resurrected Jesus, Thomas, the disciples, and the wound in ways that have an impact on familiar interpretations of this scene. They provide a powerful counterpoint to the "substructural" assumptions about the war, thus potentially challenging the national story of war wounds and their afterlife. Shay and Doerries attempt to awaken the collective through the retelling of ancient stories. This ancient Christian story may awaken a collective as well.

Different from the other chapters that focus on the biblical text in the Gospel of John, this chapter approaches the biblical story through Caravaggio's painting, *The Incredulity of St. Thomas* (see p. 16). The painter's interpretation of this biblical scene turns our attention to the open wound, the finger inserted into flesh, and the proximity of the disciples to Jesus. The somatic and affective power of the painting differs from textual engagement and resonates with the powerful live experience of sitting with members of the healing circle. It is impossible to look at the Caravaggio painting and to dismiss the wound; all eyes are directed to it. This is true of the healing circle, in which wounds are the very purpose for gathering. It is the direct statement about wounds that draws the two together. In its transmission, this biblical story has been at the forefront of debates about right belief in Christianity, but its visual rendering raises questions of a different sort, about touch, about flesh, and about wounds. Like the Caravaggio painting, WJH members help us imagine what it means to put wounds at the center of this biblical story.[13]

The Return

"He came back," she told me. Gayle wasn't talking about a literal return.[14] Her brother Bud returned from Vietnam over three decades ago. She was talking about Bud's journey of healing after his experience of war, a "return" that involved long-term addiction and estrangement from his family and friends. Like many civilian family members, Gayle had never heard him talk about his war experiences. A quiet man, he was even quieter when he returned from Vietnam, she noted. The image of the soldier returning home is a classic American image, representing heroism, sacrifice, courage, service, and honor. But when Bud returned from Vietnam, he did not come home to celebrations. And he did not really return. He had a small group of friends from the local branch of the Veterans of Foreign Wars, but he broke ties with family and friends. While he managed to keep a job as a pipe fitter at the Chrysler automobile plant in Twinsburg, he struggled with alcoholism and was in and out of rehab programs for the decades following Vietnam.

I never met Bud, but Gayle was animated when she spoke about him. Both were members of WJH. The group was started by Rev. John Schluep, a Protestant minister and noncombat veteran, who was convinced that Christian churches needed to interface with other local organizations in order to attend to the needs of veterans in their surrounding communities. Knowing that I was interested in different models of veteran healing, he approached me at a conference and began to tell me about the work he was doing with Ohio veterans. He invited me to witness the work of WJH firsthand.

Different from the others, this chapter takes as its primary literatures a set of interviews that I conducted with members of the group. I was interested in how grassroots organizations, and especially religious communities, take up the work of veteran care. I arrived with the intention of interviewing the group's facilitators. And yet it was the presence of a particular cohort of civilians and their stories that turned me to think more directly about what civilian participation in veteran healing might look like. Although I did not realize it at the time, I was picking up on Doerries' insistence that veteran healing is the work of a collective. Very few veteran groups incorporate civilian participants, beyond the clinicians or mental health providers who often facilitate the groups. The civilians in WJH spoke to me about the various ways in which they are touched by war. They also spoke about moments of healing, about wounds they did not know they had, and about the practice of gathering to hear the often-unimaginable stories of war. They provide an undocumented picture of a wider arena of healing. I interviewed seven civilians along with John and Shianne, the cofacilitators. As leaders, they provide a model, a container, in which the healing can take place, resourced by the rituals and words of their traditions.

John felt a growing sense of responsibility to address the challenges of veterans returning home. A VA psychiatrist had referred a veteran to him who was struggling with "God issues" that stemmed from his experience at My Lai almost forty years earlier. Around the same time, John read Edward Tick's book *War and the Soul*. Tick's organization, Soldier's Heart, gave John a model through which to think about veteran healing. John began to look around. Akron, Ohio, was filled with veterans of the various wars. He was concerned that the country was abdicating responsibility to its veterans. He was also leading a small monthly men's gathering at the church, and he discovered that war and the military were central topics of conversation. Several of the men had served in the military—World War II, Vietnam, and Korea. Meeting during the height of military interventions in Iraq, the group's discussions of current events began to uncover stories of past military service.

As they continued to meet, John sensed that something more needed to happen. He says, "The name Shianne Eagleheart kept coming up in the areas of trauma work and with hospital and medical and behavioral health people." After about five years, he realized, "I've got to get ahold of this person. I've got to find out who she is." A ceremonial healer in the Seneca tradition and a licensed psychotherapist, Shianne views her work with veterans as part of the ongoing work of her native peoples. The work crosses cultures, just as her healing work crosses the practices of her indigenous tradition and the practice of psychotherapy.[15] She began to cofacilitate the groups with John, and they partnered in this work for over five years.

Both are charismatic figures, although in very different ways. John is a talker, a "straight shooter," and a natural storyteller. When John wants to have coffee with you, one church member told me, you know that he is going to approach you about something serious and important. He moves from the public to the personal with an enviable ease. He "makes the rounds" at church potlucks, asking people about things that matter to them—sports, family, job searches, and potluck special recipes. Several members were drawn into the ministry through cup-of-coffee meetings with John. As they speak, it is clear that church members trust him and that they honored his vision enough to make WJH a central ministry of the church. Their "ownership" of it came later.

Shianne is commanding, but in a more still and grounded way; it is hard not to hang on her every word, since it seems to come from a deep place. She told me that as a ceremonial healer and a therapist, her work takes place on two levels: the unseen and the seen world. Encounters with her reflect this movement.

After reading a newspaper feature about the group, Gayle left a message on Bud's answering machine asking if he would be interested in attending. She was never sure if he would call back. After four days, he responded, "I don't think that's for me. I went to the wall and I made my peace. I'm OK." She told him that she would go with him. "Just think about it," she urged.

In WJH veterans are referred to as warriors. The term "warrior" places military service and combat within the setting of ancient cultures that designated an honorable role to members of the community who engaged in battle.[16] The retrieval of the term "warrior" is intended to restore honor to the role of combat veterans and calls the wider society to acknowledge its own role in both sending persons to fight and incorporating them back into society when they return. The sense that something is wrong with how U.S. society treats veterans is palpable; members express their concern that citizens abdicate responsibility for the consequences of war and make the veteran carry the burden alone. In warrior cultures expectations were placed both on the community and on the one who is sent to fight on behalf of the community.[17]

Bud called Gayle back the afternoon of the meeting. "Let's go and try," he said. They went together. On the drive home, he said he wanted to go back and asked if she would go with him. "Absolutely, I will," she said. Gayle is a Strongheart, a name given to civilian members who support those who return, who commit themselves to hold the experiences of war in a particular way—through their witness to the veterans' process of reintegration. Warriors Journey Home is unique in its inclusion of civilians. Most veterans' groups recognize how difficult it is for veterans to build trust and think that happens best with fellow service members. The presence of civilians is not without challenges, but WJH operates with a conviction that war is a collective enterprise. The warriors go out to war to protect their communities; the persons of strong heart welcome them back home and protect them as they reintegrate into society. John says, "Civilians are people of strong heart, and they have that responsibility and obligation really. . . . When a veteran returns home, we have that responsibility to protect them, to bring them back into a safe environment, a safe place."

By assigning Stronghearts a role, the group expands the circle of veteran healing to include spouses, partners, children, siblings, and others who commit to this work. Waiting for warriors to come home requires a unique kind of strength. The waiting is not passive; there is internal work that the Stronghearts need to do in order to be ready to protect soldiers when they return. One of their major roles is to listen to the stories of war that are spoken within the circle. It takes an act of courage to speak about the harm that one experienced—or inflicted—in combat, but it also takes courage to hear the stories and to withhold judgment. This involves listening even when nothing is verbalized, and participating in rituals that create a container for difficult truths to surface.

They come to WJH for a variety of reasons. Like Gayle, some are family members of veterans. Some come by way of the church, and at John's prodding. Others are concerned civilians who heard about the work of the organization and started attending. Although there may not be a direct and conscious connection to war, most do not have to go far back in their family history to find a relative who has served in the military or has been in combat. For Gayle, the military was always within arm's reach; nearly every male family member served in the U.S. military.

Bud's silence about Vietnam was not surprising, Gayle said, given that their father, a veteran of World War II, would never talk about his war experience. Bud broke that silence after four months of attending the group: "It was the first time I had ever heard him talk about Vietnam." He only spoke once after that, but Gayle believes that WJH brought her brother back. After the first meeting, Bud called his daughter Rachel. It was the first time he had called her in six years. "Aunt Gay," she told Gayle later, "I'm so grateful that you went to that meeting with him. I hope this will be something for him." He called her every week after that.

He started to call Gayle as well, on his morning walk from the parking lot to the Chrysler factory. He chided her for still being in bed: "Hey, what are you doing? If I have to be up, you have to be up." She caught glimpses of her brother and the relationship she once had with him. "I lost him, you know," she explained, just as he lost something of himself in Hanoi. Decades later he was coming to terms with that loss. His healing process was cut short. Bud died in his sleep nine months after their first visit to WJH. Reflecting on his death, Gayle remarked, "I can look back and say, 'You know what? We were close,' you know. He came back."

Circle

There is no large infrastructure to Warrior's Journey Home. It is primarily a ritual space, signaled by soft drumming, the dimly lit room, and the smell of white sage or sweet grass. Just hours before, I had sat in the multipurpose room eating a potluck lunch with members of the large Protestant church. And moments before, the facilitator had welcomed us in the church foyer and stated the guidelines for the circle process. A shared silence when participants cross the threshold, an unstated reverence, adds gravity to what is about to take place. Metal chairs are placed side by side, and they circle what looks like a makeshift memorial at the center, a composite of talking sticks, dog tags, military insignia, and candles. This night, the circle is large, they tell me, because they have gathered to honor Janie, one of their beloved members, a senior Strongheart. Many had attended her funeral the previous day, but this felt like a more fitting place to honor Janie. She had been faithful to the group, coming twice a month for over eight years. John lit the sage in her honor and held up the stick, carved for her by one of the members of the group. It was a special night. Janie, their elder, was present, watching over them, and they would continue in the work as a means of honoring her.

Each circle begins and ends with a clearing round. The facilitator stands in front of each member of the circle, offering the gift of white sage and moves from person to person, as each is invited to enter into the ritual of smudging. When lit and the flame subsides, the leaves slowly burn. Smoke encircles the sage. Through the wave of a hand, a person can draw the smoke closer, inhaling it and drawing in its scent. This waving and rising is believed to draw the prayers of the heart out and "up to the Divine Spirit."[18] Smudging is a ritual act of cleansing. It is performed as a way of preparation for healing to take place. Some describe the smudging *as* a healing.[19]

The facilitator returns to the center of the circle and picks up a tall wooden stick, holds it upright, and carries it to the members. Hand carved by one of the veterans, the stick is handled with care. The facilitator reaches around the smooth wood, as if reaching for the hand of a dance partner. When you receive the stick, you take a pause, and look in the eyes of each person in the circle, circling the room; you may offer a word, but you close by announcing your name. "I am 'x,' and I am clear."[20] You survey the circle clockwise as you look directly into the eyes of each person seated there. The eye contact is a sign of recognition and also a vow to tell your truth. Cindi, a mother of two girls and the wife of a Gulf War veteran, describes the meaning of the direct look. It says, "You can't lie. You can't hide. You're not hiding." Surgery from a non-war-related injury triggered her husband's aggressive behavior following the war, and it sent the family into a tailspin. At a crisis point, Cindi found WJH. "Truth emerges from just that one act. There is a great deal of truth," according to Cindi. By looking someone in the eye, you are not just looking *at* them, you are looking *into* them, as if to clear the way for deeper truths to emerge. Staring into the eyes of each person in the circle is, according to John, a practice of "connecting at a spiritual and soul level." Tom, one of the earliest members, notes that the clearing round marks each member's entrance into and exit from the space of healing.

Once all are cleared, the talking stick is returned to the center. Most of the veterans in the circle have fought in World War II, Korea, and Vietnam. Many vets come to the circle with stories about the unimaginable tasks they were asked to perform in combat. One, Tom recalled, had to keep a whole field of wounded soldiers alive until medical help arrived, while "another one in Vietnam, one of the guys, his job was to clean the body parts out of helicopters." Some speak; others have never spoken. There are anywhere between ten to twenty-five people attending each circle. But the circle is always larger. The truth telling in the circle is witnessed by those physically present, but there is an acknowledged *presencing* that enlarges the circle. The dog tags signal the presence of fallen warriors, many of whom fought alongside the veterans in the circle.

The circle provides a space for raw emotion, for talking, and for silence. Anyone in the circle can speak.[21] When veterans first come, many are uneasy about being there. "If you didn't want to participate, you didn't have to and that's a very comforting thing." But one veteran opening up might invite another to speak. It starts with sharing stories, but it doesn't end there. Tom was not enlisted, but he remembers his uncles returning from war and the impact on the family. A committed church member who supported John's early efforts to involve the church in military ministry, Tom believes in the group process and saw something distinctive about the bonds formed in circle: "And once you have that instant attachment, then you see it growing and you could see openness—relaxation, more openness, more actual feelings rather than stories. . . . They started talking about how they felt and that's when the real growth took place."

When the stories are told within this setting, they are accompanied by strong emotion. Whether through the smell of burning sage, the sense of the presence of the "communion of all veterans" represented by the dog tags, or the passing of the handcrafted talking sticks, participants attest to the powerful sensory engagement that they find in the circle. While the mantra for WJH is "speak, listen, and heal," the unspoken and embodied rituals of the group are what many refer to when speaking about the process as sacred.

When she went to her first circle, Cindi says she just sat and cried. She understands herself as a deeply spiritual person, but she did not need to tell me that. She has the aura of a mystic and the energy of a fierce mother bear who vigilantly protects her cubs. She invited me to her home for the interview. Although I had heard part of her story before the interview, it was moving to hear it in her home. She had fought hard for her home and to keep her family from being destroyed by the war.

She told me that she had prepared the space for me to be there. Our interview, unlike the others, is marked as a sacred space. She understands the circle to be a space that symbolizes the flow of life—both the powers of creation and destruction. All of life is happening there: "This is a place where there is pain and healing, where you hear about destruction and you hear about life. There was always a balance." The connection between the Native American tradition and the combat experience was a critical one for her, and she describes the process of the circle by recalling her time with the Lakota. She had spent time working with two Native American professors at Sinte Gleska University, a "spotted eagle university" in South Dakota. While there, she notes, "I was fortunate to go to the Rosebud in the Pine Ridge Reservation and learn from the Lakota, how they view veterans and how they help the veterans with their wounds."

She refers to the work of the circle by appealing to the Lakota term "Wakhan." *Khan*, she tells me, means energy or life, and *Wa* proclaims the creation of something but also can serve as an "I" statement. Something comes into being in circle—"So Wakhan is all that is sacred," she says. Bringing the power of ancient wisdom traditions to her postwar experience was like a spiritual homecoming for her.

Lost Souls

"Soul is the part you don't understand," Barbara tells me. When PTSD was first identified as a disorder in 1983, her husband Peter was seeking treatment through the VA. Peter was a Vietnam vet, and he has been on a journey in search of healing since he returned in 1968. High school friends, they started dating after the war and were married approximately a year after he returned from Vietnam.

After the couple retired, some of the ongoing symptoms of Peter's war experience became more pronounced. Barbara sensed a change: "I knew it was very much on his mind, and he had a lot more time to think about it." In that first year of retirement, Barbara said that he read incessantly in an attempt to understand how that history unfolded in him. It took something from him, she said. And he was able to say that he was a different person before and after Vietnam. In contrast to Bud, Peter talked a lot about his war experiences. He kept looking for the language, and she kept listening. "We always said we'd stay together because we like each other," she said. "[War] was our problem because I have lived with him for forty-three years."

A news clipping alerted them to a peace and war conference hosted by Cleveland State University's Inamori Peace Institute, and they were introduced to a healing circle there. WJH hosts bimonthly circles, but the group often partners with organizations working on veteran care. Barbara and their daughter Caitlin, a nurse practitioner and researcher at the VA, accompanied Peter to that first circle. They were expecting an informational session; instead, they entered into a circle: "So we're kind of shocked that we were going to actually do the circle that day. And so my dad sat in the middle as a veteran. There was an inner circle of chairs and then an outer circle of chairs. Then my mom and I sat in the outside." It was a turning point for the family.

There was something different about the WJH circle. The diagnosis of PTSD was instrumental to Peter's postwar healing process. But it was not comprehensive. The language of soul clicked when he first heard it in the healing circle. It was an arena that had not been touched by his years of therapeutic work. Barbara conveyed Peter's experience of hearing the language of soul for the first time. He said, "That's it. I felt like my soul left me in Vietnam."

This awakening was sparked by a term that was difficult to pin down—both in my interviews and in the literatures. The language of "soul" is prominent in WJH. The "soul" language may come from Tick's writings, which had a strong influence on John.[22] Tick provides a long and broad description of soul in his book. It serves as an umbrella term to speak about what is violated in war. It is used by Stronghearts in a similar way—as a kind of catchall term. Chuck, the group's administrator, says: "The soul of the person, the inside, the—we've got all these little catch phrases, the invisible wound, the soul. . . ."

In my interviews Stronghearts spoke of the soul in a variety of ways. The soul is ancient, deep, and lost. It precedes some modern conceptions of the person—as individual and autonomous—and modern practices of military engagement. The understanding of person and community is more full-orbed. It seems to evoke the depths of a person—as opposed to spirit language that is often associated with heights. Spirit, John says, is ascending language, and soul is descending language; the work of healing spans both. Rita Brock, in the choice of "soul" to name the work of addressing moral injury (Soul Repair), is attuned to the philosophical and theological inheritance of the term "spirit," which is often disembodied, immaterial. There is something fleshier about the soul.[23]

At first, I kept pursuing a more precise use of the term. But Barbara's statement stopped me: the soul is the part of yourself that you can't figure out. You don't understand it. Peter, in hearing the language of the soul, registered that something was missing. But he only discovered it when he was in the context of the circle. It was the setting that was important. In directing questions, I was working from the inside out, hoping to move from a definition of soul to the work of healing, but this was something enacted from the outside in. The term was given shape and expression by the context. My search for a definition was missing the point. You only knew that something was missing when it was called out, touched, and encircled. Peter discovered a language or, perhaps more aptly stated, imagery to facilitate another phase of his healing process. The soul is the part that you cannot figure out—*on your own*. The witness of the circle brought something to the surface.

WJH does not disparage the medical model of veteran healing, but the group operates with a conviction that their ancient traditions offer a more connective path to healing—less individualistic and more holistic. John sees it in his tradition, and Shianne in hers. The appeal to ancient stories and warrior cultures is expressed in this curious combination of Christianity and earth medicine in WJH.[24] Neither understand themselves as bringing religion into the group nor as basing the healing process in religion. They speak about this work in terms of spirit, soul, tradition, and medicine. This is not without tension. But what the facilitators bring are traditions that place human experiences within a broader sacred story.

The circle expands as Shianne speaks. She speaks about the present time as an unfolding of ancient prophecies. She talks about civilization and its development, a time forecasted in which great healing will come but only after a period of turbulent struggle. Transitions from one age to the next can be the most violent. Healing movements are taking place in the midst of struggle, and WJH is one such movement.

The group has grown used to working with the images of healing that Shianne offers. They are more cosmological in that they intermingle the animate and inanimate, animal and human, ancestors and living creatures, to form a vision of how all things are interrelated. Participants are particularly attuned to the healing rituals that she brings from her tradition, and several say that their initial curiosity with an unfamiliar tradition transformed into a deep reverence and respect during their time in WJH.

The work of the circle is a collective process of soul development.[25] When someone returns from combat, they often do not return alone. Souls may also take up residence, inhabiting those who return from combat. Shianne describes them, "If someone's coming back, they're coming back, and it's not just them. The guy that they held as he bled out in their arms is with them, too." She suggests that the connections may be so strong in battle that the surviving soldier *takes in* the soul of the deceased and his "unfinished business." The soul of the dead soldier and the struggles that he carried before his death may still need to be released. The survivor brings that home; the journey of healing is, thus, a double and conjoined journey: "And so the soul healing a lot of times isn't just for the person who has experienced the carnage of war." We do not know what to do with this, but veterans often express it. They say, "I feel like he's with me." This is not always a calming presence; it might be restlessness or rage that they cannot identify as their own. When Shianne speaks, there is no longer one soldier or an individual soul. Soul does not follow strict borders of subjectivity or personhood.

The presence of the ancestors is palpable for those in the circle. For some, the memory of a fellow soldier or a civilian casualty haunts them. The circle becomes a space of confrontation with the past. As each holds Janie's stick, the positive presence of the deceased is also recognized, as the dead can provide spiritual strength. The process is witnessed by the ancestors, whose spirits are invoked and invited into the circle. The military dog tags placed at the center of the circle represent the presence of the deceased warriors. Janie's walking stick passes, and her spirit is invoked. Barbara and Peter's daughter Caitlin told me that the family dinner prayer changed as a result of participating in the circles. They amended the classic Serenity Prayer: "Great Spirit, grant us the serenity to accept the things we cannot change, the courage to change the things that we can, and the wisdom to know the difference *and the allies, loved ones, and ancestors to help us.*"

Christianity is not readily recognized as a healing tradition by WJH members. In fact, it is often seen as an obstacle to drawing veterans to circle. Chuck says that many veterans are put off by the fact that WJH meets in a church. Often the one to field inquiries, he tells prospective veterans, "We are spiritual-based and spiritual is about your soul and about—maybe what you believe on a deeper level." Perhaps the stories have been told in a certain way for so long that the healing aspect is lost. Or perhaps WJH members who have been familiar with Christianity in some form expect little to nothing from that tradition. John says that the absence of attention to bodies, to the somatic, is where Christianity misses the mark. It appeals to the frontal lobe but misses a basic insight about trauma—that it lodges in the body. John acknowledges the dissonance in the religion that he represents, and he is not defensive. He is just hopeful that there is more. The teachings of Jesus become a container for John's work. He takes big terms like "salvation" and "redemption" and ties them more closely to the life of Jesus. Salvation really means healing, he insists, and not a "get out of hell free card."

Plunging our fingers into Christ's wounds

The language of souls lost and found touches on something missing from the language of trauma, something more radically communal. Souls can be found only within a setting attuned to a search process. It is only in being found that you discover what was lost. The concept of "invisible wounds" has become a familiar way of talking about war wounds. Unlike physical wounds, psychological wounds are often not available to the eye. But the imagery of souls lost and found leads to an insight more radical than even the group may register: the soul does not belong to you alone. *BEAUTIFUL*

Hurt Goes to Hurt

It is partly Shianne's past, and her own experiences of wounding, that led her to be a healer; the other part is carrying on the tradition of her native peoples. "We give the gift of healing to others," she tells me. She tells me that healing traditions will be misunderstood, and even this interview, she says, will fail in its attempts to capture its meaning. The unseen world of which she speaks can be compromised by the language of the seen world.

She did not share the details of her past, but it is clear that her personal history is bound to the history of the colonization of her peoples in this country. From one perspective, her work with veterans is miraculous, in that she offers her healing gifts to the descendants of persons who abused her peoples. The veterans in the circle are overwhelmingly white, male, and of European descent. I am curious about how this historical trauma plays out in the group. It is clear that Shianne is not resigned to that history, as if glossing over it or relegating it to the distant past; it is evident that she reckons with it in the process of her work. How do you do it? I ask. She responds, "I go to that heart and soul need. I just go there. It doesn't matter about the history of anything." She is attuned to trauma in such a way that it informs her vision. She explains, "There's just this—I see. I see it in you. I know it. I've lived it. I know what I needed. I know what it took, and I know that it saved my life, and I know we're going to lose you if we don't do—I'm really about the bottom line. That's where I live."

This can be easily misunderstood as a statement that histories do not matter, and she as much as says that. But she goes on to say that there is an ordering to the work. There will be a time, she says, when the history will be addressed, and trust, built up over time, will make this work possible. Addressing the harms of history is important; tending the wound is primary, immediate.

When veterans walk into the group, Shianne sees their hurt. And she sees with the eyes of her own wounds as if they have a direct link to someone's pain. My hurt knows your hurt, and it goes to it. *Hurt goes to hurt*. Shianne's insight reverberated through all my interviews. The phrase (and its variations) catches on. It captures something that Stronghearts experience but find difficult to name. It confuses their sense of the role that they are playing—as listener, as helper, as outsider. It challenges their conception of how they are situated in relation to war trauma. The notion of "hurt goes to hurt" does not presume that they experience what the veterans experienced, that they somehow *know* the war experience. There is explicit acknowledgment by Stronghearts that they do *not* know the experience of combat. It is not about empathy, as if the pain of another elicits something in you, drawing you to act or respond. It is that the wound of another reveals your wound.

In several of the interviews, this is a revelation: Stronghearts discover that they have wounds that needed tending, wounds they would not have registered were it not for their participation in WJH. Ann holds Janie's talking stick when she speaks with me. A mother of two middle-school children, she works full time at an insurance company. She's the crier in the group, she tells me. She cries just about every time she comes to circle. She was interested in helping veterans' families, but she never imagined that she would work directly with veterans. John invited her to circle—repeatedly. "I was completely overwhelmed, because I don't really have any background in the military," she explains. Given her soft high voice, you have a sense that the bark of military orders would undo her, yet she is surprisingly tough. In her first meetings, she was nervous about the anger and agitation she witnessed. She still feels that, but she trusts the process.

Ann presents herself as more removed from the impact of war than other Stronghearts. She is conscious of the hard work that many in the circle have done. Given that the vocabulary is pervasive, I ask her if she sees herself as wounded in some way. "I think I did and I don't—or I do and didn't realize I did," she starts out. Then she begins to tell me about her first marriage that ended after eighteen months: "I felt responsible for the entire screw-up, and I think that my ex-husband felt that way, too." She recalls an unusual circle that was composed of children of vets. They were talking about their struggles with fathers returning from war. When she left the circle, she remembered that her ex-husband's father was a combat vet in Korea. She says, "I had no idea this was really impacting me . . . I walked out of there overwhelmed with sadness and joy, because I thought, 'Gee, it really wasn't my fault, twenty-four years later.'"

The *it* was her divorce. When she heard the children of veterans, she knew something more about her ex-husband's childhood and the responses that war triggers. War was present in her first marriage, but its effects were not visible. Moments like that happen often, Chuck says, in which a door seems to open across the circle. Gayle remembered what it was like to walk around the house after her ex-husband returned from Vietnam. It was the feeling of being "always on edge." That became so familiar to her that she didn't recognize the effects. I had asked her the same question as Ann, about whether she saw herself as wounded. And like Ann, she tells me that before her involvement in WJH, she would have said that she didn't: "But I think I'm seeing more than that . . . I

think I see them, you know, gradually." They are always quick to say
that this wounding is not of the same sort or scale as what they hear
from veterans in circle. But they have been newly attuned to the channels of hurt.

John K. was drafted but unable to go into combat. He was designated as IV-F, meaning not qualified for military service, by his doctor.
Like other IV-Fs, the experience of staying home can come with sharp
criticism from civilians whose sons were sent to Vietnam. "You're kind
of in a weird place," he says, "somebody out there hates you because
they see you as being a little conniving or a draft dodger and all the
other bad things." When John Schluep approached him about participating in WJH, it was an opportunity and also a reminder of his IV-F
status. I asked him if he was able to talk about *that* in circle. "Oh, yes.
Yes, I did," he answered. It was the same circle in which one of the guys
talked about the mortar that hit the guy behind him, as his unit was
marching off the airfield. Right there, walking single file, he was gone.
"It's visceral," John K. said. The guy in the group was struggling, many
years later, with being the one who survived. The guilt of survival may
have triggered John to share his own sense of guilt—the guilt of not
going to war: "You listen to people that have bled and you'd feel like
you should've been there."

A sense of unworthiness—a "not good enough" feeling—
accompanied him ever since. During one of the circles, a veteran
approached him, took the stick from the center, and handed it to him.
"He gave me a hug and said, 'You are . . . I declare you more than good
enough." He recalls that it was very emotional and powerful because
the words were spoken by someone whom he had always felt was his
accuser, standing in judgment of him for over forty years. By bringing
his story into the circle, John K. was telling the larger story of war.
Vietnam was marked with controversy, and one of the aspects of that
was the controversy over the men who stayed at home.

As I listen, the Stronghearts are discovering wounds that they did
not know they had or did not know how to name. Ann says, "I think
that's the amazing part about the people of Strongheart is that they experience healing in the circle which none of us ever thought we needed."
The wounds did not have to be of the same order to speak to each other;
the pain of war was particular but not untouchable. Wounds can find
each other; they can recognize one another. While many WJH members attest to the ways in which war trauma transmits across generations,

they are witnessing another kind of transmission—a transmission in service of healing.

Something happens in circle. Healing takes place there. This is uncontested in the Strongheart testimonies. But there is little discussion about the source of healing. Where is it coming from? Who or what is the source of healing? Interestingly, these questions are not central for those whom I interviewed. They did not speak in terms of God healing them or of attributing the work to God. When I ask Gayle to talk about the healing process that took place in her brother, she says, "I don't know what the healing is: I just know that I recognize it when I see it. You know, there's just—I don't know how to explain it. It's just that inner feeling that you get that kind of brings things out." The divine was talked about less as a source of healing and more in terms of a witness to what is taking place—as witness to the healing rather than the ultimate source of it. It did not matter where the healing comes from. The emphasis was on presence and participation.

When circle begins, everyone shows up. There is a quality of presence that people bring to circle. It is not just about being there; it is about how you approach being there. Facilitators are directed to prepare the circle. Soul work is not about following a script or learning techniques. There is a framework to follow—the ceremony provides parameters—but the movement of spirit involves something between the lines of the script. Because of the kind of work that is being done, the great healers must be summoned. In each circle, there is a summoning of the ancestors, a call for Great Spirit, for the Holy Spirit to be present. Shianne says, "The spirits are participating. . . . You can discern and sort out however you decide, but the spirits are participating."

In Alcoholics Anonymous, there is an acknowledged higher power, however unspecified. There is a posture of dependence in the face of addiction and struggle that underlies the group. Some veterans in the circle have participated in AA and that vocabulary enters into the circle at points. In WJH the language of dependence is not prominent, and, in fact, there is more emphasis on their collective power. The higher power invoked in WJH is less of a soloist and more like an ensemble chorus. When I asked them if they saw themselves as healers, Cindi quickly says no: "So I don't do any healing. . . . The circle is what's healing, that energy. You are part of that. You're bringing something into that for healing."

Through participation in the group, attunement to another's journey unearths the unexpected within you. But this perception suggests that healing is not accomplished by standing outside it, but that one's own pain may come to the surface through the process of reaching out to another's wound. It is not just that one's "hurt" recognizes the hurt in another, but that the collective attunement to pain forges routes of healing that did not previously exist.

Razors and Doves

While WJH members testify to the changes that they experience within the circle, Shianne has a particular gift for capturing the experiences by way of vivid images. Just as "hurt goes to hurt" evokes an image of pain traveling from one person to another, she offers the images of razors and doves to describe the healing process. It is a demanding process. The circle is not simply about getting someone to tell their experience of war; that may be one element of a much more tortuous process. She describes encountering someone in that space. It is like watching razors come out of someone: "Somebody is going through something, like those razors are coming out of them, you know, it hurts. They cut up a person from the inside—destroying the soul. They are doing great damage, and they need to be removed. But there is pain as the razors break the surface of the skin. She remembers her own process and describes it as a process of confronting her own death—watching her own death. "When I had to do my healing, I had to go back to the places where I was shattered and that I died. I died there. And so you're asking me to return to the place that I died." Healing work involves witnessing your own death. The transformation cannot happen without the return to the site of death.

Something comes after this encounter, but she insists that you have to "stay with the pain to know that part." There is the moment when the clouds part after a violent storm:

> And then all of a sudden, you see the sun, and it's dropping on the leaf where the moisture is glistening. And this is the place of the new day and the new vision, and this lightness you feel like there's release. I didn't know I could feel this way. And there's something really awesome about this feeling, and it's so new. And so those are the doves.

Shianne is speaking about her own rebirth, but not exclusively. She says that she didn't know that the feeling was possible. It is unclear whether the image of doves is firsthand or secondhand. The doves come after the razors. And this experience of newness, green, new life, was not something that she could see. This is the process that she witnesses in others—death and rebirth. In the interview, she moves between a description of her personal experience and her experiences as a healer. She switches from the "I" to the "he/she/they" when she refers to the healing work, as if she, as healer, taps into the power of her own healing to guide her work with others. She recalls her own experience of death. Razors will be lodged inside indefinitely. Eventually, a person will bleed out. The work of removing them is too difficult. Her role is to hold a vision of a different ending: "But I know that the doves are coming after the razors, you know, and they're being set free."

When Shianne describes her task with someone in this process of transformation, she says it's like being a midwife: "You stayed with them while they do it. It's like a woman having the baby. She says that at the point of the worst part of the transition of labor, 'I can't do this.' And then she does it." This transformation is a rebirth, and the birth channel for entering into the world a second time is, in Shianne's account, also a death channel. The passage into new life requires encountering pain and death—a confrontation with the harm that you have done and that has been done to you.[26]

She presents this vision to me right before we enter into the circle process. As participants speak, I recall the images. I envision doves, rising up in the midst of the difficult words offered in the presence of multiple witnesses, multiple midwives.

Another dove story emerged in the interviews. Gayle shared an experience that she had after Bud's death. She was grieving his loss, and she went on retreat with a group from WJH. She was anticipating an encounter with Bud, knowing that sometimes people experience the presence of ancestors when they go more deeply into the healing rituals. Going into the sweat lodge, she was longing for a vision of him; coming out of the lodge, she says: "I was really disappointed—I mean, I tried not to show it, but, you know, I was really, truly disappointed." She was in a room gathering her things when Ann approached her, telling her there was something important that she needed to discuss with Gayle. Ann had been sitting outside the lodge, praying for Gayle and the others inside. Deep in prayer, she happened to look up: "She told me that Bud was there. And he had a wave that I have never seen him do with anyone else but . . . for Warrior's Journey . . . almost like a circular, 'Hi, Ann.'" Gayle says, "At first, I was a bit jealous because he came to her and not to me. And then, after I thought about it . . . I thought maybe it's better that way, that might be even better." Confirmation of Bud's presence also came at the ceremony that night, in the form of a gift given to her by one of the members of the community. In the drumming circle, a woman placed a barrette in Gayle's hand, telling her it was a gift: "The Great Spirit asked me—told me that you were the one that needed this."

There are many ways of dismissing these experiences. Gayle admits that she still had her mother's voice in her head saying, "Oh, that's witchcraft." But there is a point when she just decided not to try to explain anymore. "I am being fed, you know, through the Great Spirit, whether you call him God, whether you call—no matter what you call him. I felt like I had been with my brother. And now, I just need to sometimes hold it or put it in my pocket." This vision, or visitation, is communal in nature. Gayle is reminded, in Bud's visitation to Ann, that the healing circle is wide.

Gayle's vision is consistent with the invocation of the Holy Spirit and the Great Spirit as it is practiced in circle. These spirits are not absent, nor do they suddenly become present. They are always present, but the summons is a way of recognizing their presence in our midst. The question is whether we have the capacity to receive their power and recognize their presence.

In Christianity, spirit is not confined by language or place. Following his resurrection, Jesus is understood to have entered into a locked room to appear to the disciples. In the Gospel of John, he is both spectral and corporeal. He makes several postresurrection appearances, and the disciples wonder if they are seeing a ghost. As Gayle's mother whispers the warnings into her ear, I am reminded that long-standing debates and discussions about the nature of the Holy Spirit underlie her mother's concerns. They circle around the question, How do we know how and when God's Spirit is present? Gayle has stopped talking with her mother about her experiences in WJH. She wants to keep the peace. But Gayle is unwavering in her belief that the Great Spirit gives gifts in unexpected ways.

Refiguring Resurrection

Participants gather to witness the invisible wounds of war. The work of the circle is to bring the warrior back home, to facilitate a different kind of return than a physical one. This return will vary for each, and there is no set timeline; the return is not ensured. But the circle-work is focused there; it involves bringing the internal and invisible wounds to the surface in order to name them, and to release them.

They are gathered close, watching for the razors to emerge—like the disciples. This is a healing scene when read through the lens of WJH. The gathering is for the sake of healing. The work of the return is communal. It is here that the disciples learn the work of witnessing invisible wounds. And Jesus becomes the one who shows them the way. He instructs them in the work of healing. And in the process, they discover wounds that they did not know they had. It is only through a communal practice of witnessing that they can facilitate the return. The doves follow the razors. This is the good news.

The Thomas scene has been read classically as a narrative scene that demonstrates Thomas' passage from unbelief to belief. For WJH participants, Thomas' encounter is situated within a different landscape—one of wounding and healing, losing and finding. It became clear, in the interviews, that the role of belief is secondary to the work of healing. In fact, it can obstruct the healing process. The language of belief falls away. In circle, John often tells stories of Jesus as healer. Jesus did not work alone; he was a healer surrounded by a team of healers.

If we think of the Upper Room as an extension of the healing stories in the gospels, the disciples gather around wounds in a different way. In his early ministry, Jesus directed the disciples to the wounds of those who approached him to be healed. Now they gather around his wounds, first to watch his execution and second to make sense of his curious return—the marks of his resurrection. This was the way that Jesus encountered people; he tended to wounds, even naming ones that they did not know that they had.

But here Jesus appears with wounds. WJH members are wary about how the term "hero" operates, often as a way of further alienating veterans from their actual experiences of war. The hero image is what others need, but it is not always what the veteran needs. The soldier-savior trope "has emotional power and staying power because it makes sense. Soldiers *have* served, suffered, and sacrificed. Soldiers *do* demonstrate altruism in the extreme,"[27] Ebel writes, acknowledging that the actions of soldiers should not be diminished. But it is the employment of these actions to feed a redemptive national story that concerns him. America "requires this incarnation" because it relies on the soldier to sanctify the soul of the nation. Keeping with the logic of the nation, the resurrection scene features the triumphant savior, whose wounds are glorious marks of one whose sacrifice redeems the nation.[28]

Another way of interpreting the wounded warrior image is along the lines of the ancient epics. The wounded warrior goes out from the community in service of its protection; the wounds, while marking one body, are understood to represent the wounds received in service of the community. They are collective wounds, a symbol of war's communal impact. They are heroes, not because they fight for their country but because they are willing to surface truths about war that have been lodged within them. Jesus, positioning amid the ancient wounded warriors, is like Odysseus returning to his homeland after his journey through the underworld. He identifies with the wounds. But they do not need to be drawn up into the conqueror narrative. Instead, this Jesus identifies with and knows the complexities of war. And, upon returning, he is able to expose truths about what it means to go to war. A richer reading of the descent into hell could emphasize solidarity rather than sacrifice. The wounds tell truths about war.[29]

This is more consistent with the way WJH depicts ancient warriors. And yet they collectively enact something more than this. The resurrected Jesus discloses his marks to an intimate few. We can think of the women gathered around his body, wrapping it in preparation for burial. This is a different kind of preparation, in which Jesus pulls back his robe to reveal to those who knew him well the truth of his journey. He entrusts them with this revelation. The difference between this and the previous lies in the opening of this story to the collective and not to the singular figure. The emphasis is placed on the ways in which the disciples are drawn into the work of wounds.

I surface this difference by moving between Caravaggio's showing of the ancient story and the work of the healing circle. In Caravaggio's rendering, Jesus is the central figure and the disciples gather around him. There is no central figure in the WJH resurrection scene. The status of Jesus becomes indistinguishable from the others; he stands among them. What joins the circle together is the work that they are preparing to do. The journey that they will take is a journey initiated by the work of the eyes. Jesus is situated alongside the others. What sets Jesus apart in this scene is that he is instructing them in the way of wounds, exposing his wounds to make visible the invisible journey ahead. He takes them on a journey that requires a different way of seeing. The significance of altered vision in the gospel account can be witnessed in the unusual means of perception within the group. Eyes do not just see what is visible on the surface in the WJH circle. Eyes are like excavation tools, used to clear anything that obstructs the path to the soul. The curious thing about the clearing statement—"I am 'x,' and I am clear"—is that it identifies each member individually (a singularity), but it also positions each person in service of the greater work. A community forms. Barbara and Peter might say it is a search and rescue team looking for lost souls. And in the search, the question of whose souls are lost and whose found is unclear. The soul does not belong to you alone.

For participants, the dramatic center of the narrative is the discovery of wounds and their surprising communicability. It is the unearthed wounds of the veteran that reveal wounds in the civilian. The gathering around wounds opens the civilian to a process of hearing the horrors of war and its effects named, voiced. The journey of the warrior home involves naming the realities of what war does and of what is done in the name of war. But the surprising element of Strongheart participation is that wounds communicate across experiences. Eye meets eye. Wound meets wound. The wound is not only a portal, but it becomes a mirror that reflects back on the one witnessing. Stronghearts narrate the turning of Thomas' finger in the opposite direction: the finger points back, as if the wound is a mirror that exposes wounds that he did not know he had. The finger moves in both directions, as if there is a direct line between wounds. It is not so apparent, then, who is wounded.

Razors

Warriors Journey Home links the work of the eyes to the wounds. When you look someone in the eye during circle, you are stating that you are ready to enter into the work of healing soul wounds. You are searching for a path of entry. The opening of the eyes is the critical opening, as if it is a portal, an aperture, into seeing what is inside. For members of WJH, the eye becomes a portal through which the razors can be accessed. And what you see when the eyes meet in circle are the razors lodged within. Some razors have been there so long that pathways have been created around them—an internal rerouting by way of pain. The wounds are not externally visible. They can only be seen if someone looks for them and is attuned to the damage that war does to the soul. Even though the system has rerouted, the razors are still in place, doing damage there. The work of removing them requires more pain. It will involve a difficult labor process, Shianne says. There is necessary preparation, then, for seeing the razors, a kind of communal attunement needed to facilitate the process of healing.

If we return to Caravaggio's depiction, the wound is at eye level with Thomas and two others looking directly into it. Caravaggio's rendering of the wound resembles an eye, as the fold above Thomas' finger forms the lower edge of the eyelid. While the wound on the surface is the object of the gaze, the wound, as eye, can be a portal to invisible wounds. When the disciples are huddled around the wound, their eyes meet this eye-wound, and it is as if a unique portal opens, disclosing what is typically hidden from view.

Caravaggio's painting also turns us to the finger. Thomas touches the wound, but, as Caravaggio shows us, Thomas is not simply touching the surface; his finger plunges into the wound. The finger circles the perimeter of the wound in order to make way for the razors to exit. This is not an attempt to verify Jesus' identity. We then read Jesus' instruction to Thomas differently. The eye directs them in, and the finger makes room for the razors to come out. Jesus' invitation to touch is an invitation to clear the way for the exit. He is not satiating Thomas' doubt by inviting him to touch the wounds. He is inviting Thomas and the disciples into the work of healing. This is not a test of faith; nor is it a sensory accommodation of Christ to Thomas, as John Calvin presents it. Jesus is directing them to the collective work of healing by reorienting their senses, pointing them to truths that rarely come to light. They will need courage to move amid the less discernible channels in which death still has a strong grip.

Doves

Shianne's image of razors and doves prompts the most imaginative refiguring of this scene. If the wound is open, we can imagine that this figure might bleed out. But this wound does not seem to produce any liquid. Sometimes bandages are removed in order to expose the wound to open air, allowing a natural healing process to take place. Yet, unbandaged, they can also be exposed to harm again. The circle becomes the space in which the first bandages are unraveled. The wound is still fresh, but it is not reopened.

The wound is an opening out of which the razors can be released, and the disciples, then, are providing a context into which the razors can emerge. The wound is both an entrance and an exit. The entrance for healing is the eye-wound, and yet it is also the exit for the razors to be released. Those present will witness the transfiguration of this wound, as razors are followed by doves. The three figures gaze into the wound of the resurrected Jesus. But the wound is a portal for healing.

These wounds are not simply remnants of a past suffering; they mark a beginning out of which new forms of life arise. In the manual given to WJH facilitators to inform them about the healing circle process, John uses the language of crucible. He plays off the term "crux," meaning "a crucial moment in time." The event of crucifixion was certainly seen as a crucial moment, he notes. But he appeals to a crucible in one of its lesser known uses—as a container in which elements are brought together and something new is created. The circle, he says, "becomes a crucible of safety. . . . It holds elements that may or may not become dangerous." The circle is a safe place, not because safe things are brought there but because difficult truths are told there and held. He writes, "The circle is used and becomes a crucible for story telling—listening—and healing becomes very important because the environment will 'hold' the elements of the story."[30]

The site of resurrection is a site of safety. But work is being done there. If we think through the dynamics of this scene, the razors are breaking the surface of flesh as they exit. And it is this work done on the surface that is critical. Many veterans return from war, and they are unrecognizable to those they love. Embedded in Gayle's words, "He came back," is the period between Bud's departure from Vietnam and his entrance into the healing circle. She was just beginning to recognize him. Recognition did not mean that he was restored to who he was before the war; but, when the razors began to break the surface, Gayle saw possibilities of connecting with him.

The Gospel of John combines the narratives of resurrection and Pentecost. And John Schluep's invocation of the Pentecost scene brings together the Thomas and the Upper Room scenes.[31] The importance of Pentecost, John says, is that each person hears peace in his or her own respective language; languages are crossing—Great Spirit, Holy Spirit, the Christ, the ancestors—and their ears are tuned in a new way. Distinctions that were important in one context are no longer important in the context of healing. Jesus appears in the midst of the disciples, a spectral appearance, and he announces peace. And they look around, wondering how peace can come when there is wounding in their midst. They are huddled in fear. But doves follow the razors; this is the truth that they know that the world does not know.[32] The echo of the Johannine statement is powerful here; they are being ushered into truths that others do not want to have exposed, that, when they break the surface, will speak what few have the capacity to hear.

The circle provides a space in which these contrary "truths" can be held. War stories are love stories, John says. They are stories about love for country, love of family, and love of freedom. But war stories are also stories about unmentionable harm, loss, and inhumanity. The soldier-savior trope tells the first story, but this story can leave the veteran feeling betrayed by the nation that idealizes love and uses it for its own purposes, regardless of the toll it takes on the soldier.[33] And yet there *is* pride present in testimonies offered within the circle. But there is also the affective charge of fighting, the adrenaline rush that often accompanies the stories. This is physical, awakening the charge of war as a form of recall that is messier and difficult to valorize. An Iraq veteran attending circle my first visit told the group that he missed being in theater. When he was fighting, he said, it was the most alive he had ever felt. Coming home deadened him, he said, but no one wants to hear that.

The Upper Room presents a vision of a home community retooling, awakened to the challenges of homecoming. The disciples inhale a common breath, bodies awakening to life on the other side of death. The question is whether the story of life after death can account for these tensions. This is messy love, more dynamic than pure, more charged than idealized. This is the work that the disciples are being prepared for. "This Spirit, these doves, live in you," Jesus tells them, "and they are waiting to be released." Just as hurt goes to hurt, doves call to doves. The promise that Jesus made to the disciples before his death is that the paraclete would come, would inhabit them, and would bear witness to the events that took place, the things that they would not comprehend, even as they were standing there. This paraclete-territory is marked by indirect witness. When the risen Christ appears in their midst, he announces his presence by declaring "Peace" and gifting them with the Holy Spirit. One of the prominent images for God's spirit is the dove. In WJH circles, the doves ascend when razors are releasing. They arise from the site of wounds. As wound calls to wound, peace calls out to the dove. The question of God's presence in suffering is a perennial and pressing one. God's Spirit is present, but the razors may cut so deeply that the presence of God cannot be felt. Yet the doves are multiple. Doves call out to the doves to prepare a way, to facilitate a difficult passage.

The vision of razors and doves is not a culminating vision or an ending. Members of WJH show up every other Sunday at 6:00 p.m. The circle process is an intentional gathering that prepares the way for that return. Members of the circle understand themselves as part of a process that extends beyond one particular war or generation. They see it as ongoing work. Ann's husband asks why she would subject herself to this—why put yourself through it? John K. noted that it was precisely this ongoingness that made it too difficult; "I had to take a break," he tells me. Gayle keeps going, even after Bud is gone. In many senses, they continually hold vigil for the "return" of the veteran. But this is not a one-time resurrection; it is ongoing work.

Salvation

The WJH vision of the Upper Room does not feed the soldier-savior trope. It does not fortify a logic that glorifies wounds while abandoning veterans in their woundedness. Instead, it reveals curious turns in the biblical narrative, unraveling the salvific logic that constitutes the surface of America's public life.

Jonathan Ebel makes the case that American civil religion functions according to an incarnational logic. The soldiers embody—incarnate—the spirit of the nation. They are its "Word made flesh." This constellation of word, flesh, and spirit continues to play out, continuing a version of Christian logic, while less recognized as such. All that the United States stands for is made visible in the body of the soldier. A visible embodiment of America, soldiers are required to perform the identity of soldier-savior.[34]

At several points, WJH challenges such a reading. It refocuses attention on a group, rather than an individual. Rather than setting one person out, it positions persons around wounds and invites them to seek that which is lost, both in someone else and then within themselves. The parables of the lost things return, as salvation is focused on recovering what has been lost. Soul work is collective.

Ebel says that there is another side to the process of the sacred relationship between nation and soldier, which he identifies as "excarnation." This is the process of taking spirit out of the body of the soldier to use and reproduce it for the national good, to support a story of national identity. He writes, "Excarnation is necessarily selective, necessarily careless of human particularities. It is the edge of American civil religion that cuts the soldier as it attempts to heal him."[35] The ideals of the nation are not becoming flesh, as with the incarnation, but they are de-fleshed, or extracted from flesh and live on and proliferate far beyond the body of the soldier. The spirit keeps alive and reinscribes the ideals in the public sphere, but this spirit can operate apart from the actual experiences of war. While actual blood is shed and bodies engaged in combat, Ebel writes, "They must be made intelligible by *blood preserved* and *bodies kept whole*, by the witness who transforms blood into ink, the survivor whose uniformed body stands in for the fallen."[36]

Christianity contributes to the transcendent soldier narrative. The concern that both Wool and Ebel raise is whether the common every-dayness of the soldier's challenge to reintegrate is countered by the nar-rative of the nation and, in turn, by its supporting theo-logic. The hope is to find ways to tell the war story differently. The Greek epics provide a way of addressing the war experience to acknowledge its more tragic dimensions. In so doing, they reveal the limitations of a redemptive logic. While it is easy to see that a certain version of Christian theology is the problem, it is more difficult to imagine a countertheology from within Christianity. Ebel asks, "Will better theology change the con-tours of citizen's devotion to the United States and to those who wear its uniform?" He opens to it, invites it. But this theology would have to make possible a witness to the "complex humanity that continues beneath and beyond the uniform."[37]

A different theological vision arises from a reading of the Upper Room. Spirit and flesh are reconfigured. Truth telling is in service of releasing razors. Sacrificial logic unravels, replaced by a vision of com-munal care. Instead of discarding the savior trope altogether, it may need to be retrieved for the sake of the other ways in which salvation is pre-sented in the Christian gospels. Jesus came to seek and save that which was lost. This, of course, has been read in terms of the afterlife and is operationally one of the most exclusivist claims wielded in the name of Christianity. But because the martializing mythologies of religions are surfacing and the violence of fundamentalisms are proliferating, it is important not to give up the visions of salvation but to construct countervisions from within the very same traditions. Theologians need to be courageous enough to lose the victory narratives, to shed these, in order to return again to some of the fainter inscriptions that touch the surface of skin but rarely receive the attention of "devoted publics."[38]

Before his death, Jesus tells his disciples that he will be sending them a new spirit, a spirit of truth, not a spirit that the world knows.

Instead, it is a spirit that carries on his life, his memory. If we imagine excarnation as the extraction of spirit for the purposes of the nation, as Ebel presents, then a different spirit—one which the world cannot give—might reinfuse flesh with breath.

Expanding Ebel's analysis in a more theological direction, the notion of excarnation reveals not just a problem with the christo-logic, but with the pneuma-logic. The spirit of the nation hovers over the embodied realities of those who fight in its name. A Christian theology of spirit has often been a hovering theology. But a spirit released into the Upper Room is more elemental; he breathes it into the space. It reanimates the collective. He shows them channels through which difficult truths cross. They must travel different routes in search of lost souls. They must make peace with the dead and the living.

Ebel's last chapter is a benediction of sorts. He titles it "Of Flesh, Words, and Wars." He is pointing to a way of "doing civil religious hagiography" differently, questioning the role that scholars play in upholding a particular vision of the nation. He is also summoning theologians to do their work with the substructural Christian assumptions that still function below the surface of America's collective skin.[39] Theology may need, as well, to be done in a "less orthodox register."[40] This means opening to a theology of spirit that can reposition suffering so that it may be engaged rather than idealized.

Shianne is no longer with the group. It is a difficult story, and one that I am not equipped to tell. I keep hearing her words about the order of healing and about the time to reckon with the history of harm to her people, a history that lives on in the present. Perhaps that time arrived, and no one was prepared. Perhaps there were no Stronghearts for that ongoing and unacknowledged war on native peoples.

Writing the wrongs of the past and making peace require something other than a reiteration of sacrificial logic. The soldier-savior trope relies on a model of the one who dies in behalf of the many. The transformation happens outside us, it is done *for us, in our behalf.* And yet this gospel account closes with the regeneration of breath. He said a spirit would come to live in them and carry them into truths that they thought were unbearable. The "many" are learning to become those of strong heart. WJH members believe that they are participating in a greater work, an ongoing work, of which there is no promised end. What makes their work sacred is not that it wins or that it rests upon an assured end. It is sacred, because it professes a radical vision of interconnectedness, a communicability that binds all living things together at the most elemental level.

I register the pressure to tell the story of WJH in a particular way and especially so after I heard the news about Shianne. The pressure is to offer up the work of WJH as inspirational, and even ideal. American therapeutic models have their own transcending sweeps that can offer secularized versions of the redemption story.[41] But to linger with the more complex story reflects the kind of truth telling that I have been pursuing in this resurrection story. Bud's story of after-living was more like a living hell than a glorious heaven. But he knew the circle and began to trust it. He found a route home, and he was beginning to make his way there. Yet he did not win any battles over his addiction, and Vietnam still haunted him.

Tom, a Vietnam vet, is one of the long-standing members of WJH. He would probably say that WJH saved his life. Several Stronghearts refer to him when they talk about the transformation that is possible in the group. He is now one of the circle facilitators and works as a case manager at a homeless veterans' shelter in Akron. He turns to poetry as a medium of healing, and he sometimes shares his poems in circle. His poems return me to the Upper Room. I imagine Tom sitting next to Peter in circle, reading a portion of his poem, titled "Unnamed." Where did the soul go in Vietnam? What happened to it? They share this question. Tom reads: "I watched my soul, a never regained part of me, / Fly with wings, but not those of an angel / but as a dark and sad object / wondering how this could ever have happened."[42]

Then he starts to read another, one that flashes back to an ambush in Vietnam, and to one whose "glaring eyes" haunt his dreams, as she stands at the edge of her village protecting what he has just taken away from her. "How can you ever forgive me?" he asks. The question of forgiveness is released into the circle.

Nameless Woman

There will come a time, I am convinced,
when those throughout history, have abused the power entrusted to
    them
and heaped injustice and destruction and death onto the world's poor
The moment will arrive when reasons will be required,
And a bitter toll will be extracted.
And only then might those whose lives have been decimated,
Only then might they be willing to forgive.[43]

I imagine Shianne there to receive his words. This last stanza of his poem mirrors Shianne's comments in the interview about the order of healing. There will come a time, she said, in which the group would need to come to terms with other kinds of wrongs done, other unacknowledged wars. This history, too, is about the history of America and a redemptive story told about a chosen people who were promised the "new Israel" at all costs. The extermination of Shianne's peoples was part of that redemptive vision, the "necessary" acts required to build the nation. Those wounds still live on, perpetuated by multiple excarnations.

The work of healing is messy. Perhaps we can only write it in multiple drafts. Perhaps it, like writing, is a craft, practiced over time. Perhaps it is practiced indirectly until, one day, practitioners can feel their souls, rediscovered, rebirthed through a channel forged by those of strong heart.

Janie was the first one to greet Gayle and Bud when they came to the group. She was always right there to greet everyone. "She and Bud had a connection," Gayle tells me. It was Janie's dream to go visit "the Wall" to honor her son Bradley. He was a door gunner in Vietnam and died of Agent Orange after the war, before Janie attended her first circle. You could say that Janie became Bud's war mother and he her adopted son. Gayle remembers that Bud began to make plans to take Janie to the Wall. She was not physically able to make the trip, and he died shortly after that.

During all of the changes taking place in the group, it is the bond created within the context of WJH that Gayle holds on to. When I ask her about the future of WJH, she admits to being concerned. There have been losses amid the changes. But she tells me, "You know, I will be there until the end. And after that, I will find a new place, a new way."

→ your trauma is not erased, its acknowledged and through community, there is solidarity and a ability to keep living.

→ does true healing ever come at the cost of anothers life/existence/experience?

Resurrection does not mean
wounds are washed away or
erased !!!

It means there is more life to
be had post wounds. There is One who
can understand woundedness and
enter into our woundedness

Conclusion
Communal After-Living

Some wounds do not go away. They remain invisible, operating below the surface of our lives. When and if these wounds surface, they are often unrecognizable and misunderstood. As insights about the ways in which violence affects bodies, severs social relations, and transmits across generations emerge, there is a growing need to take account of wounds and their continued impact on us. I have referred to the present challenges by using the terms "after-living" and "ongoingness." These acknowledge that there is something of those wounds still persisting in life, that there is no pure space to stand apart from them, and that we need to think creatively and constructively in the midst of these realities. The "posttraumatic" identifies a way of living with awareness that experiences do not respect lines between past, present, and future, that histories of suffering persist in the present, operating powerfully below the surface of conscious life.

These wounds present a challenge to Christian theology. The logic of wounds in Christian thought is mixed. With wounds at its center, it has a curious history of erasing wounds. This erasure is often enacted through claims of resurrection. While the wounds of crucifixion stand as one of the central symbols of Christian faith, the articulations of the meaning of those wounds have often perpetuated rather than alleviated suffering. Paired with claims of resurrection, they often enact a story of life overcoming death, of the alleviation of suffering in the hereafter. But these explanations are not sufficient to speak to the ongoingness of suffering, to wounds resurfacing within life. The phenomenon of wounds returning meets us at a different point in the Christian narrative. It insists on a "language of life" on the other side of death. Conceiving life with attunement to traumatic realities requires rethinking the narrative of life through the losses, both perilous and promissory.

When Jesus miraculously appears to his disciples following his death, he returns with the marks of suffering still on his body. The marks remain. And he displays these wounds and invites the disciples gathered around him to see and to touch them. The Thomas encounter is distinctive in respect to touch. It has been an influential story in displaying the meaning of resurrection in Christianity. But the truths that it tells often have little to do with woundedness. This presence, and yet curious absence, of wounds attests to the fact that these wounds, interpreted theologically, have little to say about the material realities of wounds that we bear in life.

In Christian narrations of resurrection, wounds disappear. John Calvin serves as the representative of this disappearance. His uneasiness with these wounds reflects a host of concerns: that wounds will diminish the promise of life after death, that they will compromise the vision of the glorified Christ. He is invested in a heavenly vision of the afterlife. But we can also witness his *dis-ease* with bodies, with materiality, and with the spectral. His conception of faith privileges hearing and seeing. Those who are strong in faith will not need the carnal and sensual means of coming to belief. He downplays the aspect of touch in this resurrection encounter, reading the wounds as God's accommodation to human limitation.

And yet there is more to Calvin's writings, and I open up, within his resurrection vision, another way of conceiving of woundedness as marking limitation while opening into an embrace of creaturely life as interdependent. This "more" that I glimpse in Calvin is what I pursue in the subsequent chapters, by returning readers to this story of Thomas and the Upper Room appearances.

The Johannine appearances feature wounds returning on the body of the risen Jesus. By interpreting this narrative from various angles, I unearth a vision of woundedness that acknowledges the dynamics of how wounds function in the after-living. They surface and recede. They are not readily accessible to the eye. The dynamics of wounds in trauma sheds new light on this resurrection scene, in which Jesus is teaching the disciples a way amid wounds.

Taking seriously the imperceptible processes that shape a posttraumatic landscape, I focus attention on several aspects of the Johannine resurrection account. Jesus displays the wounds to his disciples, but their response prompts him to approach them again. The display expands to touch, as Thomas asks him not only to see but also to touch the marks. This underscores the insight that wounds cannot be easily seen or accessed. This reading takes seriously the ways in which the wounds are both concealed and revealed, engaged and covered over.

Second, I emphasize that a spirit is breathed into this space. Earlier in the Johannine account, Jesus promises his disciples that he would send them a spirit that would bear the memory of his life and yet carry this memory forward into the future. This memory bearing is somatically transmitted, as Jesus breathes new air into the territory of the Upper Room. Through the medium of breath, life is reanimated, made sacred.

Third, a new community is formed and given shape, as the disciples come to terms with the past and reorient themselves to practices of care and truth telling. New configurations of life are envisioned and carried forward.

While the story of doubting Thomas and the Upper Room serve as accounts that secure the truth of Christian faith, these foci reshape classic depictions of belief toward the work of engaging wounds. The vision of after-living is a collective vision in which the work of wounds involves reconceiving touch, not as grasping the truth of Jesus' identity but as embodying the healing vision of Jesus, whose touch was a gesture of valuing those who were devalued, giving integrity to flesh and recognizing the ways in which certain persons are marked as outsiders.[2] It is not surprising, then, that this alternative vision of Thomas' touch is informed by theological interlocutors who are attuned to the dynamics of wounds being covered over and to the operations of power that keep certain truths from coming to the surface. I draw upon the work of feminist, womanist, and black theologians to envision the encounter between Thomas and the risen Jesus. They remind us that Christian theologies are not immune from covering over wounds. They shed light on familiar modes and patterns of thinking, interrogating the assumptions and investments that underlie familiar interpretations. Their recognition of practices of theology as wounding, in its more insidious sense, holds good news and bad news in tension. This tension is evident

in readings of the postdeath scene of Macrina read with feminist concerns in mind, and in the wilderness vision of the Upper Room via the
work of womanist theologian Delores Williams.

By gathering readers around the image of the risen Jesus with
wounds, I weave a theological commentary on resurrection wounds
and insist that they can speak amid the tenuous realities of after-living.
While Christian theologies of resurrection often feature visions of an
otherworldly afterlife, resurrection accounts, whether in the gospels or
in texts such as Gregory of Nyssa's, are never exclusively about life after
death. They capture moments following loss, death, and grief. These
can be undertheologized or overwhelmed by the transcendent sweep
of future-oriented theologies, but they nonetheless offer a tapestry for
thinking about life at its most tender and tenuous points, in its complexities and messiness. These "after" moments, narrated in terms of
trauma, point to an uncertain space featured *within* the gospel narratives
themselves.

The gospel writers provide different accounts of resurrection. The
accounts reflect varying ways of making sense of the trauma of Jesus'
death and the implications of his death for their lives going forward.
While many stories were circulating, some accounts became authoritative texts for the early community. Even those differed in emphasis. The
earliest accounts in the Gospel of Mark presented the loss in raw and
unprocessed form. The disciples come to the tomb, and it is empty. "He
has been raised, he is not here," the Gospel concludes.

The later accounts diverge. Rather than his disappearance, they
emphasize Jesus' appearances to the disciples. Biblical scholar David
Carr distinguishes these early and later accounts in light of the realities
of trauma. While the early account "preserves the sting of the traumatic
loss," the later accounts attempt to remedy that sting by filling in the
gaps with Jesus' appearances to the disciples.[3] Carr writes, "They countered the shame of crucifixion with the glory of triumph over death."[4]
The later accounts expressed triumph as a means of overcoming, of vin-
dicating, the defeat that may have marked the postdeath scene.

This speaks to the historical transmission of these Gospel texts as
well. What is potentially lost in the later accounts, according to Carr,
is the capacity of these texts to guide communities responding to the
"lingering force" of death in their midst.[5] While they have the potential
to meet persons and communities in these experiences and to provide
accompaniment amid these losses, they can also enact, evidenced in the

apologetics of the later tradition, a way *around* the losses, an overcoming
of that trauma.

This impulse to overcome, narrated through the later tradition, is
also at work in the erasure of wounds. While the writings are capable
of providing a way of attending to their losses, they can also serve quite
different ends. Instead of providing a means of acknowledging loss,
these texts provide a bandage over wounds and thus foreclose practices
of attending to them. They can hover above the surface and cover over
wounds. These appearances can become about securing the identity of
Jesus as the Christ, and yet, in so doing, they cease to tell "truths" about
fear, death, loss, shame, and the lingering force of those realities. Their
potential to either engage *or* cover over wounds is part of the transmission of this sacred story.

As reflective of this later tradition, the doubting Thomas story
has been transmitted, handed down, as a story of triumph. Thus, the
wounds must, in the end, testify to the triumph of resurrection. I have
attempted to read this later gospel as an account that provides space to
attend to wounds rather than to erase them. These appearances, such as
the one to Thomas, linger longer with the postdeath realities and provide testimonies to the shame of crucifixion in order to provide a vision
of how a community is to carry forward the message of Jesus.

It matters how we tell this story. The exigencies of after-living
require a hermeneutics that engages wounds. How does a community
work through such losses? If this story is held to be sacred by a community, it is made sacred by telling truths about the wounds that we
bear in life.[6] Directing the story toward the after-living, the encounters
between Jesus and the disciples present moments in which the disciples
come to terms with razors lodged deep within, as Shianne narrates.
These texts have the capacity to touch shame, grief, and anger, but
Thomas' pointing finger is often directed elsewhere.[7] Macrina's scar,
revealed to Gregory in the moments after her death, is a mark of healing within life. A mother's touch on the skin of her daughter focuses
attention on blessing, and on ways of tending to life. The timing of the
encounter also underscores the startling revelation that resurrection is
already taking place in the midst of things. Touch, through this retelling, features agency and connection. Jesus' appearances link back to his
work of healing. Faith returns to the dust of the everyday, as Macrina
swirls dirt, tears, and prayers to create a healing balm. The parables
of Jesus also return in their countervisions to the familiar yield of the

doubting Thomas story. The search for lost souls narrated by Strong-hearts in Warriors Journey Home reminds us of the parables of lost things in the gospels, in which Jesus tells his followers that their work is to seek out that which is lost. In so doing, their own losses are unearthed and held by those who commit themselves to the work.

The power of these resurrection appearances lie in their ability to offer a vision of wounds that turns us to the world in a particular way. Without an appeal to the seductive pull of promised endings, they can turn us to life in the midst of its complexities and uncertainties. This is not weak or ambiguous theology. It is sustaining theology that probes the capacities and readiness of communities to hold pain and to stay with difficult truths. This spirit, released in the Upper Room, is often on lockdown within theologies concerned with securing truth. We witness this played out in national narratives, as veterans bear the weight of theologies operating beneath the surface of our collective skin.

I reenvision the meaning of resurrection in the Christian tradition, locating its power in confronting, rather than erasing, the complexities of life beyond "deaths," whether literal or figurative. My theological commentary on this biblical passage circles around central images in the story, and I return to them in each chapter.

The *first* is the image of wounds on the body of Jesus. In his return, he brings the memory of histories of suffering forward, and he begins to teach a way of engaging wounds. Jesus' body is marked by the social forces of his day. The crucifixion marks are signs of this denigration and humiliation. That is part of the history of this body. If we follow Christian claims about the crucifixion, we can think about the crucifixion as not only the suffering of one body but also of a body that takes in histories of suffering and bears the marks of these histories. The claim that Jesus takes on the sins of the world can be rendered, here, in socio-material terms. His body is marked. But the resurrection accounts attest to a different moment, in which the memory of that suffering returns to be engaged and the disciples are invited to receive it, to bear it. If these marks are erased, these difficult memories can be pushed below the surface.

In the return of this body, histories surface in a more perilous sense. Thomas, read through the lens of the historical wounds of race in the United States, is implicated in a history of wounding.[8] Thomas' demand to have access the body speaks to the more insidious dimension of this encounter. Thomas must reckon with his past. Figured in the body of

Jesus and the memory bearing and truth telling of the Spirit, the past becomes present in this encounter. The encounter demands something of Thomas. Jesus' invitation confronts Thomas with the truth of his participation in these histories. And the apparition texts confront those approached with a decision about how they will position themselves in relation to these bodies. They evoke response and signal responsibility.

While Jesus' body is marked by history, it is also, as described in the Gospel of John, enfleshed. Mayra Rivera's retrieval of the concept of flesh, via a Johannine poetics, invites us to think about Jesus' body as both singular and collective. He bears witness in his body to the flesh of the world, marked in multiple configurations.[9] The marks are imprinted on his flesh. But because flesh is changeable, malleable, the marks are also not fixed.[10] This body brings to the surface those histories in such a way that when Thomas gazes at this body, he is drawn into the fabric of flesh reconstituting. This is Gregory of Nyssa's vision, as well, and the miracle of resurrection told through Macrina's scar. It is also the potential yield of Calvin's graft.

The *second* is the space between Thomas' finger and the body of Jesus. The interpretive history of the Thomas account has envisioned this space differently. Some, like Caravaggio, have filled in this space, depicting Thomas' finger as plunging into the wound, and others have kept his finger at a distance. The Johannine account allows for both readings. The gap in the biblical account opens up an interpretive space in which the meaning of resurrection has been debated. Calvin's concerns highlight how the nature of faith and truth depend on a particular reading of this account. But Calvin, as biblical interpreter, takes liberties with the account, attending to some details of the text while minimizing attention to others. Calvin emerges within the Christian tradition as an authoritative interpreter, and yet it is important to remember that his concerns are rooted in the soil, reflecting the contextual realities of his day. The transmission of Calvin's thought, however, can enact a forgetting. Thus, by opening up this space, I am asking contemporary readers to consider how theology positions us in relation to the "truths" of Christian faith, turning us to or away from the soil of human experience.

The *third* is an image of a community gathered around wounds. The surface of skin becomes an image for the work of wounds. When wounds are surfaced (and this often is disruptive and unwelcomed), they appear in the gospel text in a communal setting. Not one but several disciples are present. The surface can become a site of crossing and

potential transfiguration of wounds. Different from the wounds of crucifixion, these wounds appear within the sphere of life, and they initiate
different expressions of life without erasing the difficult truths of the
past. Each chapter points to the communal dimensions of resurrection.
The solo image of Thomas, as doubter confronting the truth of the risen
Christ, gives way to a vision of sociality and responsibility. The meaning of faith is evidenced in the cultivation of practices of care and companionship. "Do not pass by this miracle," Vetiana instructs Gregory.

For those attentive to systematic theology, each of these images
contributes to doctrinal questions about God, resurrection, spirit, eccle-
siology, and eschatology. Leading with the biblical text, offering, like
Calvin, a commentary on this passage in the Gospel of John, I recover
the imagery and storied dimension of these resurrection encounters, as
well as the centrality of the bodily and the sensory. This provides a necessary corrective to a theo-logic of resurrection. Featuring the points at
which the logic breaks and can no longer hold resonates with insights
of trauma—that one cannot think one's way out of it. By recovering
the poetics of John, I open up interpretive possibilities for the sake of
accessing truths conveyed through bodies.[11]

For those working in the area of trauma, investments in this sacred
story may not follow in the same vein as theologians or biblical scholars.
However, this story speaks to central concerns in trauma. It emphasizes
the importance of a collective and the formation of a community of
witnesses. In keeping with insights from the neurobiology of trauma,
it displaces the focus from the cognitive dimension of trauma work
to a multisensory and somatic engagement with wounds. These readings feature the interaction between word and body, without displacing
either. This interaction honors the importance of narrative and insists
that traumatic experiences live on in our bodies.

Cultural narratives about suffering, its meaning and purpose,
often have their origins in religious ideas, and this is particularly true
within the context of the United States. Jonathan Ebel identifies these
as "substructural" in respect to a theology of incarnation underpinning
American civil religion.[12] For practitioners working with trauma, these
substructural beliefs may appear in the narratives of clients, whether or
not they adhere to any particular religion. Insofar as these resurrection
texts speak to Christian beliefs about the afterlife, the nature of God,
these may operate at a level that is not often registered. Touching upon
this theological territory here may be helpful in detecting, and perhaps

unlocking, the negative hold that some of these authoritative, and even abusive, narratives have.

❀ ❀ ❀

"Is the resurrection *for the good?*" This was the question posed by the contemporary Thomas in the restaging of this biblical account in *Les Revenants.* The haunting depiction of the dead appearing to the living was situated within the context of a community with unprocessed traumas. The returns of the dead brought those histories to the surface of skin, manifesting on the bodies of those living. The image of the surfacing and crossing of wounds presented a vision of interconnectedness in perilous form, as a kind of epidemic of wounds. The wounds of one appeared on the body of another, as if improperly aligning experience and subject. While individual trauma can be represented singularly, the vision in *Les Revenants* is startlingly collective.

Thomas, by barging into the church and demanding that the priest speak to the meaning of what was taking place, brought this ancient story into our contemporary situation. While it pressed the question of the meaning of the Thomas account, it also unearthed an affirmation present in multiple iterations of the Christian tradition: we do not belong to ourselves but are, at our core, intertwined. The question of how to live this out is a challenge.

The vision of the disciples in the Upper Room can provide a response to the question of goodness. In a "posttraumatic" climate, this room is a site of reckoning with pasts. It is a place where wounds are touched, and where shame, grief, and anger are released. It is a place of tenderness and courage. The resurrection scene directly speaks to the affective formation of a community struggling with death and loss. The capacities cultivated there require attunement to truths that rarely come to the surface. Infused with breath, each turns to those gathered in the room. A collective forms in the after-living. To be awakened to these realities is not easy work, but the razors will continue to cut us from within until we find ways to release them. This community meets at the junctures of histories and discerns points of crossing, embodying new configurations of life. Amid the ongoingness of violence, there are paths forged across wounds.

Notes

Introduction

1 Cathy Caruth, *Literature in the Ashes of History* (Baltimore: Johns Hopkins University Press, 2013), 7.

2 Fabrice Gobert, creator, *Les Revenants*, directed by Robin Campillo (Paris: Haut et Court Production Company, 2012). To view this particular episode: "Camille," season 1, episode 1, 2012.

3 It is the English translation that presents her comments in more triumphant terms—as prevailing vs. continuing. Sandrine's fate in the show also counters the vision of triumph. In fact, she places hope in a supernatural vision of the afterlife and desires to escape the world. The show presents, via Sandrine, a religious vision that fails to speak to the return. Ironically, it draws on the supernatural and yet rejects supernaturalist accounts of religion in the process.

4 "Victor," *Les Revenants*, season 1, episode 4, 2012.

5 John 20:19-20.

6 David J. Morris, *The Evil Hours: A Biography of Post-traumatic Stress Disorder* (New York: Houghton Mifflin Harcourt, 2015), 1.

7 Cathy Caruth, *Unclaimed Experience* (Baltimore: Johns Hopkins University Press, 1996), 9. Works such as Judith Herman's *Trauma and Recovery*, Bessel van der Kolk and Alexander McFarlane's *Traumatic Stress*, Robert Jay Lifton's *The Broken Connection*, and Jonathan Shay's *Achilles in Vietnam* are just a few of the watershed texts in trauma studies that began to theorize the effects of overwhelming events in ways that extended psychoanalysis and broadened theories of history. These literatures unearthed a more layered and complex relationship to the past, revealing its intrusive power in the present. Moving

trauma off what we could refer to as the psychoanalytic couch, they provided a vocabulary of the aftermath of violence. They corresponded with the evolving diagnosis of posttraumatic stress disorder, which became a way of speaking about the persisting symptoms of an event that exceeded the capacities of the human to process it. The "enigma of suffering," coined by Cathy Caruth, has been identified as such for the ways in which it shatters primary assumptions about what it means to experience the world. The trajectory mapped out by Freud and psychoanalysis identified temporality at the center of this enigma, as traumatic experiences came to represent a rupture of one's experience of time. The past is not remembered but relived. The past is not past. Researchers following in this lineage focused on the challenge of integrating a past that was not fully integrated and, thus, *returns* in the present.

8 This analysis of the relationship between life and death was heavily influenced by portraits of survival in post-Holocaust literature. Examples include Primo Levi, *Survival in Auschwitz*, and Maurice Blanchot, *The Writing of the Disaster*.

9 Turns to assess life, both realistically and yet more positively—hopefully— can be witnessed, as well, in a turn to spirituality within these fields, once highly suspicious of religion. But it is not religion that is fueling the spiritual sphere in these cases; the language of belief and the structures of institutional religion are not witnessed in this quest for a new language of life.

10 See Gert Buelens, Sam Durrant, and Robert Eaglestone, eds., *The Future of Trauma Theory: Contemporary Literary and Cultural Criticism: Contemporary Literary and Cultural Criticism* (London: Routledge, 2014). Postcolonial, gender, and queer studies, each informed by psychoanalysis, were also moving from categories of mourning and melancholia to thinking, in Eve Sedgwick's words, in more "reparative" ways (Sedgwick, "Paranoid Reading and Reparative Reading, Or, You're so Paranoid, You Probably Think This Essay Is about You," in *Touching Feeling: Affect, Pedagogy, Performativity* [Durham, N.C.: Duke University Press, 2003], 123–51). This turn to *life* emerged, within the clinical/therapeutic arena of trauma, largely by way of strident critiques of psychoanalysis' limited vision and is expressed in three modes: turn from the psyche/unconscious to the somatic/affective, turn from pathology to creativity, and turn from the individual to the collective. Even those heavily informed by a psychoanalytic trajectory were seeking within it a more generative expression of posttraumatic living.

11 Theologians and biblical scholars engage theories of trauma. Several Christian theologians focused their analysis rethinking the relationship between crucifixion and resurrection. Examples include Serene Jones, *Trauma and Grace*; Flora Keshgegian, *Redeeming Memories: A Theology of Healing and Transformation*; and Shelly Rambo, *Spirit and Trauma: A Theology of Remaining*.

12 The following were considered watershed theological texts, aimed at rethinking the symbol of the Christian cross: Jürgen Moltmann, *The Crucified God: The Cross of Christ as the Foundation and Criticism of Christian Theology* (New

York: HarperCollins, 1974); Rosemary Radford Ruether, *Sexism and God-Talk: Toward a Feminist Theology* (Boston: Beacon, 1983); Delores Williams, *Sisters in the Wilderness: The Challenge of Womanist God-Talk* (Maryknoll, N.Y.: Orbis, 1993); and James Cone, *The Cross and the Lynching Tree* (Maryknoll, N.Y.: Orbis, 2011).

13 Engagements with modernity divided Christians on matters of the afterlife, as some rejected the supernaturalism associated with claims about the resurrected body and with the literalism of heaven and hell, and others have reinforced these beliefs and emphasized the dangers of giving way to modern science. Claims about the resurrection of the body and the destiny of Christian believers divided Christians. For those who identified with progressive forms of Christianity, these symbols of the afterlife were largely abandoned, as attention to *this* life and to the promises of God *within history* were emphasized. This history will not be accounted for fully here, but it helps to explain why doctrines such as the resurrection of the body are largely untouched within certain circles of Christian theology. Views of the afterlife marked the boundaries of Christian belief, distinguishing Christians from *within* the faith.

14 N. T. Wright, *Surprised by Hope: Rethinking Heaven, the Resurrection, and the Mission of the Church* (New York: HarperOne, 2008).

15 Susan Brison, *Aftermath: Violence and the Remaking of a Self* (Princeton: Princeton University Press, 2002), 49.

16 "Julie," season 1, episode 3 (Lena begins to manifests wounds on her skin); "Sergei and Tony," season 1, episode 5 (there is an exchange between Camille and Simon about "the returns" in which Camille says, "Love is stronger than death. What a load of bull!"); and "Adele," season 1, episode 7 (Lena sees a marking on Camille's face).

17 The fact that Camille and Lena are twins underscores this vision of connection, as twins often signify the mystery of porous identity.

18 The study of epigenetics and trauma is uncovering precisely this kind of crossing, in which physiological effects of traumatic experiences can be transmitted across generations. Rachel Yehuda's studies of Holocaust survivors and, more recently, war veterans suggest that people can inherit the effects of past traumas that are not their own. *Les Revenants* is not speaking about another world but about an enigmatic phenomenon of how the boundaries between persons is more porous—a shared vulnerability. Yehuda with Krista Tippett: "I think that in general the concept of post-traumatic stress disorder has allowed us to acknowledge that trauma effects last. They endure. They don't all go away. And now, epigenetics allows us to extend it to generational." Yehuda, "How Trauma and Resilience Cross Generations," *On Being*, July 30, 2015. See also Rachel Yehuda and Linda M. Bierer, "The Relevance of Epigenetics to PTSD: Implications for the DSM-V," *Journal of Traumatic Stress* 22, no. 5 (2009): 427–34; and Rachel Yehuda et al., "Holocaust Exposure

Induced Intergenerational Effects on FKBP5 Methylation," *Biological Psychiatry* 80, no. 5 (2016): 372–80.

19 Another French word in translation, *sur-vivre*, became significant in early studies of trauma to name a more porous relationship between death and life. The emphasis there was placed on an excess of death in life—this word, in translation, expresses something more about life. Throughout the book, I exchange this term with the notion of "ongoingness."

Chapter 1

1 For an excellent exploration of the reception of the doubting Thomas' story, see Glenn W. Most, *Doubting Thomas* (Cambridge, Mass.: Harvard University Press, 2007).

2 John 21:25.

3 Rembrandt, *Doubting Thomas*, 1634, oil on panel, Pushkin Museum, Moscow.

4 Giorgio Vasari, *Incredulity of St. Thomas*, 1557, woodcut, Sterling and Francine Clark Institute, Williamstown, Mass.; and *Incredulity of St. Thomas*, 1572, oil on panel, Santa Croce, Florence, Italy.

5 Caravaggio, *The Incredulity of Saint Thomas*, 1601–1602, oil on canvas, Sanssouci, Potsdam, Germany.

6 In the 1550s Calvin turned his attention to writing commentaries. The exercise of preaching was, for him, a way of engaging in debates and also a means of responding to primary ministerial concerns. He preached up to five times a week, and each occasion had a slightly different focus and audience. He was said to preach in plain, straightforward language. Lester DeKoster writes, "The ministerial staff met regularly on Friday afternoons for discussions of ongoing matters, and usually a textual exposition, called the 'Congregation,' often given by Calvin." DeKoster, *Light for the City: Calvin's Preaching, Source of Life and Liberty* (Grand Rapids: Eerdmans, 2004), 69. See also Dawn Devries, "Calvin's Preaching," in *The Cambridge Companion to John Calvin*, ed. Donald K. McKim (Cambridge: Cambridge University Press, 2004), 106–24; and T. H. L. Parker, "Part Three: An Account of Calvin's Preaching," in *Calvin's Preaching* (Edinburgh: T&T Clark, 1992), 57–78.

7 First published in Latin as *Institutio Christianae religionis*. My references are taken from John Calvin, *Commentary on the Gospel according to John*, vol. 2, trans. William Pringle (Grand Rapids: Eerdmans), 1956.

8 John 20:1.

9 Calvin, *Commentary on John*, 2:250.

10 Calvin, *Commentary on John*, 2:278.

11 Calvin, *Commentary on John*, 2:265; John 20:20.

12 Calvin, *Commentary on John*, 2:274.

13 Calvin, *Commentary on John*, 2:274.

14 Calvin, *Commentary on John*, 2:274–75.

15 Calvin, *Commentary on John*, 2:275; John 20:26.

16 Calvin, *Commentary on John*, 2:278; John 20:29.

17 In his portrait of the women at the tomb in John 20:11, he writes, "As the women remaining at the sepulcher, while the disciples return to the city, they are not entitled to great accommodation on this account; for the disciples carry with them consolation and joy, but the women torment themselves by idle and useless *weeping*. In short, it is superstition alone, accompanied by carnal feelings, that keeps them *near the sepulcher*." Calvin, *Commentary on John*, 2:254.

18 Calvin, *Commentary on John*, 2:277.

19 Calvin, *Commentary on John*, 2: 274.

20 Calvin, *Commentary on John*, 2:275.

21 Calvin, *Commentary on John*, 2:276.

22 Calvin, *Commentary on John*, 2:276.

23 Calvin, *Commentary on John*, 2:277–78.

24 Calvin, *Commentary on John*, 2:278.

25 He writes, "We ought, therefore, to believe that Christ did not enter without a miracle, in order to give a demonstration of his Divinity; by which he might stimulate the attention of his disciples; and yet I am far from admitting the truth of what the papists assert, that the body of Christ passed through the shut doors." Calvin, *Commentary on John*, 2:264. According to Calvin, Christ takes all measures to ensure/confirm our belief, but we do not need to place emphasis on these measures. They will lead us astray, as they do the papists. Calvin, *Commentary on John*, 2:264.

26 Calvin, *Commentary on John*, 2:264.

27 Calvin, *Commentary on John*, 2:264.

28 Calvin, *Commentary on John*, 2:269; John 20:22.

29 Calvin, *Commentary on John*, 2:274.

30 Calvin, *Commentary on John*, 2:274–75.

31 Calvin, *Commentary on John*, 2:264.

32 Calvin, *Commentary on John*, 2:280.

33 Calvin, *Commentary on John*, 2:272.

34 Calvin, *Commentary on John*, 2:254.

35 Calvin, *Commentary on John*, 2:277.

36 Calvin, *Commentary on John*, 2:278.

37 Calvin, *Commentary on John*, 2:282.

38 Calvin, *Commentary on John*, 2:275.

39 Calvin discusses John 19:36, which refers to the blood and water out of the side wound: "That faith may no longer rest *on these elements,* John declares that the fulfillment of both of these graces is in Christ." *Commentary on John*, 2:240.

40 "And, indeed, he who, after having received those striking proofs, which are to be found in the Gospel, does not perceive Christ to be God, does not deserve to look even at the sun and the earth, for he is blind amidst the brightness of noonday." Calvin, *Commentary on John*, 2:282.

41 Calvin, *Commentary on John*, 2:278.

42 Calvin, *Commentary on John*, 2:278. And, in fact, Calvin says that Christ finds Thomas blameworthy for his failure to attribute honor to the word of God. He blames him, Calvin writes, "for having regarded faith—which springs from hearing, and ought to be fully fixed on the word—as bound to the other senses."

43 Calvin, *Commentary on John*, 2:278.

44 Calvin, *Commentary on John*, 2:265.

45 Calvin, *Commentary on John*, 2:265.

46 Calvin, *Commentary on John*, 2:280.

47 Calvin, *Commentary on John*, 2:277.

48 Calvin, *Commentary on John*, 2:277.

49 Calvin, *Commentary on John*, 2:277.

50 Calvin, *Commentary on John*, 2:277.

51 Julie Canlis writes, "For Calvin, the ladder is Christ—not in the facile explanation that 'Christ is the way,' but that our ascent is profoundly bound up in Christ's ascension, by our *participation in his ascent*. . . . The mystical ascent is this deeper and deeper burrowing into Christ (always pneumatologically conceived), not our effort to do so. His ascent is our path and goal. His narrative has become our own." Canlis, *Calvin's Ladder: A Spiritual Theology of Ascent and Ascension* (Grand Rapids: Eerdmans, 2010), 50–51; emphasis in original.

52 Canlis, *Calvin's Ladder*, 114.

53 Canlis, *Calvin's Ladder*, 114–15.

54 Canlis, *Calvin's Ladder*, 116.

55 Canlis, *Calvin's Ladder*, 115. Augustine offers a different vision. See Kristi Upson-Saia, "Resurrecting Deformity: Augustine on Wounded and Scarred Bodies in the Heavenly Realm," in *Disability in Judaism, Christianity, and Islam*, ed. Darla Schumm and Michael Stoltzfus (New York: Palgrave Macmillan, 2011).

56 John Witvliet says that Calvin's vision cannot be described as escaping from earthly realities into "heavenly repose." He continues, "At the same time, I suspect that the issue is more complex than might first be admitted. This is especially true if we remember that when we ascend to heaven, we find there, according to Calvin, Jesus Christ, who, *in his humanity*, is seated at the right hand of the Father. The presence of the human Jesus there hardly squares with a celestial, otherworldly vision of eternal repose associated with Neoplatonism." Witvliet, *Worship Seeking Understanding: Windows into Christian Practice* (Grand Rapids: Baker Academic, 2003), 127; emphasis in original.

57 Canlis, *Calvin's Ladder*, 121.

58 Canlis, *Calvin's Ladder*, 121.

59 Canlis, *Calvin's Ladder*, 114.

60 Canlis, *Calvin's Ladder*, 115.

61 Canlis, *Calvin's Ladder*, 128.

62 Canlis, *Calvin's Ladder*, 115.

63 Canlis, *Calvin's Ladder*, 145–46.

64 Roy E. Stewart is concerned that the metaphor of engrafting suggests that we, the weaker (wild) scion, could improve the root plant, Christ: "The idea of any (figurative) human scion 'improving' the (figurative) stock which is Christ is simply ridiculous, if not bordering on the blasphemous. Calvin gave enlarged currency to a singularly unfortunate piece of symbolism." Stewart, "A Study of New Testament Symbolism and Baptismal Application," *The Evangelical Quarterly* 50, no. 1 (1978): 21.

65 Canlis, *Calvin's Ladder*, 116–17.

66 While Calvin does not represent the whole Christian tradition, his commentary does reveal operative assumptions underlying the meaning of resurrection.

67 Mayra Rivera, "Ghostly Encounters: Spirits, Memory, and the Holy Ghost," in *Planetary Loves: Spivak, Postcoloniality, and Theology*, ed. Stephen Moore (New York: Fordham University Press, 2011), 360.

68 Rivera, "Ghostly Encounters," 126.

69 Rivera, "Ghostly Encounters," 119.

70 Rivera, "Ghostly Encounters," 125.

71 Rivera, "Ghostly Encounters," 124.

72 One set of reflections on hauntology has emerged from Jacques Derrida's work on the spectral. Derrida, *Specters of Marx: The State of Debt, the Work of Mourning, and the New International*, trans. Peggy Kamuf (London: Routledge, 1994). Within psychoanalysis, an influential text is Nicholas Abraham and Maria Torok, *The Shell and the Kernel: Renewals of Psychoanalysis* (Chicago: University of Chicago Press, 1994). Philosopher John Caputo has developed this notion in a more theological direction in *The Insistence of God: A Theology of Perhaps,* Indiana Series in the Philosophy of Religion (Bloomington: Indiana University Press, 2013). Special thanks to Andrea Hollingsworth for alerting me to a set of creative responses to Caputo's writing on hauntology: Erin Nichole Schendzielos, ed., *It Spooks: Living in Response to an Unheard Call* (Rapid City, S.Dak.: Shelter 50 Publishing Collective, 2015).

73 Avery Gordon, *Ghostly Matters: Haunting and the Sociological Imagination* (Minneapolis: University of Minnesota Press, 1997), xvi.

74 Gordon, *Ghostly Matters*, xvi.

75 Gordon, *Ghostly Matters*, xvi.

76 Gordon, *Ghostly Matters*, xvi.

77 Jesus tells them that the Spirit of truth will come to them. John 14:17b reads: "You know him, because he abides with you, and he will be in you." The notion of divine indwelling follows in chapter 17, as Jesus instructs them about the new configuration of relationship that will come about after his death: "I in you and you in me, that they may become completely one, so that

the world may know that you have sent me and have loved me even as you have loved me."

78 Mayra Rivera, *Poetics of the Flesh* (Durham, N.C.: Duke University Press), 2.

79 Rivera, *Poetics of the Flesh*, 152.

80 Rivera, *Poetics of the Flesh*, 154.

81 Gayatri Chakovorty Spivak, "Ghostwriting," *Diacritics* 25, no. 2 (1995): 78.

82 In a section titled "Pastoral Eschatology," Richard Mouw writes, "Rightly understood, Christian theology has a pastoral dimension to its task . . . Indeed, it is difficult to think of a branch of academic theology that has. more direct relevance to the lives of ordinary believers than eschatology." Mouw, "Pastoral Eschatology," in *Essentials of Christian Theology*, ed. William Placher (Louisville, Ky.: Westminster John Knox), 337.

83 Rivera, "Ghostly Encounters," in *Planetary Loves: Spivak, Postcoloniality, and Theology*, 133.

84 Ezek 37:5-6: "Thus says the Lord GOD to these bones: I will cause breath to enter you, and you shall live. I will lay sinews on you, and will cause flesh to come upon you, and cover you with skin, and put breath in you, and you shall live; and you shall know that I am the LORD."

Chapter 2

1 The English translation of Gregory's account, *Vita Macrinae* comes from Gregory of Nyssa, *Ascetical Works*, trans. Virginia Woods Callahan (Washington, D.C.: Catholic University of America Press, 1967), 163–91. I follow Virginia Burrus' example and shorten these references to *Vita Mac.* When I reference the Greek text, I am working with Pierre Maraval's translation and the abbreviation for the text *V. Macr.* Gregory of Nyssa. *Grégoire de Nysse: Vie de Sainte Macrine*, trans. Pierre Maraval, Sources chrétiennes, no. 178 (Paris: Éditions du Cerf, 1971). *Vita Mac*, 185.

2 Virginia Burrus, "Macrina's Tattoo," *Journal of Medieval and Early Modern Studies* 33 (2003): 403–17.

3 Burrus, "Macrina's Tattoo," 414.

4 Georgia Frank, "Macrina's Scar: Homeric Allusion and Heroic Identity in Gregory of Nyssa's *Life of Macrina*," *Journal of Early Christian Studies* 8, no. 4 (2000): 525.

5 *Vita Mac*, 182.

6 At the moment of her death, Gregory writes, "From then on, she was without breath and movement, and I recalled an injunction she had given me when I arrived, saying that she wanted my hands to be placed upon her eyes and the customary care of the body to be taken by me." *Vita Mac*, 182. Note, however, that while Macrina made this request, her eyes lowered on their own and there was "no need for any arranging hand" (182). This raises the question of the significance of Gregory's presence. Why did Macrina make this request?

7 Macina makes it clear that she wants him to be present. He writes, "When the time came to cover the body with the robe, the injunction of the great lady made it necessary for me to perform this function." *Vita Mac*, 185.

8 *Vita Mac*, 182.

9 *Vita Mac*, 185.

10 *V. Macr.* 31.12 (SC178:242).

11 *Vita Mac*, 185.

12 Ὁρᾷς, ἔφη, τὸ λεπτὸ τοῦτο καὶ ἀφανὲς ὑπὸ τήν δέρριν σημεῖον [*V. Macr.* 31.8–9 (SC178:242)].

13 *V. Macr.* 31.8–9 (SC178:242).

14 There are varying accounts of the location of the illness, but many scholars concur that the disease was located on the breast. See Derek Krueger, "Writing and Memory in Gregory of Nyssa's Life of Macrina," *Journal of Early Christian Studies* 8, no. 4 (2000): 504; Georgia Frank, "Macrina's Scar," 512. *V. Macr.* 31.16 (SC178:242).

15 *Vita Mac*, 185.

16 *Vita Mac*, 186.

17 Frank, "Macrina's Scar," 513.

18 Frank, "Macrina's Scar," 514.

19 My reading of Macrina developed through conversations with Richard Kearney and the project represented in the coedited volume *Carnal Hermeneutics*. Kearney's account of fathers and sons in his essay "Writing Trauma" prompted my reflections on mothers and daughters. Kearney, "Writing Trauma: Narrative Catharsis in Homer, Shakespeare and Joyce," *Giornale di metafiscia* 1 (2013): 7–28; Richard Kearney and Brian Treanor, eds. *Carnal Hermeneutics*, Perspectives in Continental Philosophy (New York: Fordham University Press, 2015).

20 Her name connects to Lampedes, the torch-bearing nymphs of the underworld, who are the companions of Hecate, the Greek Titan goddess of witchcraft and crossroads. They are spirits of the underworld who bear light.

21 Gregory of Nyssa, *Macrina*, 186.

22 *Vita Mac*, 164. Immediately after childbirth, Emmelia receives a vision, prompting her to assign a secret name (Thecla) to Macrina. Thecla was an early Christian martyr, famed, Gregory notes, for her virginity.

23 Cameron Partridge, "'Form Blossoming in an Unusual Manner': Reclothing Sexual Difference in Gregory of Nyssa," in "Transfiguring Sexual Difference in Maximus the Confessor" (Ph.D. diss., Harvard University, 2008), 60.

24 Partridge, "Transfiguring Sexual Difference," 64.

25 I am indebted to Partridge here for his emphasis the importance of clothing in Gregory of Nyssa's interpretation of resurrection.

26 Gregory of Nyssa, *On the Making of Man*, in *Nicene and Post-Nicene Fathers*, Second Series, vol. 5, trans. H. A. Wilson, ed. Philip Schaff and Henry Wace (Buffalo, N.Y.: Christian Literature Publishing, 1893), 27.3; Partridge,

"Transfiguring Sexual Difference," 62–63; and Caroline Bynum, "Survival, Flux, and the Fear of Decay," in *Resurrection of the Body in Western Christianity, 200–1336*, (New York: Columbia University Press, 1995), 83–86.

27 Gregory's account of Macrina's life ends much like the Johannine gospel, spurring testimonies that exceed the container of the text. He writes, "And after this, there were other events more surprising than these; the healing of disease, the casting out of devils, true prophecies of future events, all of which are believed to be true by those who knew the details accurately; amazing although they are." *Vita Mac*, 190. The Johannine gospel ends with similar claims that the events exceed the limits of what can be written: "There are many other things that Jesus did; if every one of them were written down, I suppose that the world itself could not contain the books that would be written" (John 21:25).

28 *Vita Mac*, 188.

29 "He told me the story of a miracle connected with Macrina and, adding only this to my story, I shall come to an end." *Vita Mac*, 188. The soldier is prompted to tell the story, because he is aware of the impact of her loss—on Gregory and others.

30 *Vita Mac*, 189.

31 *Vita Mac*, 189.

32 *Vita Mac*, 189.

33 *Vita Mac*, 189.

34 *Vita Mac*, 176.

35 *Vita Mac*, 176.

36 Frank, "Macrina's Scar," 514.

37 *Vita Mac*, 186.

38 Carolyn Walker Bynum writes, "The paradigmatic body was that of the holy ascetic—and not just any holy ascetic. Much of Gregory's discussion of resurrection is a discussion of the body of his sister Macrina." Bynum, *Resurrection of the Body*, 83.

39 Gregory of Nyssa, *On Virginity*, in *Saint Gregory of Nyssa: Ascetical Works*, Fathers of the Church 58, trans. and ed. Virginia Callahan (Washington, D.C.: Catholic University of America Press, 1967), 3–78.

40 Peter Brown, *The Body and Society: Men, Women, and Sexual Renunciation in Early Christianity*, 2nd ed., Columbia Classics in Religion (New York: Columbia University Press, 2008), 291.

41 Brown, *The Body and Society*, 299.

42 Brown, *The Body and Society*, 298. Brown writes, "They (the women in her community) were as close as any human beings could be to the original, open-hearted straining of Adam toward God. In that sense, Macrina stood on the frontier of the invisible world. (*Life*, 11.33-45, pp. 178–80) Time for her had already ceased to consist of a succession of expedience to dull the blow of

death: she could look directly into the immensity beyond the grave." Brown, *The Body and Society*, 298.

43 *Vita Mac*, 167.

44 *Vita Mac*, 167.

45 *Vita Mac*, 166.

46 *Vita Mac*, 166.

47 Susanna Elm, *Virgins of God: The Making of Asceticism in Late Antiquity*, Oxford Classical Monographs (Oxford: Clarendon, 1996).

48 In the medieval period, there was a religious order of women who lived separated from society but worked within public settings. Because of their status as both inside and outside society, they were thought to be particularly equipped to facilitate the passage from death into life. Considered to be the hospice workers of their day, they were well known for their work with the "'living dead' of the medieval world. . . . They were liminal figures, ideally suited to mediate during those first hours after death." Walter Simons, *Cities of Ladies: Beguine Communities in the Medieval Low Countries, 1200–1565* (Philadelphia: University of Pennsylvania Press, 2001), 78–80.

49 There are potentially two things here that distinguish the "good news" of scars: (1) the fact that they do not directly mark suffering moves us away from the notions of repetition and imitation, as if the suffering itself is redemptive; (2) this leaves the mark open to other configurations of suffering and healing.

50 Gregory's *Vita* has garnered attention at the intersection of issues of gender and genre. Interpreting this vita has been important, not only for retrieving history of late medieval women but also for thinking about present-day representations of women's bodies, authority, and divinity. The question of genre is live throughout, as Gregory struggles to name the proper form of writing—is this a letter, a treatise, or, perhaps, an elegy? It has also been noted the degree to which the account of life is overwhelmed by Gregory's account of Macrina's death, as the death scene accounts for a good portion of the vita. J. Warren Smith, "A Just and Reasonable Grief: The Death and Function of a Holy Woman in Gregory of Nyssa's Life of Macrina," *Journal of Early Christian Studies* 12, no. 1 (2004): 57–84.

51 Derek Krueger writes, "The hagiography makes the story of Macrina indelible." Krueger, "Writing and the Liturgy of Memory in Gregory of Nyssa's Life of Macrina," *Journal of Early Christian Studies* 8, no. 4 (2000): 495.

52 Francine Cardman writes, "My hopes are to find some traces of Macrina in the scant clues and tantalizing absences of the *Life*; my fears are that she is so veiled in Gregory's web of words that only the phantoms of memory survive." Cardman, "Whose Life is It?: The *Vita Macrinae* of Gregory of Nyssa," *Studia Patristica* 37 (2001): 35. Cardman is taking up concerns raised by Elizabeth A. Clark in "The Lady Vanishes: Dilemmas of a Feminist Historian after the 'Linguistic Turn,'" *Church History* 67, no. 1 (1998): 1–31.

53 Gregory of Nyssa, *On the Soul and Resurrection,* in *Saint Gregory of Nyssa: Ascetical Works,* Fathers of the Church 58, trans. and ed. Virginia Callahan (Washington, D.C.: Catholic University of America Press, 1967), 295–374.
54 Clark, "The Lady Vanishes," 23–24.
55 Luce Irigaray, *Marine Lover of Friedrich Nietzsche* (New York: Columbia University Press, 1991), 166.
56 Irigaray, *Marine Lover,* 166.
57 Irigaray, *Marine Lover,* 166–67.
58 Irigaray, *Marine Lover,* 170.
59 Irigaray, *Marine Lover,* 171.
60 Grace Jantzen's work is of paramount importance here, in that it both offers a critique of a death-centered Western tradition but also proposing a turn to life. For a good summary of these two aspects, see Jantzen, "Flourishing: Toward an Ethic of Feminist Theory" and "On Changing the Imaginary," in *A Place of Springs: Death and the Displacement of Beauty,* vol. 3 (New York: Routledge, 2010), 170–95.
61 Catherine Keller, *Face of the Deep: A Theology of Becoming* (New York: Routledge, 2003), 221.
62 Amy M. Hollywood, *Sensible Ecstasy: Mysticism, Sexual Difference, and the Demands of History* (Chicago: University of Chicago Press, 2002), 270. She writes, "When in contemporary feminist discourse, identity is defined primarily (if not solely) in terms of traumatic suffering, there is the danger that 'woman' will signify only victim and that feminist politics will be reduced to reactionary forms of *ressentiment*" (270).
63 Sharon V. Betcher, introduction to *Spirit and the Obligation of Social Flesh: A Secular Theology for the Global City* (Minneapolis: Fortress, 2014), 1–15; Betcher, "Becoming Flesh of My Flesh: Feminist and Disability Theologies on the Edge of Post-humanist Discourse," *Journal of Feminist Studies in Religion* 26, no. 2 (2010): 107–18.
64 Betcher, *Spirit and the Obligation of Social Flesh,* 21.
65 *Vita Mac,* 174.
66 She gives the account of its origins. She also makes the choice about how Macrina will be robed, as she selects Emmelia's garment to place over the body.
67 *Vita Mac,* 186.
68 Burrus, "Macrina's Tattoo," 411.
69 *Vita Mac,* 180.
70 This is a Pauline reference and one that Burrus refers back to in her interpretation of her own tattoo.
71 Recall John Calvin's image of engrafting as the central image for regeneration from chapter 1. He draws on the Johannine imagery in which the new life in Christ is actually figured as a graft, in which believers are grafted into Christ.
72 Hollywood, *Sensible Ecstasy,* 270; emphasis in original.

73 Hollywood, *Sensible Ecstasy*, 277.
74 Burrus, "Macrina's Tattoo," 412.
75 *Vita Mac*, 174.
76 The allusions to the cover of a book and Macrina's cover(ing) is intentional, and this is, again, Johannine in configuration.
77 Burrus, "Macrina's Tattoo," 405.
78 Augustine of Hippo, *The City of God*, in *Nicene and Post-Nicene Fathers*, First Series, vol. 2, ed. Philip Schaff (Edinburgh: T&T Clark, 1890).

Chapter 3

1 Wendell Berry, *The Hidden Wound* (Boston: Houghton Mifflin, 1970), 4.
2 Berry, *Hidden Wound*, 9.
3 Berry retraces stories of his friendship with Nick, and this relationship forms the backdrop of his analysis of the "hereditary knowledge of the hereditary evil" that was transmitted through generations of white families in the American South. Berry, *Hidden Wound*, 6. He writes, "When I was three years old Nick Watkins, a black man, came to work for my Grandfather Berry" (22).
4 Berry, *Hidden Wound*, 52.
5 George Yancy and Cornel West, "Cornel West: The Fire of a New Generation," *New York Times*, August 19, 2015. West refers throughout the interview to the significance of the shootings in Ferguson, Missouri, as a pivot event defining the climate in which black persons are living within the United States. He calls it the "age of Ferguson." He not only identifies it in terms of police brutality but also as a site of "black prophetic fire" in which a younger generations of activists are fighting against injustice.
6 Jennings wrote in response to Dr. Anthea Butler's posting about the killing of Trayvon Martin and the acquittal of George Zimmerman. He writes, "It touched a nerve in what Wendell Berry called *the hidden wound*—that raw, throbbing one that never grows skin thick enough to keep it from puncturing and bleeding at the slightest touch. The deep wound of our racial history has never passed—no one in America lives without it." Willie Jennings, "What Does It Mean to Call 'God' a White Racist?" *Religion Dispatches*, 2013; emphasis in original.
7 Berry, *Hidden Wound*, 18–19.
8 James H. Cone, "Jesus Christ in Black Theology," chap. 6 in *A Black Theology of Liberation* (Maryknoll, N.Y.: Orbis, 1990), 110–28. First published in 1970.
9 James H. Cone, "'The Terrible Beauty of the Cross' and the Tragedy of the Lynching Tree: A Reflection on Reinhold Niebuhr," chap. 2 in *The Cross and the Lynching Tree* (Maryknoll, N.Y.: Orbis, 2011), 30–64.
10 Willie James Jennings, introduction to *The Christian Imagination: Theology and the Origins of Race* (New Haven: Yale University Press, 2011), 1–11.
11 Jennings, *Christian Imagination*, 291.
12 Geoffrey Canada, *Fist Stick Knife Gun: A Personal History of Violence* (Boston: Beacon, 1995).

13 John 16:12-13: "I still have many things to say to you, but you cannot bear them now. When the Spirit of truth comes, he will guide you into all the truth; for he will not speak on his own, but will speak whatever he hears, and he will declare to you the things that are to come."

14 Jennings, *Christian Imagination*, 7.

15 Jennings, *Christian Imagination*, 7.

16 John 20:22-23; my trans.

17 See Yves Congar, *I Believe in the Holy Spirit*, Milestones in Catholic Theology (New York: Crossroad, 2000). "The breath-spirit (the Spirit) is qualified in various ways according to the effects that it, as a principle, produces" (4).

18 John 20:27.

19 Melissa Harris-Perry, *Sister Citizen: Shame, Stereotypes, and Black Women in America* (New Haven: Yale University Press, 2011), 36.

20 Harris-Perry, *Sister Citizen*, 35.

21 In a piece written in conversation with disability theologians, Harris-Perry, writes, "The struggle for recognition is the nexus of human identity and national identity, where much of the important work of politics occurs. African American women fully embody this struggle" (*Sister Citizen*, 4).

22 Harris-Perry, *Sister Citizen*, 36.

23 Harris-Perry, *Sister Citizen*, 43.

24 Harris-Perry, *Sister Citizen*, 43. See also discussion of shame, chap. 3, pp. 101–33. The work of womanist theologian Phillis Sheppard examines the psychic impact on African American women at greater length. See Sheppard, *Self, Culture, and Others in Womanist Practical Theology* (New York: Palgrave Macmillan, 2011).

25 Berry, *Hidden Wound*, 5.

26 Berry, *Hidden Wound*, epigraph.

27 Harris-Perry, *Sister Citizen*, 39–40. Willie Jennings raises the question of where Christian theological culpability in practices of misrecognition. He writes, "The crucial matter is precisely where Christians imagine they stand as they look out onto bodies, their own and others." (296). Jennings, "Reading Bodies from "Hidden Places: Reflections on Disability in the Christian Tradition," *Journal of Religion, Disability & Health* 17, no. 3 (2013): 295–300.

28 Berry, *Hidden Wound*, 6.

29 Willie Jennings, chap. 1, "War Bodies: Remembering Bodies in Times of War," *Post-traumatic Public Theology*, eds. Stephanie N. Arel and Shelly Rambo (New York: Palgrave Macmillan, 2016), 31–32. He writes, "The disciples of Jesus are invited in the memory work of a God seeking to embrace God's creation."

30 In *Christian Imagination*, Jennings' indictment of theology that comes from the "commanding heights" feed this image of theologies that hover above the soil. He writes, "Western Christian intellectuals still imagine the world from the commanding heights" (8).

31 John 16.

32 Cone asks in his earlier work, "How are [blacks in America] to interpret the christological significance of the Resurrected One in such a way that his person will be existentially relevant to their oppressed condition?" Cone, *Black Theology of Liberation,* 129. I am bringing this question forward, linking it to his analysis of the ongoing crucifixions in our midst.

33 John 17.

34 Avery Gordon, *Ghostly Matters: Haunting and the Sociological Imagination,* (Minneapolis: University of Minnesota Press, 1997), 64. She writes, "From a certain vantage point the ghost also simultaneously represents a future possibility, a hope" (64).

35 Cone, *Cross and the Lynching Tree,* 41.

36 Jennings, *Christian Imagination,* 7.

37 Jennings, *Christian Imagination,* 115.

38 Berry, *Hidden Wound,* 19.

39 Michael Rothberg, *Multidirectional Memory: Remembering the Holocaust in the Age of Decolonization* (Stanford, Calif.: Stanford University Press, 2009), 9.

40 Judith Butler raises concerns in this essay about the ways in which the value of human life is being determined through the lens of the media. Some lives, by being placed outside of the frame of public viewing, are deemed as unworthy of remembrance. Some lives count, she says, and others are not counted. Butler, "Precarious Life," in *Precarious Life: The Powers of Mourning and Violence* (New York: Verso Books, 2006), 128–52.

41 Rothberg, *Multidirectional Memory,* 3; emphasis in original.

42 Rothberg, *Multidirectional Memory,* 11. He asks, "Can there be a more open-ended sense of the possibilities of memory and counter-memory that might allow the 'revisiting' and rewriting of hegemonic sites of memory?" (310).

43 John 17:23.

44 Rothberg, *Multidirectional Memory,* 132.

45 Rothberg, *Multidirectional Memory,* 126.

46 Rothberg, *Multidirectional Memory,* 116.

47 Rothberg, *Multidirectional Memory,* 112.

48 Rothberg, *Multidirectional Memory,* 132.

49 Rothberg, *Multidirectional Memory,* 115.

50 Rothberg, *Multidirectional Memory,* 115.

51 This refers to Cone's appeal to witness the transformation that God enacts on the cross. "One needs a powerful imagination. It will take a powerful imagination to see both beauty and terror." Cone, *Cross and the Lynching Tree,* 37.

52 Rothberg, *Multidirectional Memory,* 313. Rothberg writes, "Memories are mobile; histories are implicated in each other. . . . The only way forward is through their entanglement."

53 Delores Williams, *Sisters in the Wilderness: The Challenge of Womanist God-Talk* (Maryknoll, N.Y.: Orbis, 1993), 167.

54 Williams, *Sisters in the Wilderness*, 161–67.

55 Williams, *Sisters in the Wilderness*, 165.

56 Williams writes, "Humankind is, then, redeemed through Jesus' *ministerial* vision of life and not through death." *Sisters in the Wilderness*, 167.

57 Williams, *Sisters in the Wilderness*, 167.

58 Williams, *Sisters in the Wilderness*, 167.

59 Williams, *Sisters in the Wilderness*, 167.

60 Williams, *Sisters in the Wilderness*, 167.

61 Rothberg, *Multidirectional Memory*, 126.

62 Williams, *Sisters in the Wilderness*, 167.

63 Williams, *Sisters in the Wilderness*, 166: "The cross thus becomes an image of defilement, a gross manifestation of collective human sin. Jesus, then, does not conquer sin through the death on the cross. Rather, Jesus conquers the sin of the temptation in the wilderness."

64 Berry, *Hidden Wound*, epigraph.

65 Jacqueline Grant, "The Sin of Servanthood and the Deliverance of Discipleship," in *A Troubling in My Soul*, ed. Emilie Townes (Maryknoll, N.Y.: Orbis, 1993), 199–218.

66 Williams, *Sisters in the Wilderness*, 175.

67 Williams, *Sisters in the Wilderness*, 175.

68 Williams, *Sisters in the Wilderness*, 175.

69 Williams, *Sisters in the Wilderness*, 164.

70 Williams, *Sisters in the Wilderness*, 165; emphasis in original.

71 Womanist JoAnne Terrell writes, "For Williams, the story of Hagar, the Egyptian slave and surrogate for Sarah (Gn 16; 21:8-21), is a compelling analogy to the experiences of African American women. Hagar's story has implications not only for a communitarian survival ethic in the African American community but also for reconceptualizing the nature of God" (116). Terrell, *Power in the Blood?: The Cross in the African-American Experience* (Maryknoll, N.Y.: Orbis, 1998).

72 Emily Holmes, "Delores Williams' Theology of the Wilderness Experience: Incarnation in the Wild," *Union Seminary Quarterly Review* 58, nos. 3–4 (2004): 13–26. She writes of Williams "The metaphor of wilderness becomes an internal and mental expression of the challenges of the socio-economic world" (18).

73 Holmes, "Williams' Theology," 22.

74 Holmes, "Williams' Theology," 25. Holmes writes, "Redemption, in Williams' view, happens in and through the incarnation and ministry of *healing that results from it*" (emphasis in original).

75 Rothberg, *Multidirectional Memory*, 3.

76 Williams, *Sisters in the Wilderness*, 160. One of the aspects that Williams lifts up is the cooperation of human initiative *and* divine intervention.

77 Williams, *Sisters in the Wilderness*, 160. She writes, "In a Christian theological context wilderness-experience more than black experience, provides an avenue for black liberation theologians, feminist theologians and womanist theologians to dialogue about the significance of wilderness in which each identifies as the biblical tradition most conducive to the work of his or her theological enterprise."

78 Williams, *Sisters in the Wilderness*, 161.

Chapter 4

1 Jonathan Shay, *Achilles in Vietnam: Combat Trauma and the Undoing of Character* (New York: Atheneum, 1994), xxi.

2 Shay, *Achilles in Vietnam*, xxi. Shay writes, "I have brought them together with the *Iliad* not to tame, appropriate, or co-opt them but to promote a deeper understanding of both, increasing the reader's capacity to be disturbed by the *Iliad* rather than softening the blow of the veterans' stories."

3 Shay, *Achilles in Vietnam*, xxi.

4 Edward Tick, *War and the Soul: Healing Our Nation's Veterans from Posttraumatic Stress Disorder* (Wheaton, Ill.: Quest Books, 2005).

5 Participating in the performance, I began to question whether the sacred story within Christianity could function similarly, to open up discourse about a more complex path to healing. Given the practiced dimension of all religious traditions, the enactments of a sacred story are part of the lived practice of faith.

6 Zoë Wool wrote after observing veterans at Walter Reed Hospital, "Notions of sovereignty, exception, and sacrifice are mobilized to fit soldierly acts of life and death into a reducible relationship between citizens and the state, one that leaves no messy remainder." Wool, *After War: The Weight of Life at Walter Reed* (Durham, N.C.: Duke University Press, 2015), 129.

7 For a description of what tragedies enact, read Bryan Doerries, prologue to *Theater of War: What Ancient Tragedies Can Teach Us Today* (New York: Knopf, 2015), 3–8.

8 Jonathan Ebel, *G.I. Messiahs: Soldiering, War, and American Civil Religion* (New Haven: Yale University Press, 2016), 7.

9 Ebel, *G.I. Messiahs*, 8.

10 Dan P. McAdams, *The Redemptive Self: Stories Americans Live By*, rev. ed. (Oxford: Oxford University Press, 2013).

11 McAdams, "Culture, Narrative, and the Self," chap. 11 in *Redemptive Self*, 268–88.

12 See Stanley Hauerwas, *War and the American Difference: Theological Reflections on Violence and National Identity* (Grand Rapids: Baker Academic, 2011); Daniel M. Bell Jr., *Just War Is Not Christian Discipleship: Recentering the Tradition in the Church Rather than the State* (Grand Rapids: Brazos, 2009); Ted Grimsrud, *The Good War That Wasn't—and Why It Matters* (Eugene, Ore.:

Wipf & Stock, 2014); and Oliver O'Donovan, *Just War Revisited* (Cambridge: Cambridge University Press, 2003). Many of these works are influenced by the writings of John Howard Yoder, *When War Is Unjust: Being Honest in Just-War Thinking* (Minneapolis: Augsburg, 1984); and John Howard Yoder, *The War of the Lamb: The Ethics of Nonviolence and Peacemaking*, ed. Glen Stasson (Grand Rapids: Brazos, 2009).

13 As Glenn Most has pointed out, the insistence that Thomas touches the wounds does not come from the text but from its transmission history, from the influence of paintings such as this. The Caravaggio rendering has strongly influenced the interpretation of this passage, so much so that its depiction is often mistaken for the biblical rendering. He writes, "Visual artists had almost always been depicting Thomas in the very act of penetrating Jesus' wound with his finger, and in so doing they contributed decisively to the widespread conviction that this is what he really did." Most, *Doubting Thomas* (Cambridge, Mass.: Harvard University Press, 2005), 224.

14 David Finkel, "The Return: The Traumatized Veterans of Iraq and Afghanistan," *The New Yorker*, September 9, 2013.

15 Seneca was the largest of six nations that together formed the democratic Iroquois or Haudenosaunee (People of the Longhouse) Confederacy. Historically, the Seneca Nation controlled trade and traffic in the western portion of Iroquois territory, now western New York, where they currently hold three territories. They continue to support their community of nearly 8,000 enrolled citizens. "Culture," Seneca Nation of Indians, accessed August 10, 2016, https://sni.org/culture.

16 Edward Tick uses the model of warrior cultures and adapts it to modern warfare. Edward Tick, chaps. 2–4 in *War and the Soul*, 25–78. The contemporary use of this term in veteran communities inherently critiques current U.S. military practices in which military personnel are treated as paid servants of the state, as mercenaries who are paid to fight and kill. John Schluep writes, "Historically, the warrior in other cultures was an important member of society. When warriors were called to serve in war they returned from battle with a clear responsibility to teach and guide the society. For the returning veteran there was not an automatic reintegration; but rather a ceremony and ritual to bring the warrior home. This ceremony and ritual involved the community and the veteran in a cleansing." Schluep, *Soul's Cry* (Tallmadge, Ohio: Good Place Publishing), 4.

17 Shannon French studies the codes of warrior cultures to assess the ethical shortfall of warring practices. French, *The Code of the Warrior: Exploring Warrior Values Past and Present* (Lanham, Md.: Rowman & Littlefield, 2003).

18 John Schluep, *Broken Wings*, training manual, Warriors Journey Home, 5.

19 Christina Conroy, a theologian working with the history residential schools and First Nations peoples in Canada, describes the process by saying that it is "as practical as it is mystical." Canadians are familiar with the practice of

taking off their shoes before entering a house. This ritual is practical in this way—as an act of preparation to enter into a space. Christina Conroy, personal correspondence with the author, July 21, 2016. See Conroy, "Theology After Residential Schools," in *Theology After Residential Schools* (Ph.D. diss., Emory University, 2016). John Schluep writes, "Smudging and smoke are not necessary but provide a symbolic ritual of an internal and spiritual preparation." Schluep, *Broken Wings*, 7.

20 Schluep, *Broken Wings*, 6.

21 Schluep, *Broken Wings*, 5. Schluep writes, "A circle is used because in a circle no one is above anyone else and all are equal distance from the center."

22 Edward Tick, *War and the Soul: Healing Our Nation's Veterans from Post-traumatic Stress Disorder* (Wheaton, Ill.: Quest Books, 2005).

23 Rita Nakashima Brock and Gabriela Lettini, *Soul Repair: Recovering from Moral Injury After War* (Boston: Beacon, 2012). Brock is also the founder of the Soul Repair Center, located at Brite Divinity School in Fort Worth, Texas.

24 Shianne warns against referring to her tradition by using the term "Native American spirituality." She is deliberate about teaching people about the practices of her tradition but is concerned about the quick-fix buffet approach to practices and rituals. She is careful to emphasize the Native tradition(s) while avoiding the terms "religion" and "spirituality" that lead to so much misunderstanding. When people refer to her tradition as "Indian religion," she responds, " 'No, it's not a religion.' And because it's creation, it's one that enfolds in the moment in relationship to the Divine, in the circle, in the natural world, so it's a way of life." The gift of native peoples to warriors is earth medicine.

25 Shianne emphasizes how important it is to provide veterans with structures for support. She shares, "And the ways that we do that within our indigenous communities is to create opportunities for ceremonies that heal the soul, and that's the place where they will have the opportunity to tell their story and go wherever they need to go and what's creating the greatest despair because everyone who returns has some level of despair they're dealing with." For more information about Shianne's work through the Red Bird Center, visit http://www.redbirdcenter.org/.

26 Dori Laub speaks about multiple witness positions in his trauma work. The third witness position is a cocreative process in which both participants enter into a new form of relationship, constituted in part by a history that is not fully known or grasped. Laub's reworking of the therapeutic relationship in light of trauma provides a way of reflecting on Shianne's work. Shianne is witnessing her own process of rebirth as she witnesses someone else's release. Laub, "An Event Without a Witness: Truth, Testimony, and Survival," chap. 3 in *Testimony: Crisis of Witnessing in Literature, Psychoanalysis, and History* (New York: Routledge, 1991), 75–92.

27 Ebel, *G.I. Messiahs*, 7; emphasis in original.

28 See Wool, "The Economy of Patriotism," chap. 3 in *After War*, 97–129. Wool says this narrative crushes many struggling veterans under its weight: "Sacrifice was a claim, a claim that people other than injured soldiers made about, and on, the past acts of violence legible on soldiers' bodies" (103).

29 One strain of Christianity claims that Jesus traveled to the depths of hell and claimed victory there. Even before the visible appearance to the disciples, he claimed victory over death. The "harrowing of hell" is a story of what happens after his death. He emerges from the depths victorious. Another account says that the journey through hell was not a victory but, instead, a demonstration of God-forsakenness in the depths, an extension of the suffering on the cross. The images of triumph are displaced, and the picture is more solemn. These display an interpretive range in the Christian proclamation of redemption—the vision of the warrior-victor and the warrior who knows the experience of death in full.

30 Schluep, *Broken Wings*, 5.

31 See Callid Keefe-Perry's brief discussion of John Schluep's work as "theopoetics" in *Way to Water: A Theopoetics Primer* (Eugene, Ore.: Wipf & Stock, 2014), 175–76.

32 I present this in the language of the farewell discourse in the Gospel of John where Jesus tells his disciples that the Spirit of truth will come, and the world does not know this spirit. John 14:17: "This is the Spirit of Truth, whom the world cannot receive, because it neither sees him nor knows him. You know him, because he abides with you and will be in you."

33 James Hillman, "War is Sublime," chap. 3 in *A Terrible Love of War* (New York: Penguin, 2004), 104–77.

34 Ebel, *G.I. Messiahs*, 21. He writes, "Through them we know the nation. Through them we can be saved. In the beginning is the Word. Then the Word is made flesh."

35 Ebel, *G.I. Messiahs*, 196.

36 Ebel, *G.I. Messiahs*, 197; emphasis added.

37 Ebel, *G.I. Messiahs*, 198.

38 Ebel, *G.I. Messiahs*, 196.

39 Ebel, *G.I. Messiahs*, 193. "Martial mythology" is still very live. Ebel writes, "I have argued that these soldiers and their observers practice American civil religion as they imagine and enact soldiering, and that the space between the imagined and the enacted, though it continues to fill with myths, symbols, and echoes, is a deep and dangerous place."

40 Ebel, *G.I. Messiahs*, 197.

41 McAdams, *Redemptive Self*, xiv; and Barbara Ehrenreich, "Positive Psychology: The Science of Happiness," ch. 6 in *Bright-Sided: How Positive Thinking Is Undermining America* (New York: Metropolitan Books, 2010), 147–76.

42 Tom Saal, "Unnamed," Warriors Journey Home, http://warriorsjourneyhome .org/images/UntitledPoem.jpg.

43 Tom Saal, "Nameless Woman," Warriors Journey Home, http://warriorsjourney home.org/images/NamelessWoman.jpg.

Conclusion

1 Cathy Caruth writes, "This language of life must be reread, and understood anew, through the losses, and disappearances, of an era in which the possibility of the future is fundamentally in doubt." Caruth, *Literature in the Ashes of History*, xi–xiii.

2 See Mayra Rivera's distinction between grasp and touch in *The Touch of Transcendence: A Postcolonial Theology of God* (Minneapolis: Fortress, 2007).

3 David M. Carr, *Holy Resilience: The Bible's Traumatic Origins* (New Haven: Yale University Press, 2014), 231.

4 Carr, *Holy Resilience,* 231. Daniel Alan Smith says that the early gospel tradition (the Markan disappearance tradition) was quickly replaced by the appearance tradition (the later gospels, including John), revealing a growing apologetics around the resurrection. Smith explains, "The empty tomb story [Mark], practically from the very beginning, was thought to be in need of apologetic and theological support from the appearance tradition." Smith, *Revisiting the Empty Tomb: The Early History of Easter* (Minneapolis: Fortress, 2010), 178.

5 Carr, *Holy Resilience*, 232.

6 Mark D. Jordan, *Telling Truths in Church: Scandal, Flesh, and Christian Speech* (Boston: Beacon), 2004.

7 See Stephanie N. Arel's work on shame in *Affect, Shame, and Christian Formation* (New York: Palgrave Macmillan, 2016).

8 Rivera writes, "Words mark, wound, elevate, or shatter bodies. Social discourses divide the world and mark bodies differently" Rivera, *Poetics of the Flesh*, 2. The effects of these wounds are often difficult to trace and words often break apart when the stories of harm are being told, whether from within or without.

9 See Mayra Rivera's discussion in chap. 4, "Incarnate Philosophy," *Poetics of the Flesh*, 59–86.

10 Rivera, *Poetics of the Flesh*, 134. Rivera writes, "Flesh reminds us that the boundaries between individual bodies and the world are porous, provisional, elusive."

11 Rivera, *Poetics of the Flesh*, 4. "I want images of corporeal life that convey the effects of imperceptible processes that accumulate in our bodies, that materialize in and as our flesh." Rivera, *Poetics of the Flesh*, 103.

12 Ebel, *G.I. Messiahs*, 20.

Bibliography

Abraham, Nicholas, and Maria Torok. *The Shell and the Kernel: Renewals of Psychoanalysis.* Chicago: University of Chicago Press, 1994.

Arel, Stephanie N. *Affect, Shame, and Christian Formation.* New York: Palgrave Macmillan, 2016.

Augustine of Hippo. *The City of God.* In *Nicene and Post-Nicene Fathers*, First Series, vol. 2. Edited by Philip Schaff. Edinburgh: T&T Clark, 1890.

Bell, Daniel M., Jr. *Just War Is Not Christian Discipleship: Recentering the Tradition in the Church Rather than the State.* Grand Rapids: Brazos, 2009.

Berry, Wendell. *The Hidden Wound.* Boston: Houghton Mifflin, 1970.

Betcher, Sharon V. "Becoming Flesh of My Flesh: Feminist and Disability Theologies on the Edge of Post-humanist Discourse." *Journal of Feminist Studies in Religion* 26, no. 2 (2010): 107–18.

———. *Spirit and the Obligation of Social Flesh: A Secular Theology for the Global City.* Minneapolis: Fortress, 2014.

Blanchot, Maurice. *The Writing of the Disaster.* Lincoln: University of Nebraska Press, 1986.

Bouwsma, William J. *John Calvin: A Sixteenth-Century Portrait.* Oxford: Oxford University Press, 1987.

Brison, Susan J. *Aftermath: Violence and the Remaking of a Self.* Princeton: Princeton University Press, 2002.

Brock, Rita Nakashima, and Gabriella Lettini. *Soul Repair: Recovering from Moral Injury After War.* Boston: Beacon, 2012.

Brown, Peter. *The Body and Society: Men, Women, and Sexual Renunciation in Early Christianity*. 2nd ed. Columbia Classics in Religion. New York: Columbia University Press, 2008.

Buelens, Gert, Sam Durrant, and Robert Eaglestone, eds. *The Future of Trauma Theory: Contemporary Literary and Cultural Criticism*. London: Routledge, 2014.

Burrus, Virginia. "Macrina's Tattoo." *Journal of Medieval and Early Modern Studies* 33 (2003): 403–17.

Butler, Judith. *Precarious Life: The Powers of Mourning and Violence*. London: Verso, 2004.

Bynum, Caroline Walker. *The Resurrection of the Body in Western Christianity, 200–1336*. New York: Columbia University Press, 1995.

Calvin, John. *Commentary on the Gospel according to John*. Vol. 2. Translated by William Pringle. Grand Rapids: Eerdmans, 1956.

Canada, Geoffrey. *Fist Stick Knife Gun: A Personal History of Violence*. Boston: Beacon, 1995.

Canlis, Julie. *Calvin's Ladder: A Spiritual Theology of Ascent and Ascension*. Grand Rapids: Eerdmans, 2010.

Caputo, John. *The Insistence of God: A Theology of Perhaps*. Indiana Series in the Philosophy of Religion. Bloomington: Indiana University Press, 2013.

Cardman, Francine. "Whose Life Is It?: The *Vita Macrinae* of Gregory of Nyssa." *Studia Patristica* 37 (2001): 33–50.

Carr, David M. *Holy Resilience: The Bible's Traumatic Origins*. New Haven: Yale University Press, 2014.

Caruth, Cathy. *Literature in the Ashes of History*. Baltimore: Johns Hopkins University Press, 2015.

————. *Unclaimed Experience: Trauma, Narrative, and History*. Baltimore: Johns Hopkins University Press, 1996.

Clark, Elizabeth A. "The Lady Vanishes: Dilemmas of a Feminist Historian after the 'Linguistic Turn.'" *Church History* 67, no. 1 (1998): 1–31.

Cone, James H. *A Black Theology of Liberation*. Twentieth Anniversary Edition. Maryknoll, N.Y.: Orbis, 1990.

————. *The Cross and the Lynching Tree*. Maryknoll, N.Y.: Orbis, 2011.

Congar, Yves. *I Believe in the Holy Spirit*. Milestones in Catholic Theology. New York: Crossroad Publishing, 2000.

Conroy, Christina. "Theology After Residential Schools." Ph.D. diss., Emory University, 2016.

DeKoster, Lester. *Light for the City: Calvin's Preaching, Source of Life and Liberty*. Grand Rapids: Eerdmans, 2004.

Derrida, Jacques. *Specters of Marx: The State of Debt, the Work of Mourning, and the New International.* Translated by Peggy Kamuf. London: Routledge, 1994.

Devries, Dawn. "Calvin's Preaching." In *The Cambridge Companion to John Calvin,* edited by Donald K. McKim. Cambridge: Cambridge University Press, 2004.

Doerries, Bryan. *The Theater of War: What Ancient Greek Tragedies Can Teach Us Today.* New York: Vintage, 2015.

Ebel, Jonathan H. *G.I. Messiahs: Soldiering, War, and American Civil Religion.* New Haven: Yale University Press, 2016.

Ehrenreich, Barbara. *Bright-Sided: How Positive Thinking Is Undermining America.* New York: Picador, 2010.

Elm, Susanna. *Virgins of God: The Making of Asceticism in Late Antiquity.* Oxford Classical Monographs. Oxford: Clarendon, 1996.

Felman, Shoshana, and Dori Laub. *Dori Laub, Testimony: Crisis of Witnessing in Literature, Psychoanalysis, and History.* New York: Routledge, 1991.

Frank, Georgia. "Macrina's Scar: Homeric Allusion and Heroic Identity in Gregory of Nyssa's *Life of Macrina.*" *Journal of Early Christian Studies* 8, no. 4 (2000): 511–30.

French, Shannon E. *The Code of the Warrior: Exploring Warrior Values Past and Present.* Lanham, Md.: Rowman & Littlefield, 2003.

Gordon, Avery. *Ghostly Matters: Haunting and the Sociological Imagination.* Minneapolis: University of Minnesota Press, 1997.

Grant, Jacqueline. "The Sin of Servanthood and the Deliverance of Discipleship." In *A Troubling in My Soul: Womanist Perspectives on Evil and Suffering,* edited by Emilie Townes, 199–218. New York: Orbis, 1993.

Gregory of Nyssa. *The Life of Saint Macrina.* In *Saint Gregory of Nyssa: Ascetical Works.* Fathers of the Church 58. Translated and edited by Virginia Woods Callahan. Washington, D.C.: Catholic University of America Press, 1967.

———. *On the Making of Man.* In *Nicene and Post-Nicene Fathers,* Second Series, vol. 5. Translated by H. A. Wilson. Edited by Philip Schaff and Henry Wace. Buffalo, N.Y.: Christian Literature Publishing, 1893.

———. *On the Soul and Resurrection.* In *Saint Gregory of Nyssa: Ascetical Works.* Fathers of the Church 58. Translated and edited by Virginia Woods Callahan. Washington, D.C.: Catholic University of America Press, 1967.

———. *On Virginity.* In *Saint Gregory of Nyssa: Ascetical Works.* Fathers of the Church 58, Translated and edited by Virginia Woods Callahan. Washington, D.C.: Catholic University of America Press, 1967.

Grimsrud, Ted. *The Good War That Wasn't—and Why It Matters: World War II's Moral Legacy.* Eugene, Ore.: Cascade, 2014.

Harris-Perry, Melissa V. *Sister Citizen: Shame, Stereotypes, and Black Women in America.* New Haven: Yale University Press, 2011.

Hauerwas, Stanley. *War and the American Difference: Theological Reflections on Violence and National Identity.* Grand Rapids: Baker Academic, 2011.

Herman, Judith. *Trauma and Recovery: Aftermath of Violence from Domestic Abuse to Political Terror.* New York: Basic, 1992.

Hillman, James. *A Terrible Love of War.* New York: Penguin, 2004.

Hollywood, Amy M. *Sensible Ecstasy: Mysticism, Sexual Difference, and the Demands of History.* Chicago: University of Chicago Press, 2002.

Holmes, Emily A. "Delores Williams' Theology of the Wilderness Experience: Incarnation in the Wild." *Union Seminary Quarterly Review* 58, nos. 3–4 (2004): 13–26.

Irigaray, Luce. *Marine Lover of Friedrich Nietzsche.* New York: Columbia University Press, 1991.

Jantzen, Grace. *A Place of Springs: Death and the Displacement of Beauty.* Vol. 3. Edited by Jeremy Carrette and Morny Joy. London: Routledge, 2010.

Jennings, Willie James. *The Christian Imagination: Theology and the Origins of Race.* New Haven: Yale University Press, 2010.

———. "Reading Bodies from Hidden Places: Reflections on Disability in the Christian Tradition." *Journal of Religion, Disability & Health* 17, no. 3 (2013): 295–300.

———. "War Bodies: Remembering Bodies in Times of War." In *Post-traumatic Public Theology,* ed. Stephanie N. Arel and Shelly Rambo, 22–35. New York: Palgrave Macmillan, 2016.

———. "What Does It Mean to Call 'God' a White Racist?" *Religion Dispatches.* 2013. Online.

Jones, Serene. *Trauma and Grace: Theology in a Ruptured World.* Louisville, Ky.: Westminster John Knox, 2009.

Jordan, Mark D. *Telling Truths in Church: Scandal, Flesh, and Christian Speech.* Boston: Beacon, 2004.

Kearney, Richard. "Writing Trauma: Narrative Catharsis in Homer, Shakespeare and Joyce." *Giornale di metafisica* 1 (2013): 7–28.

Kearney, Richard, and Brian Treanor, eds. *Carnal Hermeneutics.* Perspectives in Continental Philosophy. New York: Fordham University Press, 2015.

Keller, Catherine. *Face of the Deep: A Theology of Becoming.* New York: Routledge, 2003.

Keefe-Perry, Callid. *Way to Water: A Theopoetics Primer.* Eugene, Ore.: Wipf & Stock, 2014.

Krueger, Derek. "Writing and the Liturgy of Memory in Gregory of Nyssa's *Life of Macrina.*" *Journal of Early Christian Studies* 8, no. 4 (2000): 483–510.

Levi, Primo. *Survival in Auschwitz.* London: Collier Macmillan, 1986.

McAdams, Dan P. *The Redemptive Self: Stories Americans Live By.* Oxford: Oxford University Press, 2006.

Moltmann, Jürgen. *The Crucified God: The Cross of Christ as the Foundation and Criticism of Christian Theology.* New York: HarperCollins, 1974.

Morris, David J. *The Evil Hours: A Biography of Post-traumatic Stress Disorder.* New York: Houghton Mifflin Harcourt, 2015.

Morrison, Toni. *Beloved.* New York: Knopf, 1987.

Most, Glenn W. *Doubting Thomas.* Cambridge, Mass.: Harvard University Press, 2005.

O'Donovan, Oliver. *Just War Revisited.* Cambridge: Cambridge University Press, 2003.

Parker, T. H. L. *Calvin's Preaching.* Edinburgh: T&T Clark, 1992.

Partridge, Cameron. "'Form Blossoming in an Unusual Manner': Reclothing Sexual Difference in Gregory of Nyssa." In "Transfiguring Sexual Difference in Maximus the Confessor." Ph.D. diss., Harvard University, 2008.

Rambo, Shelly. *Spirit and Trauma: A Theology of Remaining.* Louisville, Ky.: Westminster John Knox, 2010.

Rivera, Mayra. "Ghostly Encounters: Spirits, Memory, and the Holy Ghost." In *Planetary Loves: Spivak, Postcoloniality, and Theology,* edited by Stephen D. Moore. New York: Fordham University Press, 2011.

———. *Poetics of the Flesh.* Durham, N.C.: Duke University Press, 2015.

———. *The Touch of Transcendence: A Postcolonial Theology of God.* Minneapolis: Fortress, 2007.

Rothberg, Michael. *Multidirectional Memory: Remembering the Holocaust in the Age of Decolonization.* Stanford, Calif.: Stanford University Press, 2009.

Saal, Tom. "Nameless Woman." Warriors Journey Home. Online.

———. "Unnamed." Warriors Journey Home. Online.

Schendzielos, Erin Nichole, ed. *It Spooks: Living in Response to an Unheard Call.* Rapid City, S.Dak.: Shelter 50 Publishing Collective, 2015.

Schluep, John. *Broken Wings.* Training manual. Warriors Journey Home. Print, 2009.

———. *Soul's Cry.* Tallmadge, Ohio: Good Place Publishing, 2008.

Shay, Jonathan. *Achilles in Vietnam: Combat Trauma and the Undoing of Character.* New York: Atheneum, 1994.

Sheppard, Phillis Isabella. *Self, Culture, and Others in Womanist Practical Theology.* New York: Palgrave Macmillan, 2011.

Simons, Walter. *Cities of Ladies: Beguine Communities in the Medieval Low Countries, 1200–1565*. Philadelphia: University of Pennsylvania Press, 2001.

Smith, Daniel Alan. *Revisiting the Empty Tomb: The Early History of Easter*. Minneapolis: Fortress, 2010.

Smith, J. Warren. "A Just and Reasonable Grief: The Death and Function of a Holy Woman in Gregory of Nyssa's *Life of Macrina*." *Journal of Early Christian Studies* 12, no. 1 (2004): 57–84.

Terrell, JoAnne Marie. *Power in the Blood?: The Cross in the African-American Experience*. Maryknoll, N.Y.: Orbis, 1998.

Tick, Edward. *War and the Soul: Healing Our Nation's Veterans from Post-traumatic Stress Disorder*. Wheaton, Ill.: Quest Books, 2005.

Upson-Saia, Kristi. "Resurrecting Deformity: Augustine on Wounded and Scarred Bodies in the Heavenly Realm." In *Disability in Judaism, Christianity, and Islam: Sacred Texts, Historical Traditions, and Social Analysis*, edited by Darla Y. Schumm and Michael Stoltzfus. New York: Palgrave Macmillan, 2011.

Williams, Delores S. *Sisters in the Wilderness: The Challenge of Womanist God-Talk*. Maryknoll, N.Y.: Orbis Books, 1993.

Witvliet, John. *Worship Seeking Understanding: Windows into Christian Practice*. Grand Rapids: Baker Academic, 2003.

Wool, Zoë Hamilton. *After War: The Weight of Life at Walter Reed*. Durham, N.C.: Duke University Press, 2015.

Wright, N. T. *Surprised by Hope: Rethinking Heaven, the Resurrection, and the Mission of the Church*. New York: HarperOne, 2008.

Yehuda, Rachel. "How Trauma and Resilience Cross Generations." *On Being*. July 30, 2015. Online.

Yehuda, Rachel, and Linda M. Bierer. "The Relevance of Epigenetics to PTSD: Implications for the DSM-V." *Journal of Traumatic Stress* 22, no. 5 (2009): 427–34.

Yehuda, Rachel, Nikolaos Daskalakis, Linda Bierer, Heather Bader, Torsten Klengel, Florian Holsboer, and Elisabeth Binder. "Holocaust Exposure Induced Intergenerational Effects on FKBP5 Methylation." *Biological Psychiatry* 80, no. 5 (2016): 372–80.

Yoder, John Howard. *The War of the Lamb: The Ethics of Nonviolence and Peacemaking*. Edited by Glen Stasson. Grand Rapids: Brazos, 2009.

———. *When War Is Unjust: Being Honest in Just-War Thinking*. Minneapolis: Augsburg, 1984.

Index